Management
Productivity
Multipliers

Management Productivity Multipliers

Tools for Accountability, Leadership, and Productivity

GERALD KRAINES, MD

SENIOR VICE PRESIDENT, PARIVEDA SOLUTIONS

CAREER PRESS

This edition first published in 2021 by Career Press, an imprint of

Red Wheel/Weiser, LLC

With offices at:
65 Parker Street, Suite 7
Newburyport, MA 01950
www.careerpress.com
www.redwheelweiser.com

ISBN: 978-1-63265-183-9

Library of Congress Cataloging-in-Publication Data available upon request.

Cover design by Kathryn Sky-Peck
Cover image by iStock.com
Interior by Maureen Forys, Happenstance Type-O-Rama
Typeset in Warnock Pro and Avenir Next

Printed in Canada
MAR

10 9 8 7 6 5 4 3 2 1

I dedicate this book to
Cynsie Kraines and Robert Krock.

CONTENTS

LIST OF ILLUSTRATIONS

ACKNOWLEDGMENTS

I WANT TO ACKNOWLEDGE the enormous contributions of two people in writing this book:

My wife, Cynsie Kraines, often says that I have studied life and leadership, whereas she has lived life and leadership. I have learned so much from her about how value-adding leaders "really" add value. She has been the backbone and source of energy for 30 years in building our firm, The Levinson Institute, which is now part of Pariveda Solutions.

My "James Boswell" and VP, knowledge management, Robert Krock, who after 30 years knows what I am going to say before I say it, often before I even think it. Documenting the principles over the past 30 years and writing this book without Robert's contributions would have been impossible.

As many of my clients and colleagues over the years know, I have learned as much from them as they have from me. Much of this book emerged from working with Denis Turcotte, Eduardo Padilla, Mikael Gordon, Jim Allen, Karen Rosene-Montella, Fabiaan van Vrekhem, Warren Knowlton, Gerry Yonas, John Dyer, Barry Hurewitz, Brian Gifford, Zoran Veselic, Ben Duster, Rafa Ramos, Steve Jenkins, Mario Botas, Francisco Martínez Colunga, Rob Hennemuth, Nick Stanage, Anne Bakar, Ferio Pugliese, Mark Fuller, Mike Broz, Eddie Opler, and many more than can fit on this page.

Finally, I want to acknowledge and thank Bruce Ballengee, Pariveda Solutions' president and CEO, and Kerry Stover, Pariveda's COO, for incorporating and agreeing to steward the Levinson IP and its purpose: "to have a profound impact on society by bringing 'basic laws of human nature' into our work organizations." For Cynsie and I now lead Levinson by Pariveda!

FOREWORD

I HAVE KNOWN and admired Gerry Kraines for the past 40 years. That span of time covers my first class at The Levinson Institute prior to Gerry's owner-ship and has seen me working for four companies in a variety of capacities—from a plant manager, to division CFO, to divisional vice president of sales, to vice president of group manufacturing, to a divisional president of a *Fortune* 500 company, to running multibillion-dollar businesses while living in Europe and working for a large glass conglomerate, to running two companies on my own. One of these was a very large public materials company based in Europe and the other was a portfolio company of one of the largest private equity firms. All of the above needed fundamental and profound change and I often relied on Gerry's wisdom to help me in making that happen.

First, I must say that Gerry "gets it." He very quickly understands the cor-rect answer and course of action where real people are involved. His ability to listen first to understand before speaking is a good lesson to take to heart. Even though he instinctively understands the solution, one of the things I have always admired most is his willingness to use the journey to the answer as a teaching moment. Often, that journey has its own unique twists and turns. I learned that by taking the time to make the journey with him, real synergies and better-than-expected outcomes often happen.

He worked extremely well with the various teams I constituted, often when fundamental restructuring, hard work, and shortened timeframes were involved. Gerry quickly earned the trust of team members and helped them in their own journeys to better understand more optimal use of the human resources at their disposal. Where fundamental change was needed—as it often was—Gerry provided excellent learning templates for my teams. Many of these had come from past work he had done in making critical assessments of people's skills and potential levels. In other cases, he was very receptive to working with us in creating *de novo* solutions.

Through it all, his fundamental compassion for people and the wonderful way in which he engaged our business leaders to arrive at their own solutions became a hallmark of our times together. My sense was then, and is now, that Gerry has never been confronted with a real-life assignment where he was unable to see the path forward. Also, I would have to believe that where leaders took his processes to heart and were willing to embrace the learning, excellent and fundamental change could occur. It certainly did in the areas in which we worked at Owens Corning, at Pilkington Glass/Libbey-Owens-Ford, at Morgan Crucible (now Morgan Advanced Materials), and at Graham Packaging.

I always came away from the times we worked together much better for the knowledge we had gained and saw my business leaders and their people becoming significantly more effective. Gerry is correct that many CEOs and senior division heads are reluctant to take the time to understand the power of his methodology. In my opinion of the CEOs today, I believe only a very small fraction are truly transformational. This is disturbing. However, for those who are capable, motivated, and willing to do it, it will certainly make a big difference. Gerry's teachings can greatly help their efforts.

One specific area is related to accountability in organizations. I gained so much in working with Gerry to better hold my organizations and their leaders accountable. I and the key people accountable for cascading it down throughout the organizations owe him a tremendous debt of gratitude. It worked and continues to work well.

I have always believed that Gerry is at his absolute best in the field working with a variety of leaders in many and varied environments. In these settings, he is able to bring to the table collective wisdom and teachings and adapt these and the new learning that usually ensues, to create even better future paradigms. I see this as a win-win and a beautiful way to move the needle forward.

WARREN KNOWLTON

FORMER CEO, Graham Packaging Company; and former CEO,
Morgan Crucible (now Morgan Advanced Materials)

MARCH 2020

Management
Productivity
Multipliers

INTRODUCTION

A Systems Approach

WHAT MAKES PROFESSIONAL ATHLETES so successful and so respected? Is it all due to nature and to natural talents? How much of a role do instruction and coaching play in developing outstanding, record-breaking skills? Is it the 20,000 practice repetitions that we read so much about?

What role does one's anatomy play in aligning one's skeletal structure and muscles to be optimized for a particular sport? Are there specific physiological systems—such as cardiovascular, neurological, endocrine, digestive, and metabolic—that predispose for success?

Does the act of visualizing performing a task create greater success while performing a specific skill? How strongly does motivation from extrinsic factors (e.g., external rewards, money, and social recognition) and intrinsic factors (e.g., desire to win, sense of pride, and mastery) contribute to outstanding performance? Does the ability to focus by tuning out distractions make a significant difference?

It may seem an overstatement to compare a work organization's productivity with that of an athlete's productivity and health, but it is not in the least. At Levinson and Co. and Pariveda Solutions, we understand how to diagnose the sources of work-related symptoms and know how to optimize organizations and workplaces to maximize productivity.

After almost 50 years of consultation and research, we understand a great deal about how nature intends for people to organize, behave, and interact around different kinds of working environments. After all, work organizations are human creations and must reflect properties found in humans themselves. There is a genuine science emerging about the proper "anatomy" and "physiology" of highly capable, effective, and accountable companies and even

1

government agencies. And, if these principles and practices are applied properly, any organization can be brought up to its maximum potential health and peak productive effectiveness.

Often, approaches to improving organizational effectiveness or "curing" areas of dysfunction focus on treating the symptoms, not on diagnosing the underlying causes. Even the most well-known and respected consulting firms tend to rely more on benchmarking to offer remedies, rather than on examining root causes through scientifically informed lenses. This rarely results in finding the actual sources of the problem or in meeting the unique needs of the client. Instead, so-called remedies merely offer a Band-Aid or short-term approach, which eventually may make matters worse.

On the other hand, we know in medicine that an accurate diagnosis is 90 percent of the cure. The same applies to helping an organization to reach its peak performance.

Our firm has approached optimizing organizational and leadership health much differently than others. That is why so many of our consultants are physicians and psychologists—many have Harvard Medical School appointments—and technologists.

Physicians are taught to examine their patients as complex human systems. They know that evolution has tested and selected the optimal anatomies and physiologies for humans to function as well as they do. When people do not feel or function well, physicians have been trained to examine all of the structures, processes, and systems that might be contributing to the symptoms and figure out which of them need to be restored to their optimal state and in what way. We have over five decades of experience of converting symptoms and data into knowledge of the underlying principles.

Both Dr. Harry Levinson, Levinson and Co. founder, and I adhere to the premise that managers are capable of learning and first applying principles to their own leadership behaviors and to requisitely aligning every aspect of their organizations with their strategies. The *Wall Street Journal* once referred to Levinson and Co. as "that bastion of organizational and executive-development consulting."[1] We prefer to think of ourselves as the thinking manager's resource.

Optimized organizations create conditions where people can work at their full potential and deliver maximum value in their roles. Their employees feel valued because they are freed up from having to waste time and energy "working the system." Optimized organizations have capable and efficient processes attached to logical structures, so it is always clear who is accountable for what and those who are accountable have the required resources and authorities. Optimized organizations have managers who add value and lead effectively to ensure their people will be successful and thus create environments in which people welcome being held accountable.

With the concepts in *Management Productivity Multipliers,* managers and consultants alike will be able—just as a physician—to metaphorically take a history, conduct a review of systems, perform a physical exam, and order the equivalent of lab tests and X-rays. You will be able to efficiently and thoroughly explore all relevant factors that may account for the problems you want to solve. You can even take advantage of the most advanced organizational and talent development software technology available, SONARIO®, to collect and synthesize all of the information and analyze it in order to treat and restore the organization as a total system.

The entire approach in this book is directed toward making your organization sustainably optimized. My goal is for all of your managers and employees to learn how to be proactive and adaptive as new demands and prospects inevitably present themselves. I want to go well beyond helping you to function at peak performance today. When you transfer all of the knowledge and tools in this book to your organization, it (and your people) will always be able to function optimally and know how to prepare—in advance—for new threats or new opportunities and for an overall productive future. This is a long-term, strategic investment in a system of productivity multipliers.

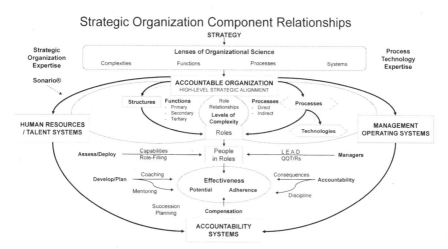

This graphic provides a high-level overview of the components in the Levinson by Pariveda consultancy model.

CHAPTER 1

Accountability

I HAVE ALWAYS been intrigued by why so many people have studied and written about leadership for so many decades and centuries, as though none of them felt those before them got it right. Each of these pundits operates with a different set of assumptions about what it takes to get people to follow their leaders, to take orders and do whatever it requires to implement them.

It reminds me of the old joke about three blind men trying to make sense out of an elephant: the trunk feels like a hose, the legs feel like tree trunks, and the tail feels like a snake. Each examines a piece or component of the elephant, but none understands how they all fit together as a whole animal.

Similarly, my impression of most management fads is that they are appealing and prescriptive, but they are one-dimensional, superficial, and they fail to address the needs of the whole organization. Instead, they offer simplistic and ultimately ineffective solutions to complex, systemic problems.

Reject simplistic solutions. Organize and lead based on sound, proven, and commonsense leadership principles.

In this book, I focus on four requisite components of managerial, accountability leadership systems and illustrate how to get each of them right and properly integrated into a whole. While understanding and implementing this model can feel daunting and requires a fair amount of heavy lifting, the returns are extraordinary: gains in productivity of approximately 100 to 300 percent. Although the components (i.e., principles, methods, practices) are simple to understand, it will take serious thought and work to join them all together seamlessly to achieve these results.

Four Building Blocks for Creating Highly Productive, Accountable, Strategically Aligned Organizations

What are the four components and underlying principles that must be incorporated into the design and implementation of such a productive, integrated managerial system?

1. **Accountability.** Managerial systems are inherently accountability decision-making hierarchies, whereas partnerships, academic departments, churches, and governance entities are inherently political decision-making systems. Therefore, I will begin by examining the nature of accountability only in managerial employment organizations and the conditions necessary for it to be experienced as trust inducing and fair by the employees who work there.

2. **Leadership.** The leadership component of every manager's role requires both setting direction and leveraging the potential of employees to achieve that direction, while simultaneously creating the maximum amount of value for the organization. I will explain how managers can fully *leverage* the potential of their people by *engaging* their commitment, *aligning* their judgment, and *developing* their capabilities, captured in the simple acronym L.E.A.D.

3. **Organizational Alignment.** A basic principle for all managerial systems is that accountability without authority is fantasy and stress. Too often organizations fail to align authorities with accountabilities. This results in a great deal of noise and wasted energy. I will present a set of core architectural principles of organizational design (structures, processes, and systems), which can ensure optimal market-centric and accountable strategic alignment.

4. **Human Resource Systems.** Roles can be defined by the complexities of their work, their functions and processes, the nature of their work, and their working relationships. HR systems must both capture these role specifications and enable the assessment of employees' capabilities to meet those requirements. Additionally, accountability without consequences is meaningless. Therefore, accountability systems require that employees be accurately and fairly assessed as to how effectively they fill their roles (i.e., "earn their keep"), if we are to tie consequences (both positive and negative) appropriately to how well people meet their accountabilities.

Myths, Biases, and Realities about Accountability

When I ask groups of employees to describe what they believe implementing a "culture of accountability" would feel and look like, the majority of them say it would make them nervous—even fearful—because they assume it would be a system to decide who to blame when something goes wrong. Most say that they rarely experience the conditions in which they have the authority, resources, and means to deliver successfully on all of their accountabilities. Employees say they often feel "set up to fail, not to succeed."

I find that many organizations—in their attempts to increase productivity and accountability—focus on the quantity of delivered outputs, relative to the originally assigned outputs, as the measure of an employee's worth. If an employee delivers amounts greater than assigned, she gets a bonus. If an employee fails to deliver what was assigned, he is often penalized.

This approach of relying only on things we can measure creates a number of unintended negative consequences. First, employees understand quickly that to maximize their take-home pay, it is in their interest to "under commit" to their managers when the quantity of outputs is being discussed. "If I low-ball what I say I can deliver, then I have a buffer if things go south and have a potential huge upside if I'm lucky." Managers understand this and often attempt to coerce their subordinates to commit to "stretch goals," asserting this increases their motivation. What it actually does is increase employees' feelings of mistrust and resentment because they realize that they are being set up to fail.

Second, because employees' earnings are tied tightly to their own outputs, they have little incentive (actually, a negative incentive) to lend a hand to teammates who are falling behind. Similarly, they tend to avoid collaborating cross-functionally on initiatives that will not result in increasing their own outputs. Therefore, when managers ask their employees to support others who may be falling behind, many employees respond reflexively by demanding, "Show me the money!"

Evaluating and rewarding employees based on their outputs alone creates an adversarial relationship between managers and their subordinates. It also works against strong, collaborative teamworking.

So, if accountability and consequences should not be tied solely to things we can count, what other things must we hold employees accountable for?

Consider the following scenario:

Fred and Mary are two salespeople with roughly the same territories with similar demographics and competitor profiles. Each committed to sell 1,000 products over the year. In the first month, by chance, Fred saw a massive influx of the company's ideal customers and a dramatic reduction in the number of competitors. During the same month, also by chance, Mary saw a significant exodus of her ideal customers and a dramatic increase in the number of competitors.

Fred was able to sell 2,000 products during the year. He never told his boss about his good fortune and rewarded himself by playing golf every afternoon. Mary alerted her manager immediately about the dramatic changes in her territory and committed to an aggressive and creative plan to minimize the loss of sales revenue. She demonstrated great initiative, worked day and night to implement it, and she was finally able to sell 700 products, whereas the manager previously felt more than 350 sales was optimistic.

Which salesperson was more effective? Fred doubled his original commitment, but not through any personal effectiveness. It was just dumb luck. In fact, if he worked full days, he should have quadrupled his original commitment.

Mary sold only 70 percent of her original commitment but alerted her manager as soon as she realized it would no longer be possible (i.e., "no surprises") and then developed and implemented a highly effective plan to reduce the likely shortfall by half.

If these employees were paid by output-based commissions, Fred would get a windfall and Mary would get less than originally planned. If they were compensated based on their demonstrated effectiveness, the story would have been reversed.

Results vs. Effectiveness

Two dimensions of what employees should be held accountable for emerge from the anecdote above.

First, when there is a change in circumstances that might have a significant impact on what employees can deliver relative to original commitments, they must alert their managers as soon as possible. When an employee gives her word, she must keep her word, no surprises! In Fred's case, the manager might have changed his deliverable from 1,000 products to 3,000 or more. In Mary's case, the manager might have changed her minimum deliverable to 350 products.

Second, managers are in the best position to observe their people. As such, they can and must evaluate how effectively each subordinate worked to overcome specific obstacles and identify and exploit opportunities. In Fred's case, he both surprised his boss by not informing him of the expanded opportunities (instead, he exploited them for personal gain) and failed to optimally and effectively exploit all of them for the company's gain. Mary did not surprise her boss. She agreed to a renegotiated lower target, and still was extremely effective in finding ways to minimize the potential losses. She more than earned her keep.

Employees are accountable for both keeping their word—without surprises—and earning their keep.

After I moved from the clinical practice of medicine to leading a management consulting and leadership development firm, it took me several years to understand why both of these aspects of accountability were necessary. I realized that what distinguishes a managerial system from a partnership is that managers get much of their work done through the subordinate resources assigned to them. Moreover, they are accountable for those subordinates. Managing partners are not accountable for the other partners in the firm; they are only accountable for running the practice administratively. Each partner's earnings are tied—by design—to the revenue he brings in individually.

Additionally, outputs from managerial systems are created by many employees working in common on different segments of the same processes. To ensure these processes are in control and that they deliver timely, quality outputs, each employee needs to adhere to process limits. Partners are individual contributors who have a great deal of discretion regarding limits and they experience directly the consequences (on their own bottom lines) of doing something well or doing something poorly.

Oscillating between Creativity and Control

There is an inherent tension in all managerial systems between wanting employees to exercise creative initiative when planning and delivering on their assignments and, simultaneously, doing so within the limits necessary to achieve process control. If an organization leans too heavily on controls, then it becomes heavily bureaucratic and allows little room for innovation. If an organization errs on the side of giving its employees too much autonomy or empowerment, it often ends up with chaotic processes and no one to hold accountable.

Root Causes of Management Fads

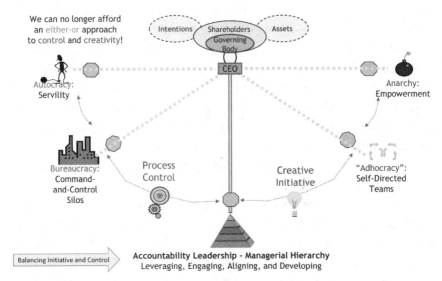

The most successful and productive organizations balance creative initiative and process control.

Therefore, accountability in a managerial system requires that employees make honest and ambitious commitments, which then obligates them to deliver exactly as agreed unless they give a "heads up" and renegotiate when in doubt. It also requires that the organization's policies and processes allow for a certain degree of discretion within limits. This enables each employee to be creative and innovative when figuring out how to maximize outputs and optimize resource utilization, while still maintaining process control.

This fact helped me to understand why there are such wide swings in the management-fad pendulum. The pendulum swings perpetually between bureaucracy and autocracy, on the one hand, and self-direction, empowerment, and anarchy, on the other.

Responsibility or Accountability?

Early on, I also learned that organizations that struggle with creating a fair-minded culture of accountability often conflate the notions of accountability and responsibility. They even use these two words interchangeably. In conversational English outside of the workplace, however, these words have very different meanings and connotations. "She's a really responsible young woman" is how we describe someone who has and conscientiously adheres to high personal standards, values, and morals. "He met his accountabilities," on the other hand, implies that he honored a commitment he made to someone else. He took on and met an obligation.

These non-workplace uses of the words have different consequences. If someone behaves in a personally irresponsible manner, we would hope that she would feel embarrassed, regretful, or inadequate. On the other hand, if someone fails to honor a commitment, he would expect to be "called to account" by the injured party.

The sense of responsibility resides inside a person. The state of accountability is attached to a role relationship.

Sadly, many employees say that they rarely experience the conditions in which they have the authority, resources, time, and means to deliver successfully on each of their accountabilities. As I pointed out earlier, employees often say they feel "set up to fail, not to succeed." This phenomenon caused me to examine the minimum prerequisites for employees to experience accountability as fair and feel "set up for success."

Accountability without authority is fantasy and stress.

Prerequisites for a Culture of Accountability

The obvious first prerequisite is that employees must be clear on what they are being held accountable for. How often do you receive an urgent e-mail originally sent to your boss? Your boss forwards it to you with the cryptic message, "Fix this!"

What exactly does that mean? Now? In a week? Temporarily? Permanently?

Managers must communicate their expectations unambiguously and make sure their subordinates understand them.

I find it useful to specify each output by two dimensions:

- Quantity: How many of the outputs are required? What is the size of the output?
- Quality: How well must it be completed? What parameters of the solution must be addressed to what degree?

The second prerequisite is that managers must (after candid and active two-way discussion) specify:

- Time: What is the longest time allotted for completion? By when must it be completed?
- Resources: What authorities, resources, and resource constraints apply? What limits must be adhered to?

This is often the tricky part of getting agreement about assignments or "QQT/Rs."[1] The manager and her subordinate may not agree on how much time—coupled with how many resources—it should take to deliver the output. The manager may fairly estimate it would only take T (amount of time) with R (amount of resources) to complete the assignment if he were to do it by himself.

However, managers' views are often biased by the reality that they are more capable and experienced than their subordinates, who may reasonably and legitimately believe it would take longer and require more resources for them to complete the assignment. Resolving these different perspectives requires active communicating, explaining, listening, and, ultimately, understanding. In this way, managers can and should push for the most ambitious commitments possible from their subordinates—while at the same time, the employees must feel that the commitments are potentially achievable.

Furthermore, managers are not always fully aware of the number of assignments their subordinates are carrying in their "baskets" of deliverables. This may significantly constrain the amount of time and attention they can free up to focus on new assignments. Once again, getting all of this information out in the open and clear requires active communication so managers can judge the viability of completing the entire set of QQT/Rs, not just a newly delegated QQT/R.

The guiding principle here is that while managers should always press for the most ambitious commitments possible, subordinates should always push back when they feel the proposed QQT/Rs are simply not achievable. This is the only way an organization can manage for reality.

To achieve consistency across the organization, I recommend using these QQT/R specifications and language for all tasks, assignments, projects, programs, initiatives, etc.

Managers must clearly specify all assignments by their Quantity, Quality, Time, and Resource constraints and get agreement from their subordinates about them being achievable.

The third prerequisite for meaningful accountability is that managers convey the purpose and context behind the QQT/Rs. When managers delegate assignments, they are not just trying to keep their subordinates busy. Remember, what is unique about managers' roles is that they have subordinates assigned to them as resources to assist them in completing their own assignments.

Every delegated QQT/R is, in fact, a component of a manager's plan to deliver on her own accountabilities. In order for managers' plans to come together optimally, they need each of their subordinates to understand the higher-level purpose that their assigned QQT/Rs are serving. In this way, managers can expect their subordinates will always consider the ultimate purpose when they are planning and implementing their own QQT/Rs. Of course, this requires that employees should always keep their managers' intentions and rationale in mind as they plan and implement their own assignments.

When these three prerequisites are met, employees become more confident that they are not being set up for failure.

> *"I know what I am accountable for delivering and why it has been assigned."*

> *"I know I have sufficient time and resources to complete this and all my other QQT/Rs—unless circumstances change, at which point I would be obligated to inform my manager and recommend changes in my QQT/Rs."*

> *"I am clear about what success looks like from my manager's perspective."*

This modus operandi is a prerequisite for building a culture of trust, which—as we will see in Chapter 2—is itself a prerequisite for engagement.

The fourth prerequisite has an important impact on creating a culture of fairness. I have explained why accountability in a managerial system has two components: honoring commitments without surprises and working effectively to overcome obstacles and identify and exploit opportunities for creating value. How is any one employee to know whether and how well she has met those expectations?

> *"How will my manager determine whether all of my commitments have been honored? How will my manager determine that he was given an adequate 'heads up' if problems arose? And how will he assess the effectiveness that I have demonstrated in my role in*

dealing with the degrees of difficulty I encountered and in identifying and creating new opportunities?"

When employees do not know how they will be measured and judged, they are left in limbo. They will have no basis for judging how fair the culture of accountability will end up.

"Will I be at my manager's mercy if we don't have good chemistry?"

"If my manager has much higher standards than other managers, will my teammates and I suffer from lower ratings than people with the other managers?"

Therefore, the organization and each of its managers must clearly articulate how outputs and throughputs will be measured. Of equal, perhaps even greater, importance, the organization must make clear the standards for judging effectiveness and how they will be applied in a consistent and fair manner across the entire organization. In a culture of accountability, roles and accountabilities vary, but all people are held to the same high standards.

The fifth and final prerequisite has to do with consequences. Accountability without appropriate consequences is fantasy. "Calling someone to account" must be tied to some degree of costs or gains. There need to be positive consequences for employees who keep their word, no surprises, and who earn their keep. Similarly, there need to be negative consequences for those who do not.

This means that there must be clear and internally consistent policies and processes governing how and when consequences are applied if one seeks to create a culture of fairness. It also means that managers themselves must be held accountable for applying both positive and negative consequences fairly, i.e., appropriate to how well their subordinates meet or do not meet their accountabilities.

For a culture of accountability to be trust-inducing and fair, managers must:

- *Clearly communicate what is being delegated;*
- *Ensure that the assignments are feasible given their time and resource constraints;*
- *Clarify the purpose and context that assignments are intending to serve;*
- *Make clear how assignments will be measured and how employee effectiveness will be assessed; and*
- *Ensure that the consequences (both positive and negative) are appropriate to the outcomes.*

In my experience, organizations that do not implement these five prerequisites of fair, trust-inducing, and meaningful accountability, but still complain about people not being accountable, have only themselves to blame.

Several years ago, the CEO of a high-tech company had his head of HR reach out to me (after my second edition of *Accountability Leadership* was published[2]) to "implement a culture of accountability." When I explained to the CEO what this would involve, he said, "Oh no, that's much too much work. I just want people to take accountability." What he really meant was that he hoped people would feel responsible enough to figure out what needed to be done and then tie things together on their own to deliver on his strategy. This was a clear-cut case of managing for fantasy.

There is no easy solution for establishing a value-creating, trust-inducing, and fair culture of accountability. Yet, the principles are clear. They are simple to articulate. The implementation of these principles does, however, require serious commitment and consistent and systematic leadership. This is no different, however, from what it takes to build a consistently winning football team, year after year. It is all about consistency, diligence, and implementing the basic block and tackling, day in and day out. However, it is worth the work, for the results and sense of gratification are spectacular.

Accountability Hierarchies: Fiction and Fact

A great deal has been written about the stifling nature of hierarchical organizations. The tendency in business literature and many schools of management is to equate hierarchy with bureaucracy. The military is often—and unfairly—held up as an example of a "command and control organization" that inhibits initiative and creativity. The underlying assumption appears to be that managers, because they have authority to delegate assignments to their subordinates and hold them accountable, will inevitably micromanage them. They will communicate not only what their QQT/Rs are but will also be unable to resist instructing them on how to complete every step. When this occurs, one does indeed have bureaucracy.

However, I assert that bureaucracy is a form of "bad hierarchy." Managerial hierarchies structured, led, and populated properly will do the opposite. "Good hierarchies" will ensure that managers and employees at every level have both the capabilities and authority to exercise considerable discretion as to how they complete their QQT/Rs—as long as they do so within process limits. Good hierarchies recognize that people are employed precisely to apply their creative initiative in order to help their managers be successful. Simultaneously, each manager is working to help her own manager succeed. This continues all the way up to the CEO to deliver on what the owners expect.

A cynical view of bad hierarchy is that employees exist to make their bosses look good. A balanced view of good hierarchy is that each employee at each level is accountable for helping his manager succeed. Once again, every position needs to be considered as a judgment and decision resource dedicated to supporting its manager's role in completing its work successfully.

Another misconception of hierarchies comes from the expression *chain of command.* This conjures up an image of an ill-tempered CEO on the top floor of a tower pulling at an unbroken chain. The chain cascades down and across the entire organization, with direct links to hundreds, even thousands,

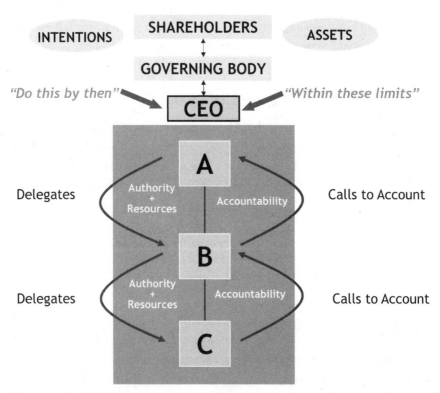

These are the A-B-Cs of accountability hierarchies.

of employees. It is as if the CEO's yanking on the chain will pull every single one of them up and off their chairs.

The reality is something vastly different. Instead, visualize a series of overlapping three-level links between a manager (of managers) linked below to a (subordinate) manager linked to its subordinate (who may or may not be a manager).

Manager A holds subordinate manager B accountable for C. Then, manager B holds subordinate manager C accountable for D. And so on down the line. This means that the CEO does not hold employees several levels below directly accountable. Rather, it means that the CEO must hold her subordinate executives accountable for holding their subordinate managers accountable for that employee.

This brings us back to our first principle that managers are *accountable for* their immediate subordinates. They will be *held accountable* by their immediate managers. Hence, this is the derivation of an accountability hierarchy.

For this reason, I find it confusing and unhelpful to ask the questions, "Who is that employee accountable to?" and "Who does that employee report to?" When any employee down the line is ineffective, the more relevant and informative question to ask is "Who is accountable for that employee?"

One of my long-term client CEOs recently took over a failing manufacturing company with a horrible safety record. At the outset, he made it unambiguously clear to everyone that addressing safety was his highest priority. Five weeks later, after one of the plant managers was found doing little to address poor safety conditions, the CEO pulled in the VP of manufacturing (the plant manager's boss) and bluntly asked his executive, "If I have to do your job for you, why do I need you?" The executive learned his lesson very quickly and immediately implemented a successful performance improvement plan for the plant manager.

Not only did the plant's safety record dramatically improve, but its delivery performance and quality also improved significantly. It has a remarkable and immediate effect on the workforce when they see accountability is more than just a slogan.

Requisite Managerial Authorities

Managers are—and must be held—accountable, for their subordinates' outputs, adherence to defined limits, and effectiveness in filling their roles. What authorities, then, must managers have with which to hold their subordinates accountable?

When there are vacancies in subordinate positions, what authorities do managers need when selecting candidates to fill the roles? Should they be able to hire anyone they want? Or do more-senior managers and HR advisors have proper roles in identifying a pool of qualified candidates from which to choose? Should they have the authority to "twist the manager's arm" to select a particular employee? I remember the time when a manager complained to me that he was pressured to fill a vacancy with a notoriously ineffective worker who was just removed from a role, because HR and legal did not want to deal with the legal hassle of terminating his employment. Should the hiring manager have the authority to say "no" to candidates who he feels are not capable of filling the role effectively?

Managers must have the authority to veto proposed candidates to fill vacancies if the manager deems them unqualified, because managers are ultimately accountable for ensuring those roles will be effectively filled.

What happens to managers' ability to hold their subordinates accountable for their outputs when many of those assignments were delegated by more-senior managers who reached down in the organization and around the immediate manager? In these cases, the immediate managers often have little control over how achievable those assignments were and whether the subordinates' basket of QQT/Rs was too overloaded to complete all of them. For this reason, managers need to establish the boundary conditions governing who can delegate assignments to and request services from their subordinates. Employees have the same obligation to push back and get their own managers engaged when they feel pressured to take on work from anyone else.

Managers must have the authority to assign subordinates' QQT/Rs or make the final decisions about assignments to them from others.

Evaluating Subordinates and Providing Feedback

Effectiveness appraisal systems in most organizations fall short of inducing a trust-inducing and fair culture of accountability. Most systems actually undermine managers' ability to hold their subordinates accountable for earning their keep. The problem is that "effectiveness in role" is inherently subjective; it cannot be easily measured the way outputs and throughputs can. Nevertheless, effectiveness in role can be observed. It presents itself in a myriad of different ways, each of which translates into some form of value creation. Employees add value in their roles when they apply their creative initiative, judgment, and discretion to solve the challenges they are confronted with.

The level of value that employees create becomes apparent when they decide how ambitious a QQT/R they are willing to commit to. It also shows up when analyzing the best ways of completing assignments and adjusting approaches when encountering unexpected hurdles—while always being cognizant of operating within resource, time, and process limits. At the same time, additional value is created when employees make adjustments to their own plans in order to support employees lateral to them (team and cross-functional peers) in order to optimally support the higher-level goals defined by their managers' context.

Additionally, highly effective employees often demonstrate extraordinary initiative by resolutely and persistently attacking the most difficult problems until the problems are resolved. They often take it upon themselves to lead when "balls get dropped," even when they are not accountable for solving the problems. Often, highly effective employees will continually take the initiative to identify new ways to enhance process-and-asset capabilities and reduce the amount of asset consumption.

The difficulty with most existing performance management systems is that they do not even attempt to evaluate the degree of an employee's "value creation"—relative to the requirements and expectations of the employee's specific role (i.e., complexity level). Moreover, they do not take into account the widely varying standards and subjectivity that each manager brings to the evaluation process. This often breeds a strong sense of unfairness in employees whose managers have impossibly high expectations. Finally, managers are rarely held accountable for defending their assessments of employee effectiveness to their own managers and peers in relation to the standards set by the CEO for the entire organization.

On the other hand, when an organization's assessment systems do meet these criteria (more details in Chapter 4), the immediate managers are in the optimal position to accurately assess (and defend) their subordinates' effectiveness in filling their roles. And since managers are directly accountable for developing subordinate effectiveness in role, the very process of evaluating their current strengths and gaps in role is the necessary preparation for subsequent feedback and coaching.

Managers must have the authority to evaluate and provide feedback regarding their employees' effectiveness in role. And managers must be held accountable for doing so in a consistent, fair, and trust-inducing manner.

Accountability and Consequences

When the managerial authority prerequisites enumerated above are in place, managers must then have the authority to apply consequences (both positive and negative) appropriate to how well or poorly their subordinates meet their accountabilities.

Managers need to have the authority to, at least, recommend merit awards for employees who demonstrated improved value creation over the past year and to ensure appropriate increases in base pay for elevated and consistent delivery of greater value than created during the previous year.

On the other hand, when employees knowingly abdicate their obligation to keep their word, no surprises, they undermine both trust and the very integrity of the accountability system. They literally break the "linked chains" of accountability and trust and undermine process control, quality, and delivery performance. This represents more than ineffectiveness. This amounts to insubordination and requires some form of discipline, both to illustrate the cost of that abdication to the organization and the importance of maintaining trust.

In addition, with consistently ineffective employees, after providing proper feedback and development efforts and documenting examples of the employees' inability to work at the required level of effectiveness, managers need to have the authority to initiate removal from role. This does not necessarily require termination of employment. Employees who fail to meet the effectiveness requirements of a particular role may have been giving it their best effort, but they might lack the potential to handle the complexity of work or the baseline experience and skilled knowledge required. In many ways, that could be more the fault of the selection process and the manager than the employee. If there are no other vacant roles for which such an employee is qualified, however, she may need to be "disengaged" from the company, but not "terminated for cause."

Managers need the authority to reward effectiveness, discipline and mitigate insubordination (when possible), and initiate removal from role of consistently ineffective employees who show little progress with coaching.

What Does This Mean for You?

How well does your organization provide the authorities managers need to hold their subordinates accountable? Think about it.

- Do managers in your organization possess each of these authorities with respect to their people in subordinate roles?
- Do managers appropriately exercise these authorities with respect to their people in subordinate roles? What percentage of managers appropriately exercise these authorities?

- Are managers held accountable by their own managers when they fail to appropriately exercise these authorities when they should have? If not, why not? What needs to change culturally to resolve this disconnect?
- What do you need to do differently, whether or not the organization as a whole addresses this?

While you may have limited authority to change or influence the entire organization's culture of accountability, you can choose to implement these practices in your unit.

Accountability in a Broader Context

In my four decades of consulting with thousands of executives around the world, I have come to see that creating a mature culture of accountability has an enormously positive effect on the people working in those organizations, regardless of the industry, country, or cultural attitudes. It has become enormously clear to me that a foundation for all meaningful human relationships is trust. And trust must be earned.

"Keeping your word" is one of the most fundamental rules of human civility and is entirely appropriate to expect in work organizations. By embedding this as a core value and operating principle in work organizations, people feel they can depend on others and then develop respect for each other. Moreover, managers who are themselves held accountable for ensuring this dependability and reliability also earn the trust and respect of the people who work for them.

Similarly, fairness is a critical determinant for people deciding whether to invest their personal commitment into a relationship—with another person, manager, or place of employment. "Earning your keep" is both a sustainable and straightforward way to describe the basic concept of fairness. It is not a harsh or unreasonable slogan; it is rooted in the most mature cultural mores and values. After all, it's just a variation of the Golden Rule.

Leadership: Where Managers Meet Their Accountabilities

Every role in a work organization unleashes a certain level of value that is necessary to achieve the work organization's strategic goals. Therefore, managers are accountable for selecting, developing, and leading employees who are capable of effectively filling the subordinate roles the managers have been assigned.

Managers must set the direction for their teams and units. They must also leverage the potential of their employees to pursue that direction.

How exactly do managers do this? To begin, they must harness the inherent enthusiasm of those employees by tapping into their individual and collective aspirations. Then, they must clearly communicate the direction and the purpose the unit is taking to enable them to make optimal enterprise-wide decisions (as opposed to expedient ones). Finally, they must develop within each employee the knowledge and skills necessary to master their roles and deliver on their full potential.

As we continue to explore the various productivity multipliers, the next chapter will explore these core tasks of managerial leadership summarized in the acronym L.E.A.D.

CHAPTER 2

L.E.A.D.

NO GENERAL CAN win a war alone. No captain can sail a schooner single-handedly. No architect can build a skyscraper by himself. No executive can single-handedly operate an extensive work organization. Leadership of any kind—managerial, military, moral, religious, political, or academic—requires leveraging the intelligence, skills, behaviors, passion, collaboration, and potential of many individuals in order to accomplish something greater than the leader or the individuals could achieve on their own. At its best, leadership leverages the full potential of the people who have been organized to accomplish a specific goal.

There are thousands of courses, articles, and books on leadership; many can be found on the Internet. They usually begin with the worn-out question, "What is the difference between a manager and a leader?" This is the wrong question to ask. Instead, we should ask, "What is the work of leadership that every manager should be accountable for?" As I spoke about in Chapter 1, managers are accountable for not only their subordinates' outputs and adherence to limits, but also for their subordinates' effectiveness.

This places active and ongoing requirements for managers to assess the effectiveness with which their subordinates are planning and executing their work, collaborating with others, overcoming obstacles, identifying and exploiting new opportunities, and adding value in a variety of additional ways. It requires providing continual feedback and coaching to enhance and reward subordinate strengths and to explain and develop approaches for reducing the gaps in their effectiveness. Most of all, managerial leaders need to have a clear-cut framework for creating the conditions in which the people in their units can thrive.

The goal of the leadership component of every manager's role is to fully lever-age the potential of the employees for which he is accountable.

This reality presents a dilemma. On one hand, managers are accountable for what their subordinates do and for ensuring that they adhere to policies and other limits when they do it. In some ways, this feels almost like a policing role. On the other hand, managers are accountable for helping to release their subordi-nates' creative initiative, which is itself a more intimate and generative role. It is as though each manager must play both roles of "good cop, bad cop" simultaneously.

So, how can we make sense out of these two types of relationships that managers have with employees in roles subordinate to them?

Two Distinct Leadership Relationships

Leadership role relationships and human relationships coexist in all organiza-tions. Role relationships must be defined by the requirements of an organiza-tion. Simultaneously, human relationships need to be healthy and mature in order to support the leveraging of each employee's full potential. However, the role relationship—the accountability relationship—must always come first. It must supersede the human relationship because that is the primary property of every managerial role.

Consider the following scenario.

Chances are that there was a time when you (or one of your teammates) were promoted from being a member of a team to becoming a manager of that team. My guess is the relationship between you and your former teammates changed, radically. In what ways did your former teammates act differently toward you? Did they share with you the latest misdeeds of their peers? "Jim has been coming in late and sometimes hungover. Abby has been 'borrowing' equipment to use at home. And Justin has found an unused office where he can take long afternoon naps."

I will bet that your ex-teammates no longer invited you out for a beer after work the way they used to. Did they share with you the same off-color jokes or their negative opinions of more-senior leadership? Perhaps it was more subtle. Did they simply feel that they needed to keep themselves more distant from you now that they considered you "management"?

My experience tells me that your behaviors and communications with them probably changed as well. You probably found yourself creating more dis-tance from them. Were you less inclined to share your thoughts about senior management? Were you also less likely to ask them to go out for a beer? Did you experience discomfort when needing to criticize one of your former teammates for the lack of quality or timeliness of her work? Did it seem that the close friendship with some of them was difficult to maintain?

These changes are inevitable because the change in your role relationship (when you moved from teammate to accountable manager) caused a disruption in the human relationship. Friends accept their friends for who they are. As a manager, you no longer have that luxury. You are now accountable for what your former friends do and how well they do it. You know that you may be called to account by your own manager if you fail to call to account your former teammates and friends—your new subordinates—when they are not meeting expectations.

Additionally, because of your new role relationship, you now have authority to affect their lives in significant ways. Your subordinate team members may feel vulnerable and instinctively create distance from you to protect themselves. They may "circle the wagons" to keep the new boss—you—at bay for mutual protection.

Nevertheless, managerial leaders need to have a healthy human relationship with their employees. However, it is one based on a different premise. Managers intuitively understand that their own success hinges on the individual and collective success of their subordinates. It is in managers' self-interest, therefore, to do whatever they can to set their people up for success.

In the 1950s, Dr. Harry Levinson observed that a *psychological contract* emerges between managers and their subordinate employees: people will commit to their managers and organization's success in direct proportion to how effectively the organization commits to employees' success.[1] The more the entire organization and each of its managers invests in creating the conditions for their people to succeed, the more strongly motivated the employees are to reciprocate.

Therefore, managers need to balance the tensions created by the competing role and human relationships with their employees. Both are necessary for organizations to realize their full enterprise value. And, most importantly, these two relationships need not be mutually exclusive. Trust and reciprocity are necessary for both relationships to thrive as the following conversation demonstrates.

> *"The fact that I am your manager and am now accountable for*
> *what you do and how well you do it prevents me from letting our*

*old friendship get in the way. While I care about you and will
commit to helping you succeed, I must be candid with you about
gaps in your effectiveness, even if it angers you or hurts your feelings. By doing so, you will be able to develop even greater effectiveness and add more value in your role, which, in the long run,
benefits both of us."*

Managers must balance these two types of leadership relationships with
their subordinates: the role relationship and the human relationship. However, the role relationship—the accountability relationship—must always take
precedence.

Where Managerial Leadership Begins

I find it useful when exploring new concepts and perspectives to understand
the roots or etymology of the words we use to describe them. The word *lead*
comes from an old English-Germanic root that means to "show the way." This
makes sense because the front end of every manager's work is to set direction for achieving whatever he is accountable for. Without good strategy, the
expression "garbage in, garbage out," unfortunately, applies.

The problem is that good strategy alone, while necessary, is not enough to
deliver the full enterprise value of that strategy. Numerous studies have shown
that many CEOs who have failed had perfectly sound strategies. They fail
because they do not understand how to systematically and accountably execute
on those strategies. In 1999, noted business consultant Ram Charan's cover
article in *Fortune* magazine identified 25 CEOs who had recently failed terribly
and publicly.[2] However, when he evaluated their stated strategies, he found that
over 85 percent of them were quite robust, but not executed properly.

This is the backdrop for understanding the purpose and role of managerial
leadership: setting direction (i.e., strategy) and leveraging the potential of one's
resources (i.e., people, processes, technologies, assets, money, etc.) to execute
on that goal.

Leadership at its core is about exerting leverage.

As you know, a lever is a simple tool that enables someone to lift a heavy
object higher than she could on her own. Archimedes asserted that with the
proper leverage, he could move the universe. Similarly, managerial leadership—when properly practiced—enables employees in a team, department, or
company to accomplish far more than they could on their own.

When I refer to leveraging employees' potential, I am referring to a unique aspect of human capability: the innate mental or cognitive ability to diagnose and solve problems. Many employees have the capacity to deal with complexities far greater than their current roles require. However, for a variety of reasons, that capacity may lie dormant and not be used to effectively meet the role's accountabilities. Employees may not be strongly motivated or informed enough about the rationale for their accountabilities and end up feeling disgruntled and disenfranchised, and "flying blind." They may lack a unique aptitude or talent required for the role. Or, employees may exhibit behaviors that are disruptive and undermine their effectiveness.

If any of these constraints occur, employees will not deliver the full value they have the potential to create and, thus, their potential will be wasted. And who suffers? The employees certainly are frustrated because they intuitively know how much better they could (or should) perform. Their paychecks will probably suffer, and their careers may be stalled because the organization is aware that they are not "giving it their all." Their departments and their managers suffer because they are not getting the full value from that position. Their families may also experience adverse effects from the employees' frustrations and demoralization. Even society as a whole suffers. Think about the memorable UNCF slogan from 1972 that still resonates today: "A mind is a terrible thing to waste."

The purpose of managerial leadership roles is to simultaneously unleash, harness, and direct the full power of employees' potential value to the organization and to simultaneously ensure employees keep their word, no surprises, and earn their keep.

Demonstrating Effectiveness in Role: Four Requirements

To understand the L.E.A.D. framework, I will begin by explaining the types of capabilities required for employees to be effective in their roles.

Since the creative work of every role involves diagnosing and solving the problems necessary to deliver on assignments, the first and most critical capability is brainpower. As explained earlier, it is often useful to think of one's current *potential* as the amount of mental processing ability an individual can bring to bear when exercising judgment and discretion. To use a computer metaphor, the speed of a processor can be a limiting factor in determining how complex an operating system or a program one can use. It is one's raw, innate ability to handle complexity (think central processing unit or CPU). Later in the book, I discuss a scientific approach to identifying the degree of complexity of work required for every role.

1. *The first requirement one needs to be effective in a role is to have the potential to handle the complexity of work of that role.*

    Yet, even with a powerful CPU, if the energy source is not sufficient to power the processor, no work can be done. It is the same with all employees. If they are not motivated enough to apply their judgment and discretion to the problems at hand, it does not really matter how bright they are. They will simply not exert the energy, time, and focus necessary to solve the most complex problems the role is accountable for.

2. *The second requirement one needs to be effective in a role is strong commitment. Employees must be motivated to apply their brainpower to unravel the complexities of their accountabilities in order to optimally complete them. Such motivation comes from a strong work ethic, in general, and from valuing the nature of work of the role, in particular.*

    As with a computer, if it is not fed accurate and useful data and if its programs do not specify the types and forms of conclusions required, we find ourselves back to the "garbage in, garbage out" cliché. We hire employees to do more than what a simple rules-based program or machine could do autonomously. We need them to constantly entertain alternatives about the best way to complete their assignments, not just take the most expedient path. By best, I mean striving to achieve the output specifics that will best serve the organization's higher-level goals, i.e., optimally "fit for purpose." Thus, a critical managerial practice—perhaps the most critical— is the ongoing setting of context, in two-way conversations surrounding assignments. Managerial context acts like a GPS system for employees to gauge all decisions in relation to their managers' intentions.

3. *The third requirement for employees to fully and effectively add value is accurate information about the intentions behind their assignments. Employees need rich and thorough context from their leaders about the rationale underlying their assignments in order for them*

to complete them in such a way that best meets their managers and organizations' needs.

Finally, if we do not have the proper operating systems and applications required for the specific work that needs to be undertaken, we will still be saddled with suboptimal solutions. Employees—even if they are bright enough, motivated enough, and informed enough about context—who lack the skilled knowledge, experience, and mindset required by their roles may still be ill-equipped to master the work of their roles.

4. *The fourth requirement to be able to master one's role is to have sufficient skilled knowledge, experience, and mindset about the functions, processes, and cultural norms of the role and the organization to accurately and efficiently apply judgment.*

A Leadership Framework: L.E.A.D.

To meet these four requirements, we need a model or framework that informs managers about the critical leadership practices that must be employed. The goal is to ensure that each of their subordinates and their subordinate teams are working at or above the level of effectiveness required of their roles. Specifically, what must managers do to harness the full potential of the employees who work for them? Keep in mind that every manager must be held personally accountable for delivering value-adding leadership.

I find it useful to identify three broad categories of leadership work, each translating into a commonsense set of pragmatic practices. Applied consistently, collectively, and carefully, these three leadership actions leverage potential.

1. **Engaging the commitment** of an organization's owners, customers, and employees is the first prerequisite. It is critical that they all trust and are committed to you and your organization. Otherwise, there will be no opportunities for creating value, achieving a fair exchange of value, and, ultimately, implementing strategy. In this book, I focus on the role of managerial leadership in engaging enthusiastic employee commitment. In particular, I draw upon the notion of achieving a "healthy psychological contract" between managers and their teams and the organization and its employees.

2. **Aligning judgment** of all stakeholders, including employees, is equally essential. If your strategies are not aligned with what the owners expect and what customers are willing to pay for, there is no basis for doing business and thus providing the owners with a return on their investment. Moreover, if your employees are not aligned with how their work is intended to support the strategy and if the structures and processes within which they work do not align their accountabilities with requisite authorities, they will be unable to deliver what the customers want.

3. **Developing capabilities** of the organization as a whole, and of every employee in the "pool of talent," is also a core managerial leadership accountability. When people, organizations, and nations settle for the status quo, they will inevitably begin falling behind. The world, its technologies, its products and services, its competitors, and its customers' needs are constantly evolving, which requires continual adaptation to survive, let alone thrive. The organizational demand for highly capable employees, who can not only master the work at hand, but also drive innovation and value creation, is unrelenting.

Leadership is the means for

The purpose of leadership is to leverage potential by engaging commitment, aligning judgment, and developing capabilities.

It rests on the shoulders of managers to understand their organization's evolving talent needs and to coach and mentor their own employees to be able to meet current and future needs.

To fully leverage employees' potential, managerial leaders must engage their commitment, align their judgment, and develop their capabilities. The acronym L.E.A.D. is central to the practice of leadership.

Why Leadership as Leverage?

Early on in my transition from being a full-time practicing physician to becoming a management consultant and, dare I say, leadership expert, I was puzzled by the management approaches of the many senior executives I had advised and worked with over the years. They never seemed to understand that their ultimate success really hinged upon leveraging the judgment and initiative of the many employees below them. Often, these executives were bright and ambitious, so it seemed all the more curious that they would insist on micromanaging the work of scores of people two, three, and even four levels down. My curiosity got the better of me. I began asking them about details of their career paths and their philosophies of leadership.

One very senior executive described to me that he joined the organization fresh out of graduate school, where he was an excellent student. Because he had great political instincts, early in his career he figured out how to "work the system." Whenever he got a tough assignment, the executive knew how to get others to "lend" resources to him. He knew how to cut corners with respect to policies, regulations, and process standards. He knew how to convince peers to defer to him. And he knew how to take credit for the work of others.

As a result, the executive got more recognition from above, faster promotions, and bigger assignments. Because he was perceived as someone who could be counted on to get results, senior management never looked at (or simply overlooked) how he got those results and how he sub-optimized the rest of the organization at the same time. When I asked him about his philosophy of leadership, he said simply "Things only get done by the 15 to 20 percent cream of the crop, so just let the cream rise to the top and ignore everyone else."

The problem for this executive (and for many others like him) is that the higher he rose in the organization, the more he "became the system." He had little conception of how to systematically and proactively organize and delegate work to capable talent, who he had to develop, and create the conditions where they could be successful in keeping their word, no surprises, and earning their keep. His mental model and behaviors leading to his career success would no longer enable him to remain successful.

The reality is that when managers reach down into their organizations to personally direct the work of others—often several levels below them—they are not adding the full value expected of roles at their own level. And they are not extracting the expected (and paid for) value from the managers and employees at the lower levels. They appear to operate with the assumption that most employees have limited capacity to think and solve problems on their own, so they must be handfed instructions about "how to connect the dots." As the executive in the illustration above once stated, "Eighty percent of employees are just commodities." This is not the message that shareholders want to hear. They understandably want to realize the full value of every person their company employs and pays for.

This is where the concept of leverage comes in. As I mentioned in Chapter 1, all employees are in reality resources delegated to managers to enable them to deliver on their assignments and add value appropriate to their roles' level of work complexity. Managerial leadership, in turn, has two basic components that require judgment and discretion: setting direction and leveraging the potential of their resources to successfully pursue that direction.

The most complex aspect of this work lies in setting direction—in deciphering the complexities underlying the task at hand and modeling plans and strategies that will ensure the most capable, efficient, and accountable means for implementing those plans. Specifically, managers must break down their own overall plans into sub-plans and outputs they will, in turn, delegate to their subordinates, with the "right" degrees of complexity that their subordinates are able to handle.

> *"As a manager, I must first figure out how to best achieve my accountabilities and then break them down into sub-tasks that I can delegate to my subordinates. They then will be accountable for figuring out how to best achieve those sub-tasks. However, in order for this to occur, I must recruit and develop subordinates who have the potential (i.e., problem-solving ability), skilled knowledge, and motivation to successfully plan and implement their assignments. And, I must set clear context surrounding their QQT/Rs so they can incorporate my intentions into their plans."*

Managerial leaders must leverage their subordinates' potential to solve and implement the smaller components of the manager's own plans.

What Engaging Commitment Really Means

When I entered the Public Health Service in 1972, I was enrolled in a course on leadership. The instructor began by asserting that the job of a manager is to motivate his people. Initially, I thought that seemed reasonable, but the more I thought about it, the more I was offended. He believed that I needed someone else (i.e., my boss) to motivate me. I thought of myself as an intrinsically motivated individual. I wanted to do good work, challenging work, work that I could be proud of. I was not comfortable needing to have a manager who felt that I could be motivated *only* with enticements or bribes, on the one hand, and threats or coercion, on the other. If I needed to be manipulated with carrots and sticks, it must mean my manager thinks of me as nothing more than a jackass.

As I stated earlier, Dr. Harry Levinson identified in the early 1950s that the levels of employee engagement, morale, and commitment to an organization's success vary directly with the level of commitment by the organization and its managers to their employees' success. After 50 years of working with companies, their managers, and their employees, we have identified four broad categories of organizational conditions (described below) that correlate strongly with an organization's overall level of engagement.

Personal Safety and Security

The importance of personal safety and security may seem obvious. However, it is worth digging into more deeply. Employees may wonder, "Can I really trust a company that fails to be hyper-diligent about keeping me safe and healthy?" Companies that are unwilling to invest in making sure that their employees are not exposed to dangerous or unhealthy working conditions are tacitly communicating that their employees are disposable or dispensable commodities that can be put at risk. Coal miners have known for decades that many of their companies expose them needlessly to mining collapses and black lung disease, but the miners simply had no alternatives to working there. When employees realize that their workplaces allow avoidable injuries that could prevent them from earning a living and supporting their families, they feel trapped, demoralized, and resentful. Productivity suffers and retention becomes a serious problem.

Similarly, employees often see their leaders making expedient, short-term decisions that might adversely affect their jobs or the sustainability of their organization (and their own future careers). They inevitably lose any trust that those leaders have the employees' best interests in mind. And when they see that those decisions were often made to increase the executives' bonuses, any remaining sense of respect, trust, or fairness is crushed.

Trust and fairness (or reciprocity) are at the root of meaningful and endur-ing engagement. All managerial leaders must maintain healthy and mature psychological contracts with their employees and continually renegotiate them as conditions change.

Personal Value

All employees (and all human beings) are complex, intentional, value-driven creatures. They make decisions and act based on the perceived personal value derived from those decisions and actions. While many people seek employ-ment because they need to provide for their families, wages alone do not gener-ate the enthusiastic commitment to do whatever it takes to make their manager and the organization successful. Employees need to experience receiving per-sonal value from their workplace to be strongly invested in doing their best work for their managers.

Personal value can accrue from many different types of experiences.

> *"If my job is interesting and the work is challenging, if it has a purpose that I can relate to and I can see my impact on achieving it, I will want to capitalize on that opportunity to deliver value for the organization and myself. And if my manager and the orga-nization actively invest in my growth and my having a rewarding career by providing coaching, feedback, mentoring, training, and advancement opportunities, I want to do whatever I can to 'earn the right' to advance as my potential matures. And if the culture is respectful and the processes are highly collaborative, I am likely to form rewarding and mutually gratifying relationships with coworkers that will make it enjoyable to come to work and work hard together."*

The greater the personal value employees derive from working in an organi-zation, the more enthusiastic they become to contribute as much value as pos-sible in return.

Value-Adding Leadership

Leaders who have given the most of themselves to their teams have received the most from them in response in terms of greater performance and effort. Mutual giving brings a higher level of engagement and learning. This means that giving yields an exponential degree of receiving. There is a powerful psychological principle at work here that underlies the psychology of giving. When we experience ourselves as givers, we receive a deep and enduring affirmation of our value to others. In transcending the self, we obtain the most profound experience of self.

There are myriad ways that highly effective managers can provide *value-adding leadership*. In return, their employees experience a strong desire to deliver comparable or even greater value. At the highest level, effective leaders articulate the purpose and "goodness" of the organization's mission and strategy. Leaders provide a vision to which employees can aspire and contribute. In this sense, they are inspirational. They communicate context clearly, so that their employees can both understand and feel a part of the bigger picture. By seeing both the relevance and importance of one's assignments in contributing to the greater whole, employees assign greater importance to their own work and become more highly motivated to give it their all.

And when managers consistently take the time to set context and ensure that their team is cognizant of higher-level thinking and then invite their team's input into testing and improving upon that thinking, employees feel greater ownership over the resulting plan and its logic. The more employees can see their "imprint on their managers' blueprint," the more it becomes *their* collective plan for success.

It is worth repeating that accountability without authority is fantasy and stress. Because trust and fairness are integral to engagement, when employees feel they are being set up to fail, they often spend a great deal of time trying to protect themselves. This can occur when their accountabilities have not been clearly specified or when the resources and authorities delegated are insufficient to deliver on by the time allotted. When managers do not take the time to explore the impact of new or adjusted assignments on their subordinates' entire bucket of assignments, employees feel they are being pushed "out on a limb being sawed off behind them."

When employees find themselves thwarted by red tape and excessive bureaucratic constraints or being held up by other parts of the organization on whom they are dependent, they feel frustrated, powerless, and once again set up to fail. Effective managers need to be close enough to the working conditions of their employees to become aware of the barriers or disconnects they encounter and to be proactive in asking when they need help. Knowing their managers have their backs is a powerful generator of enthusiastic commitment.

Creating a sense of fairness requires transparency on the part of managers, as well as their subordinates. The requirement that there should be no surprises works both ways. When managers and their subordinates agree on QQT/Rs, which should always be ambitious yet achievable commitments from the employees, it is not fair for managers to come around later, remove resources, and still expect employees to deliver on time as agreed. This means that if either anticipates possible future changes that could affect existing commitments, they need to inform the other as soon as possible to give them time to plan for contingencies.

Fairness is often put to the test when managers must decide on consequences for their employees' demonstrated effectiveness during the year and at year's end. All human beings thrive on recognition for their positive contributions to others. Employees expect to receive tangible appreciation from their managers for a job well done whether it is a simple "atta boy" or "atta girl," a public thumbs up, or a financial merit award. Employees naturally seek and expect appropriate reward and recognition for their contributions. Additionally, it is considered unfair when employees who consistently fail to deliver on their commitments or fail to add the level of value required benefit from the same rewards as effective employees. Managers and employees alike expect that everyone in the organization should be required to earn their keep. A sense of fairness demands a meritocracy!

Meaningful recognition should extend beyond praise and bonuses, as well. Highly effective employees expect that, based on their demonstrated success and initiative, they should be given greater opportunities and challenges that will enable them to grow and master new areas of work.

Highly effective employees who demonstrate the potential to do even more complex work reasonably expect to be moved near the front of the queue in being considered for promotions as vacancies occur.

The more ways that leaders add value to their employees—via inspiration, communication, preparation, and recognition—the more enthusiastically those employees will want to reciprocate by committing their attention, creativity,

focus, and time to deliver comparable value to their managers and the organi-
zation at large.

Values-Based Culture

Human beings are social creatures. We form relationships with others and seek
to belong to like-minded communities. We want to feel safe, respected, trusted,
treated fairly, and to engage in mature interactions with the people in our communities. Whether or not we are consciously aware of these expectations, we
all want our workplaces to foster trust, respect, justice, and mature behavior.
We seek employment in *values-based work cultures* that both articulate and
actively demonstrate these values.

The purpose of leadership is to leverage the potential of a manager's employ-
ees. The first managerial task is to engage the enthusiastic commitment of sub-
ordinates to apply their full potential to solve problems, complete assignments,
and add value in a variety of ways. Since people are intrinsically motivated, the
challenge is to build a trusting and fair relationship in which people feel safe and
secure, from which they derive personal value, with leaders who add significant
value, in a work culture that is based on sound and mature values.

The Role of Context in Aligning Judgment

Human beings have a far greater capacity for accurate and nuanced communication than lower-order animals. Yet, we usually do it quite poorly and never
realize it until it is too late.

> *George Bernard Shaw famously said, "The single biggest problem*
> *with communication is the illusion that it has taken place."*

> *Lily Tomlin once joked, "I always wanted to be somebody, but now I*
> *realize I should've been more specific."*

> *Oscar Wilde once said, "When people agree with me, I always feel*
> *that I must be wrong."*

> *Albert Einstein was quoted as saying, "Everything should be made*
> *as simple as possible, but not simpler."*

People usually have specific assumptions and intentions when they choose to
express something to others. However, those intentions are often the result of a
great deal of thinking and musing, not all of which reaches the level of conscious

awareness. Furthermore, those intentions are often muddled together with other expectations and thoughts. Therefore, when a manager communicates with a subordinate, only a piece of her thinking is usually communicated. And because it seemed clear in the mind of a manager, she simply assumed that the subordinate took in more than the words that were spoken. Managers expect, somehow, that the subordinate *must have* understood the meaning behind the words. Managers can be such narcissists!

In Chapter 1 on the nature of accountability in managerial systems, I stated that managers must clearly specify *what* is to be accomplished, *by when* it must be completed, and *within what* resource constraints it must be constructed. The *what* referred to specifying the *quantity* and *quality* of the output. The *by when* defined the longest time the manager would give the employee to complete the assignment. The *within what* is meant to spell out what resources and authorities would be delegated and what limits must be adhered to in order to ensure process control.

This sounds quite thorough, doesn't it? Yet, how often have you discovered that a QQT/R that was returned to you—even if it met the explicit specifications—was not really what you had in mind or that it would not accomplish what you needed it for? Or perhaps the assignment you believed you had accurately delivered to your manager was not at all what he wanted?

I find it useful to imagine our minds, with all of the active mental processing going on within them, to be like an iceberg. One only sees the top tenth of the iceberg even though we understand that 90 percent of it is below the surface. Our conscious thoughts are like the metaphorical 10 percent above the surface. Yet, most of our mental processing—accessing memories, conjuring up assumptions, weighing alternatives—is actually going on beneath the surface, i.e., below the level of conscious awareness. To ensure that one's subordinates fully understand the rationale underlying their assignments, managers need to actively engage them by setting two-way context to extract and make explicit much of that thinking. They need to tap into the "core of the iceberg" and make what was implicit . . . explicit.

Remember that every role (with each employee in it) is actually a "judgment resource" that managers must deploy to best achieve their own accountabilities. Therefore, when a manager delegates a QQT/R to a subordinate, the assignment is really a segment of the manager's overall plan for meeting his own deliverables. For a manager to ensure that the subordinate's QQT/R accurately supports her own plan and that it integrates well with the other elements of her plan, the manager must take the time to explain both that plan and the rationale behind it. This is the work of setting context.

As with all forms of communication, there is a discipline to context setting. To ensure the alignment of subordinates' outputs with managers' intentions, all managers and subordinates must learn and continuously apply context setting.

It begins with *upward context.* Managers need to explain the problem that the immediate manager is trying to solve. Typically, this starts by describing in detail what his own manager assigned to him, based on her manager's plan and logic. "My own manager is trying to find a new way to accomplish X with Y with fewer resources over the next T years. His plan and logic for doing so are P and L, and the QQT/R_{Mgr} he assigned to me is in support of his plan."

Next, the immediate manager should explain his own thinking about how to achieve his QQT/R_{Mgr} and invite his subordinates to ask questions and offer suggestions to improve upon the plan. "I believe that if we could improve the efficiency of these three-unit operations (x, y, and z), we could eliminate these two other steps (m and n) without compromising quality or productivity. This would accomplish two-thirds of the gains my manager asked me to achieve with my QQT/R_{Mgr}."

Once the manager decides on and communicates her plan, she needs to define which elements of that plan she intends to delegate to each subordinate. Initially the manager should describe the broad parameters of those assignments and ask the subordinates to develop and propose the most ambitious outputs (the Quantity and Quality elements of QQT/Rs) that they could commit to that would support the implementation of the manager's plan.

When the subordinates—in response—propose the specifics of their own QQT/Rs to support the manager's plan, a new phase in the conversation begins. Managers need to judge whether the subordinates' proposed QQT/Rs are sufficient to implement the managers' plans and whether the subordinates are requesting more time and resources than they require or are available. Once again, the leadership aspects of managers' roles are about fully leveraging the capabilities of their subordinates. Therefore, they should be constantly weighing how big a challenge each of their subordinates ought to be able to handle. And just as managers should challenge lowball proposals from below, their subordinates are equally obligated to push back if they feel their managers' expectations are impossible to meet. Remember, accountability without authority is fantasy and stress.

Setting upward context is the means by which managers ensure their subordinates understand the rationale behind their assignments, thus enabling them to make more nuanced decisions when planning and implementing their QQT/Rs. Managers will hold their subordinates accountable for the degree to which their outputs accurately fit the managers' purposes for assigning them.

The communication process then extends to *downward or teamworking context.* When managers develop plans that require delegating different QQT/Rs to several subordinates, they will likely have developed a sense about how each of those assignments is likely to interact with the others. Often, these likely second- and third-order interactions are intuited rather than consciously thought through. If several subordinates return to their manager because they cannot agree on how to proceed when their work conflicts with each other's, the manager would need to revisit his original logic in order to decide on the path forward. This frequently results in a bottleneck with many employees queuing up outside the manager's door.

To avoid these delays and facilitate the successful collaboration of teammates in identifying optimal solutions between them, managers must set teamworking context upfront. It starts with reaffirming the upward context and how each of their QQT/Rs is intended to contribute to the higher-level solution. Managers then need to articulate the relative priorities of each subordinate's QQT/R and the likely interdependencies between them. It is useful to then brainstorm various scenarios with the team (about potential conflicts and new opportunities that could arise) that might require adjustments by members of the team. With that context, each member of the team is then expected to both meet her own accountabilities and, simultaneously, achieve the best overall outcome for the manager.

This practice is exactly what top sports team coaches do. Consider any team sport, and what makes a team great. A star athlete is a wonderful asset. Yet a great team works as a team. Its coach discourages grandstanding, ball-hogging, and selfish play, understanding that team wins, rather than personal records and achievements, are what really matter. Therefore, each player must be aligned with that team goal. Each player also must know his position and remain constantly aware of how his position relates to the other positions in various situations—and always act with his own objectives and the team's overall objectives, simultaneously, in mind.

A batter hits a high-bouncing grounder between first and second base. The players automatically execute a whole series of maneuvers. The first baseman lunges for the ball, misses it, and goes skidding along on his belly. The outfielder closest to the ball, probably the right fielder, charges for the ball, as the center fielder moves to back him up in case it takes a bad bounce and he misses it. The second baseman runs over to cover first base while the first baseman gets up off the turf. The shortstop covers second base and readies himself for the throw from the outfielder, who hopes to hold the base runner to a single. Meanwhile, the pitcher backs up the shortstop in case the throw from the outfielder is high.

The average Little Leaguer grasps this. Yet this level of teamworking functionality remains elusive to most managers and employees for a very simple reason: lack of context. A game, any game, sets the context within which people must function and interact. The rules, boundaries, positions, and plays all contribute to clear context. Within such a clear context, people understand the overarching goal, their role in achieving it, others' roles in achieving it, the relationships between those roles, permissible moves, and the leader's expectations governing all of this. That creates alignment.

Setting downward context is the means by which managers ensure their subordinates are well equipped to make adjustments in relation to each other to overcome obstacles and capture opportunities that contribute the most accurate solutions and greatest overall value for their manager.

Developing People's Capabilities

I now want to explore both a narrow and a precise meaning of human potential in a work organization.

Potential is a person's raw, innate cognitive ability to unravel variables and solve problems. It represents an individual's ability to handle varying degrees of complexity.

If employees have the brainpower to be successful in their roles, the motivation to effectively apply their problem-solving ability, and the context to ensure their deliverables are accurately "fit for purpose," what remains is for them to become fully skilled and knowledgeable about the functions and processes of the role. Managers are accountable for their subordinates' effectiveness and for leveraging their potential. Hence, managers are accountable for developing their subordinates to be as effective as possible in filling their roles.

This brings us back to the concept of assessment of effectiveness described in Chapter 1.

Employees demonstrate effectiveness by adding value in their roles while applying their creative initiative, judgment, and discretion to solve the challenges they are confronted with.

Since we can readily measure outputs and throughputs, it is not difficult to determine whether employees honor their explicit commitments (i.e., QQT/Rs). Did they keep their word, no surprises? However, we cannot measure the degree of effectiveness one demonstrates in role. It is a construct. It requires a model for describing how complex the work of any particular role is. To master a role with high degrees of complexity is more difficult and results in adding more value than mastering a role with modest degrees of complexity. It requires more brainpower to master roles that are more complex.

Yet, we all know very bright people who cannot seem to work their way out of a paper bag. Someone could be bright enough to be a PhD nuclear physicist, but I would not want her to do brain surgery on me. Every role has both functional and process accountabilities that require knowledge to perform and enough skill to perform well. Unlike potential (i.e., innate brainpower), skilled knowledge must be acquired. We can learn how to do things in a variety of ways: by observing others doing them, by apprenticing under others with the skilled knowledge, by reading books and going to classes, and by coaching. We can even figure things out for ourselves by trial and error, but that is often the least efficient and most time-consuming way to acquire skilled knowledge.

So, how can managers fairly and accurately judge the effectiveness with which their subordinates fill their roles? They can judge by careful observation and comparison with the implicit and explicit expectations of the subordinate roles. Consider these questions:

- What is the degree of difficulty of the tasks assigned to subordinates?
- How ambitious are the commitments they are willing to make to do more with less?
- Are there unanticipated obstacles encountered along the way?
- How creatively are they mitigated?
- How proactive are they in anticipating and preventing problems?
- Do they take the initiative to identify new opportunities to create more value or enhance resource capability or reduce the amount of resources required?

- How responsive are they to requests for assistance from teammates or cross-functional peers?

- How much initiative do they take to persevere in solving extremely thorny problems?

- How much initiative do they demonstrate to take the lead in getting people together to solve problems for which they are not even accountable?

- How innovative are they in developing new ways to create things better, faster, or cheaper?

I have already discussed three dimensions of the work employees demonstrate in their roles, which taken together, provide a useful assessment of employees' overall effectiveness in role. These categories of work are:

- Mastering the role as defined;

- Exhibiting extraordinary initiative over and above the defined role; and

- Demonstrating disruptive behaviors that negate some of the value otherwise added to the role.

Degree of mastering a role (i.e., flawlessly delivering the defined accountabilities of the role) directly reflects the level of skilled knowledge and commitment to apply them. An employee who is not yet consistently delivering results commensurate with having fully mastered the role must have gaps in skilled knowledge or commitment or both. Coaching is the practice of identifying the gaps resulting in the assessment of incomplete mastery, providing feedback to the subordinate to create awareness, and then jointly creating a development plan to reduce the gaps.

Degree of extraordinary initiative—over and above role mastery—usually results from having potential greater than what the role requires ("headroom") or applying exceptional commitment or both. Many employees have excess headroom but do not yet demonstrate such incremental value-adding contributions. Managers should bring to their subordinates' attention opportunities where they can take more initiative to "think outside the box" (beyond what is defined for the role) and identify ways to add additional value.

Disruptive behavior also requires managerial development in the form of feedback and counseling. Often employees who exhibit these types of behaviors are unaware of the behaviors themselves or the adverse effects they have on others and on their own personal effectiveness. This type of feedback is often the most difficult for managers to provide. However, describing these behaviors and their effects and expecting employees to take responsibility for changing is critical—both for the employee's benefit and for the effectiveness of the entire team.

Managers are inescapably accountable for the effectiveness of their subordinates. Leadership requires the ongoing assessment of, and feedback to, subordinates as to how well they are filling their roles (i.e., degree of value-add relative to the complexity of the role); managers must provide developmental support to help subordinates narrow the gap between their potential and demonstrated effectiveness.

Implications for Organization and Leadership in Managerial Systems

In order to release, harness, and capture the greatest value from each of their employees, managers need to understand that the leadership aspect of the

ASSESSING PERSONAL EFFECTIVENESS
Value-Added... Relative to the Role's Requirements

Just beginning to master the **Basic Role** and adding **Less Value** than someone fully proficient

Fully **Mastered** the **Basic Role** and adding **Full Value,** consistent with deep skilled knowledge and strong commitment

Applying **Remarkable Initiative** and adding **Incremental Value** over-and-above what is required of the fully mastered role

Reduced overall effectiveness and **Value Contribution** in role by virtue of **Behaviors** that **Disrupt** the work of the unit

Maximum effectiveness in a role requires full role mastery (holding the role up), extraordinary commitment (pulling the role up), and the absence of disruptive extremes (pulling the role down).

managerial role is in the service of leveraging their potential. On the one hand, managers need to set direction and develop plans and strategies. That is the front-end part of leadership. However, to execute on those strategies they must leverage their employees' potential. And by leverage I mean they must accurately assess the innate capability of each employee to solve problems and identify how much of that capability is currently being converted into value-adding work—or not. This then sets into motion the three aspects of leadership leverage: engaging commitment, aligning judgment, and developing capabilities. L.E.A.D.

It turns out there are naturally occurring structures, identifiable for every managerial hierarchy that, applied correctly, can ensure the greatest leverage by managers of their subordinates' potential. These properties inform us that managerial systems are not only accountability hierarchies; they are also complexity hierarchies. We will continue this discussion in Chapter 3.

CHAPTER 3

Work, Complexity, and Levels

IN CHAPTERS 1 AND 2, I explored two fundamental aspects of the relationships between managers and their subordinate employees: accountability and leadership. Throughout the book, I revisit these properties. In particular, I illustrate the impact that organizational design and talent capabilities have on accountability and leadership.

Up until this point, I have defined *potential* in a unique and precise way as a person's innate mental capacity to handle complexity and solve problems. I now want to look at the organizational science concerning the nature of work complexity—especially its implications for organizing roles and selecting talent to fill those roles.

Yes, Some Roles Are More Complex than Others

A basic principle in designing accountable organizations is that accountabilities are attached to roles—*not* to individuals. The individuals in those roles are held accountable for meeting the requirements and obligations of those roles and for completing the roles' QQT/Rs. Unfortunately, most companies design and redesign their structures around their people and the capabilities of those people instead of the work and the requirements of work roles. Not surprisingly, companies often end up with imprecise role requirements. This makes it extremely difficult to accurately evaluate the effectiveness with which those employees fill those roles.

Nevertheless, most organizations recognize that different roles do indeed require employees to have different degrees of potential or problem-solving abilities. In fact, job-grading systems exist to provide a logical compensation structure for paying employees competitively, relative to the complexity of the work of their roles as found in the marketplace. This is a practical reality. People have choices as to where they work and experiencing felt-fair pay is a crucial factor in making those decisions. Existing job-grading and market-based compensation systems roughly serve their purpose when hiring employees. However, once inside an organization, few can claim their employees experience their internal compensation structures to be rational or fair.

Most employees have a sense about which roles in their organization are more difficult and more complex than others. They are also able to perceive when they themselves are underemployed—i.e., if they believe they have the potential today to work in bigger roles. Similarly, they will often point out other employees who appear to be in over their heads because they just cannot seem to take control of their roles' complexities. They have no choice but to whittle the role down to a more manageable size. This situation is often referred to as the Peter Principle.

Employees have an intuitive sense about the relative complexity or weight or degrees of difficulty of the roles in their organization.

Additionally, most employees have a sense of when there are too many or too few managerial layers in their organization. By exploring the signs and symptoms offered as evidence of either of these conditions, we can gain powerful insights as to the nature of complexity of work in roles and the primary value that managers should be creating when they set context for their subordinates.

You and your coworkers probably have sensed when there are too many managerial levels. It usually feels bureaucratic. Managers tend to micromanage. Decisions take forever because of paralysis by analysis. It is often unclear where the authority lies to make decisions. People are highly political. Bloated functional silos compete for dominance. There is a great deal of finger pointing when things go wrong, and they often go wrong. The net result is that those extra layers of managers add more noise than value. Those extra layers are worse than redundant; they actively inhibit the release of potential.

You may also have experienced the opposite circumstance in which an organization has too few levels. This may be the case when an organization has grown so rapidly that it outstripped its skeletal structure. It may also occur when a management consulting company used a blunt ax to reduce costs by drastically eliminating levels. This results in wide spans of control, leaving employees without managerial guidance. Employees feel that they are out on a limb with a sink-or-swim approach to survival. Most efforts are highly reactive with constant fire drills. There is no systematic quality control. Paradoxically, missing layers also reduce the effectiveness of the weary, overworked managers who remain.

Both too many and too few managerial layers undermine the value that managers should be adding to their subordinates. As a result, all employees and their work suffer.

What is at issue here? Is there a magic number of levels for all companies? Or is there a discoverable number of levels that is optimal for any particular managerial hierarchy? If so, should that number be based on spans of control or number of employees or total revenue or something entirely different?

Doing One's Level Best

Dr. Elliott Jaques first discovered the answer to these questions in the mid-1950s. Jaques was a noted scientist and psychoanalyst with an unusual background. He had degrees in engineering, medicine, and psychology. He also became famous for inventing the term *midlife crisis* in 1957 when he presented a paper in London. Yet, Jaques's most remarkable contributions centered around the nature of work itself, the underlying properties of work organizations, and the nature of human potential.[1]

It is intuitively obvious that roles higher in a hierarchy will have work that is more complex than roles lower in the hierarchy. Executives are paid larger salaries for their more difficult, complex work. One should even reasonably assume that the complexity of work increases gradually and progressively as one moves up each role in the chain of command.

However, there is a not-so-obvious question, as well. How much more complex must a manager's role be than a subordinate's role to be able to make a real difference when setting context by offering sufficiently greater perspective? When communicating the rationale and intentions underlying their subordinates' delegated assignments, managers need to be able to speak from a distinctly higher and more complex viewpoint. Context needs to provide employees with new and clear insights about the bigger picture that must be taken into account when implementing their assignments.

To fully understand this, all employees—including managers—are accountable for applying their judgment and discretion to formulate plans to deliver assignments that are fully fit for purpose. Managers bring to bear a required measure of "thinking" capability appropriate for their roles when discerning variables and considering alternative solutions. Typically, they then break their overall plans into shorter, less complex steps, many of which they then delegate to their subordinates.

Their subordinates are in less complex roles yet must possess the necessary degrees of potential to deal with the complexities of the less complex QQT/Rs assigned to them. Value-adding managerial context needs to enhance the employee's ability to discern variables and choose wisely among alternative solutions to select the ones that will best support their managers' intentions. Managers need to inform and elevate their subordinates' understanding of the thinking at a higher level of complexity if they are to ensure the optimal fit for purpose of their own deliverables.

Managers need for their employees to do more than take the most expedient route when completing their own QQT/Rs. Managers need for them to understand how each of their assignments is intended to fit together into the managers' overall plan and make whatever adjustments are necessary to ensure their fit for purpose.

The Evolution of Timespan

Most job-grading systems obscure the optimal and desirable "complexity distance" between managers and their subordinates to ensure value-adding context. The methods used to create them are simply too crude. They do not accurately evaluate the degrees of role complexities and inform management as to how to structure managerial levels in an optimal and productive way.

At this point, I want to offer a metaphor to help explain what I mean by a higher level of complexity. In nature, there are many examples of entities whose properties change under different conditions. For example, various characteristics of water were found to correlate with temperature once the thermometer was invented in the mid-1600s. As the measured temperature of a glass of water was lowered by degrees, the subjective sense of coldness increased. When the temperature rose, the subjective sense of hotness increased. However, when water is cooled down below 0 degrees Celsius (32 degrees Fahrenheit), it will also change state from liquid to solid and become ice. It will continue to be solid even as the temperature is lowered further. Conversely, when water is heated above 100 degrees Celsius (212 degrees Fahrenheit), it will be converted from liquid to steam (gas) even if the temperature continues to rise. Water changes state below 0 degrees and above 100 degrees Celsius.

Jaques discovered, when examining the "buckets of QQT/Rs" assigned to roles by their managers, that the length of time (T) established for the longest QQT/R in any role correlated closely with the subjective sense employees had about the weight of responsibility of their roles. He labeled the length of time of the longest assignment targeted for completion, *timespan.*[2] Roles that have assignments with longer times targeted for completion feel bigger, heavier, and more complex than roles lacking such long-term QQT/Rs. Because employees are accountable for completing all of their QQT/Rs by the times specified for each, the QQT/R with the longest T in the basket determines the overall timespan of discretion for the role in managing and completing all of its assignments.

You can test this yourself. What is your organization's (and CEO's) longest-term strategy? What is the timeframe of that deliverable? Ideally, it would be explicit.

However, it may only be implicitly understood between managers and their subordinates. Is it two or five years? Or is it 10, 20, or more years? What are the longest deliverables in the buckets of QQT/Rs of the CEO's immediate subordinate executives? What is your own manager's longest QQT/R? What is your own longest QQT/R? Among your subordinates' assignments, are there any longer than your own longest QQT/R? If you diagram these roles with their timespans of discretion, the times should progressively increase as you move from the lowest to the highest roles.

Do they?

The timespan of discretion for a role is determined by the length of time a manager allows for the completion of the longest QQT/R in a subordinate's bucket of QQT/Rs.

For example, a business-unit head within a sector of a large corporation may be accountable for increasing market share and free cash flow in her existing market and developing new products and services required to enter into adjacent markets in order to achieve 20 percent penetration in them over the next eight years. She may delegate to her VP of new product development QQT/Rs to improve features of existing products for the current market and to develop new applications that would be highly useful in the adjacent markets over the next four to five years.

The VP of new product development may then delegate to one manager the accountability for adding new features to existing products over the next two years and to another manager the accountability over two years for developing new uses of existing technology platforms for the adjacent markets. They may then each delegate three- to 12-month QQT/Rs to their subordinate engineers that would be necessary to support their own deliverables. At the same time, the corporate CEO may be asked by the board to expand markets in Asia and Latin America for the company's four different lines of business over the next 20 to 30 years.

Naturally Occurring Managerial Levels

When this approach to measuring degree of role complexity is applied to organizations where most employees recognize there are too many layers of management, a curious pattern emerges. Asking employees up and down the hierarchy whether they experience the manager on the org chart as their real manager (i.e., is that the role that determines your QQT/Rs, evaluates your performance, and holds you accountable?), the answer is often, "No, the person above me on the chart does have regular interaction with me, but it is really his boss (or his boss's boss) who calls me to account."

Several years ago, a major global automotive corporation had 13 layers of management. However, careful analysis and confidential interviews revealed that the employees identified only seven of those managerial layers as containing value-adding, accountable managers. This resulted in massive delays in decision-making, pervasive micromanagement, overly burdensome bureaucratic processes, and significant silo-protecting political behaviors. Consequently, the company was restructured with eight levels.

Over the past 60 years, this pattern of excessive, non-value-adding layers of managers has been discovered in thousands of organizations. There are many different reasons explaining how they got that way. However, it always results in a significant reduction in overall organizational effectiveness. Some of the historical causes were acquisitions that were just folded intact into the existing hierarchy, additions of new layers when spans of control were too wide, creation of new roles and layers to offer promotions to key employees when there were no vacant positions. The logic was understandable. However, it was flawed. It did not take into account discoveries about the natural structural properties of managerial systems, which I call laws of organizational science and engineering.

One lens for understanding this phenomenon is the amount of context leverage managers need to exert in order to elevate the thinking of their subordinates. Managers need to equip their subordinates with the proper perspectives when planning their QQT/R implementation in order to ensure they factor in the higher-level purpose.

Managers need to communicate their context—using their own higher-level thinking—in terms that their subordinates can understand and use. Managers, therefore, need to operate with a higher level of mental complexity than required of subordinates at lower levels. Managers literally need to think differently.

One implication of this is that when managers and their subordinates are operating with the same level of mental complexity (i.e., they have similar ways of thinking and mental processing), setting context is reduced to merely conveying information or data. The manager is not conveying greater meaning or increased understanding. It is more like receiving information from an older sibling rather than advice from a wise parent.

Therefore, a manager's thinking must be one level above (and distinct from) her subordinates' thinking to fully leverage their potential. Conversely, if the manager's role is too far removed from its subordinate role (i.e., separated by two or more levels), it will be difficult for the manager to set context clearly enough for the subordinate to find it useful. The manager's way of thinking would not be concrete or specific or relevant enough for the subordinate to be able to use it effectively when making decisions about how to implement his QQT/Rs. Meanwhile, those managers often complain that they are being "pulled down into the weeds" to do the work and thinking of their subordinates. What these harried managers are really doing, however, is the work of the missing subordinate-level manager.

With too many layers (compression), the extra managers create friction. With too few layers (gaps), managers experience a disconnect from their subordinates. Therefore, organizations need to structure roles and levels in such a way that manager and subordinates' roles are always separated by precisely one level of complexity.

This brings us back to the science. Jaques discovered in the 1950s that there are universal timespan breakpoints. Roles below a particular time horizon require a different thinking pattern than the roles above that time horizon. This higher-level pattern continues until the first role above the next breakpoint.

An inevitable conclusion in finding that all managerial hierarchies have naturally occurring, discrete levels of complexity of work is that people must also have uniquely different patterns of thinking.[3] Structuring organizations with more or fewer levels than required by their CEO role's level of complexity undermines the ability of managers to leverage their subordinates' potential. Setting context effectively requires that managers translate the complexities of their levels into the type of complex language that can elevate their subordinates' understanding.

From the Bottom Up: Value-Adding Work at Each Level of Complexity

Doing work requires deconstructing complexities, making decisions, and then implementing those decisions. There exist measurably distinct levels of complexity in every organization. The highest-level roles—those with the greatest complexity—add the greatest value by focusing on the long-term time horizons. Nevertheless, these executive roles must, simultaneously, establish effective subordinate organizations and talent and hold them accountable for focusing on the mid- and near-term time horizons. The level of role complexity determined by the CEO's timespan defines the total number of levels an

FUNCTIONS BY LEVELS OF ROLE COMPLEXITY

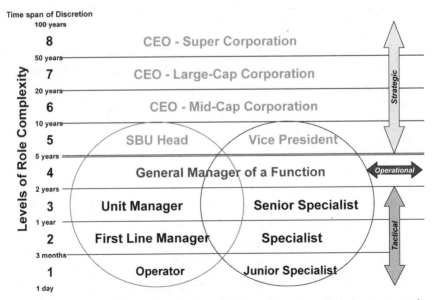

Naturally occurring, discrete levels of complexity require uniquely different types of thinking.

organization requires. The CEO's subordinate executive roles should be established within the next-lower level and each subsequent group of subordinates one (naturally occurring) level below.

The level of role complexity that is determined by the CEO's timespan decides the total number of levels an organization requires.

What follows is an exploration of an eight-level organization where I discuss in detail the nature of work found at each organizational level. I begin with the front-line worker at Level 1.

Level 1 work occurs when the procedures and the rules are already defined, and employees must figure out how to best deploy the procedures in accordance with the rules. "I have some discretion around making the process go a little faster by adjusting speed and the sequencing of products for production." However, basically, the decisions required are about how to maintain quality and control.

Typically, a machine operator, a tradesperson, a store clerk, a telephone operator, a lab technician, and similar roles all require training in procedures that they must skillfully apply when completing relatively straightforward tasks. The types of judgments required involve evaluating current state of work progress to determine which elements need to be adjusted to achieve the best outcome.

When a worker encounters an exception or obstacle, there may be a list of troubleshooting steps she could apply to bring the process back into the normal flow. However, if none of those efforts succeed, the front-line worker would then be expected to ask his manager to investigate the situation.

The timespan of these Level 1 roles can range anywhere from a day (a yard worker given assignments each day) to a week (a machine operator who needs to produce a certain quantity in a week's time) to a month (a foreman who develops the monthly shift schedule or a skilled technician who needs to identify and address variations in a machine's calibration over a four-to-six week period). Degrees of skill and knowledge can expand over time with training, coaching, and from personal experience gained by trial and error and by observing others. However, the timespans remain the same, unless, of course, the role itself changes.

Level 1 roles have timespans ranging from one day to three months and are accountable for applying existing procedures to known problems.

At Level 2, roles have timespans greater than three months, up to a year, and require a different pattern of thinking.

When an operator asks a first-line manager or supervisor to examine a problem she cannot personally resolve, what is really being requested? The manager may not have encountered that particular problem before either, but still is expected to identify the root cause or barrier and figure out how to overcome it.

Level 2 work requires that employees make connections on their own. They need to gather relevant information, analyze it, begin to make connections, generate hypotheses, and, based on those hypotheses, construct a solution that is not already in the procedure. Once a Level 2 manager identifies a new way to enhance the procedure, he may then incorporate it in the working methods of his subordinates going forward.

Where employees in roles at Level 1 are expected to use their judgment to solve problems by applying known procedures, employees in Level 2 roles (e.g., first-line managers, engineers, and accountants) are expected to apply their judgment to diagnose and resolve problems in previously unknown situations. Precisely because the types of Level 2 accountabilities are more complex, they are typically longer term. This is because it requires more time to effectively analyze the situation, understand the variables that contribute to the problem, and craft and implement solutions.

The timespans of these roles range from three to 12 months. A junior accountant may be accountable for managing and adjusting the general ledger for each quarter over a four-month period. An electronic engineer may be tasked with designing a new way to automate a variable pump in six months. A product development senior engineer may be accountable for embedding and testing new features in an existing application by its next release in a year.

Level 2 roles have timespans ranging from three months to one year and are accountable for identifying and analyzing process variation in order to understand root causes and design and implement solutions.

Level 3 work requires creating complicated sequences of hypotheses about "what if. . ." scenarios, generating alternative future pathways, and then modeling and choosing among those options to ensure an optimal benefit/risk ratio. These projects often take one to two years to implement.

Most roles at Level 2 work on assignments delegated to them by their Level 3 managers. It is useful to think of Level 3 roles as leading the organization's tactical efforts over its next one to two years. They are accountable for identifying opportunities for, and developing improvements in, the processes that their Level 2 employees are running and maintaining. They are also accountable for ensuring their three-level units collaborate effectively with other Level 3 units in achieving seamless end-to-end value-stream workflows.

To meet their continuous process improvement deliverables, Level 3 managers first need to identify (with their Level 4 managers) improvement targets, based on changing customer needs, improved competitor products and services, internal productivity, technology, and profitability requirements, etc. They then must develop alternative options or pathways for achieving those targets, often reconciling costs, time, feasibility, risk, and a slew of other variables against each other. Level 3 is where one begins to see cost-benefit trade-offs and contingency planning. It requires algorithmic-type thinking and decision-tree-like logic.

The timespans of these roles range from one to two years. A production manager accountable for the finishing line of a paper mill may have several 15-month targets for reducing scrap, increasing productivity, and improving quality. An IT project manager may have 20 months to design and implement a transformation of existing software to operate on a new platform. A product development manager may be accountable for the design, implementation, and regulatory approval of an upgrade to an existing medical device over the next two years.

Level 3 roles have timespans ranging from one to two years and are accountable for collaborating across the value stream, driving tactical projects and initiatives, implementing continuous process improvements, and providing input to their Level 4 functional heads about longer-range development programs.

Level 4 roles within a business unit tend to be heads of functions (often with director or vice-president titles), immediately subordinate to a Level 5 business-unit head. While business-unit heads typically are accountable for driving five-to-10-year long-range strategies, their Level 4 executives operate as linchpins in the mid-term, two-to-five-year horizon.

They are accountable for the operational linking of the Level 5 (L5) strategies developed by their managers to the Level 3 (L3) tactical implementation of those strategies below. Level 4 managers translate Level 5 strategy into their own Level 4 operational plans, and then delegate the tactical implementation of those plans to their Level 3 subordinate managers. Level 4 managers are also accountable for providing input to the L5 business model development from each of their functional perspectives.

Level 4 (L4) managers provide the connection, a sort of transformation bridge, from current state to future state. To accomplish this, they need to anticipate the functional capabilities that will be required in a few years' time that cannot be achieved simply by driving continuous process improvements at Level 3 and Level 2. As they develop and implement these new capabilities, they need to work with their L4 functional head peers to transform the value chain at L3 by synchronizing and integrating each of their changes.

Level 4 roles have timespans ranging from two to five years and are accountable for linking Level 5 business-unit strategy and models to Level 3 value-stream tactical implementation of that strategy. Level 4 roles are accountable for creating new types of capabilities that will be required for Level 3 work in the next several years.

Level 5 work is markedly different and bigger. The objectives at that level are truly strategic in that Level 5 executives must conceptualize the capabilities and requirements of their businesses and corporate functions necessary to compete successfully in the five-to-10-year future horizon.

By visualizing, designing, and transforming their organizations to meet the future state requirements, Level 5 managers are defining their entities' new. identities. "This is who we will become, how we will think and work differently, and how we will dominate our evolving marketplaces in the future." This often involves major changes in technology, in the way people are trained, in the way work is organized, and in the way processes are organized. Level 5 work requires conceptualizing new models for creating value. Level 5 business unit heads define these business models and drive the business results in terms of free cash flow, ROI, and market share.

Level 5 roles have timespans ranging from five to 10 years and are accountable for developing and implementing long-range business unit and corporate functional strategies designed to dominate their position in their industry. In effect, Level 5 defines its entity's future identity.

Level 6 work is also strategic. However, it looks much further out into the 10-to-20-year future. "We know the markets we are in today and working to dominate over the next 10 years. And we know what our existing ranges of products and technologies are over this period. We now need to anticipate and begin to invest in developing the types of products and services that the marketplace will require beyond 10 years."

How dramatically will the competitive, economic, technological, and demographic ecosystem change by then and in what ways? Level 6 managers have to ask the following—sometimes daunting—questions.

■ Do we currently have the foundational technological and commercial capabilities that we will need to build upon to meet those future market demands?

■ On the other hand, are the required capabilities likely to be sufficiently different that we will have to drastically transform what we do, what we produce, and how we produce it?

■ What new technologies and businesses do we need to acquire if we cannot create them organically?

■ Can we realistically catch up? Or do we need to merge with other entities that already are ahead of us?

Level 6 executives should not be personally involved in running their current businesses; that is the accountability of their subordinate L5 business-unit heads. Instead, they should be focused on maximizing the long-term asset value of their businesses. Level 6 managers should be focused on investing, acquiring, merging, and divesting assets.

Level 6 executive roles have timespans ranging from 10 to 20 years and are accountable for establishing a solid position in their business sectors by creating, expanding, and acquiring adjacent assets, businesses, and technologies. These executive-level managers also need to integrate and drive synergies among their L5 business-unit portfolios.

Level 7 executive work involves driving long-term 20-plus-year industry-wide strategies in large cap global companies. Their decisions require creating multiple and evolving complex enterprise models and projecting them forward over several decades. These Level 7 (L7) roles require sophisticated modeling of alternative future scenarios and the underlying ecosystem forces driving changes that could profoundly alter the organization's current business strategy and economic strategy.

L7 executives must envision future capabilities—which currently do not exist—that will be necessary to create or acquire entities in order to fulfill exacting requirements of the future. Much of the work involves choosing which existing business-unit portfolios to invest in, harvest, and divest in order to free up the equity needed to start up multiple new initiatives and investments. At Level 7, executives must also influence international political and economic decisions, which will shape the ways in which future markets evolve.

Level 7 executive roles have timespans ranging from 20 to 50 years and are accountable for envisioning their industry's evolving ecosystems and developing and implementing long-range investment and divestment strategies to provide sustainable, profitable growth.

Level 8 work involves orchestrating the investment and realignment of multiple L7 companies embedded in multiple industry divisions globally.

Level 8 organizations are considered mega-corporations and often have articulated long-term, multi-generational strategies. The corporate executive work focuses more on choosing which industries and future technologies to invest in or to divest with the goal of ensuring sustainable and predictable overall growth and free cash flow.

Level 8 executive roles have timespans beyond two generations and must continually assess and reassess in which of their multiple industry business divisions to invest, acquire, merge, and divest. They must also proactively drive governmental, regulatory, and industry policies, standards, and behaviors in order to create the most receptive environments for their industry lines.

These illustrations of the types of work found in naturally occurring, value-adding organizational levels of complexity were framed in terms of commercial managerial systems. Nevertheless, the nature of work is consistent. It is similar in both governmental and military work organizations, as well.

The discovery of these discrete levels of complexity is foundational and determines how companies need to be structured.

Levels of role complexity also have a profound effect on many other aspects of managerial leadership systems: designing functional alignment and

ORGANIZATIONS BY LEVELS OF ROLE COMPLEXITY

Naturally occurring, discrete levels of complexity exist in all managerial hierarchies.

process structures; types of teams; talent capabilities, assessment, and deployment; and context setting. The starting point in making these connections is to examine how the types of decisions change and increase in complexity from level to level.

Let the Manager Beware!

Companies need to be concerned, not only with over-promoting people, but also with the longer-term consequences of under-promoting them. "Am I keeping people in roles that are too small for them?" is a question that needs to be asked periodically. Operate this way over time and count on everyone suffering the consequences. In addition to feeling underappreciated and underutilized, people chronically bored and frustrated will not sustain morale, commitment, and confidence. In the short term, organizations might realize net gains by filling their positions with people possessing excess capacity. However, in the long run, this works against organizations, because opportunities almost always turn up elsewhere for these better-qualified people. (The only exception might be when the higher-capacity person is moved into a lower rung deliberately as a developmental move and thus part of a longer-term career development strategy.)

An even more urgent problem for organizations today is that they have a hazy notion (if that) of defining roles objectively. Without the insights and scientifically driven discoveries about work and levels of complexity (a productivity multiplier), it is no wonder that most organizations have as much trouble as they do.

The typical company tends to organize around the people it has—periodically shifting their logic for structure as people fall in and out of favor. As a result, the company delegates only whatever work its current—and seemingly haphazardly selected—workforce can handle. This non-system of role-establishment and role filling usually results in a decidedly unscientific guessing game. Rather than organizing proactively, with sound engineering principles, to be in alignment with company strategy, such organization is carried out in a purely ad hoc manner and productivity suffers.

CHAPTER 4

Capabilities, Potential, and Effectiveness

THINK FOR A MOMENT about a time when you were in a role that just was not "big enough" or challenging enough for you. How did you experience that situation? Were you bored? Frustrated? Underappreciated, undervalued, and underpaid? Resentful that your manager didn't appreciate your "potential"?

Now think about a colleague who was in a role that was "too big" for her. How did she behave? Was she stressed out? Insecure? Defensive? Micromanaging?

To answer either of these questions, you must have some type of internal radar and "yardstick" that informs you about how "big" (i.e., complex) a role is and how capable a person is of handling the complexities of a role. If we did not have the ability to assess these attributes of work roles and people's potential, we would have many more instances of mismatches of people and their roles. In this chapter, I present a model and the science behind it that explains how we sense people's potential and how we can do so with even more accuracy.

In Chapter 1 and again in Chapter 3, I explored two fundamental properties of all managerial systems. They are, simultaneously, accountability hierarchies and complexity hierarchies. In this chapter, I explain that managerial systems are also judgment hierarchies.

In managerial work organizations, managers are accountable for the work of their immediate subordinates, and managers are held accountable for doing so by their own immediate managers. The concept of manager A "resourcing" a subordinate manager B with a subordinate C and then holding B accountable for C is fundamental to designing and implementing a hierarchy and culture of accountability.

I then explained the existence of naturally occurring, distinct levels of work complexity in all managerial hierarchies, irrespective of the number of managerial layers any organization appears to have. Every role within one of these requisite levels requires a particular pattern of thinking and decision-making by their employees, which is different from that required by employees in "true" levels above or below that level.

For managers to be able to add the greatest value to their subordinates when setting context, they must have the ability to understand and explain the issues surrounding assignments they delegate from one higher level of complexity. For this reason, managerial roles must be established precisely one level of complexity above their subordinates' roles.

When manager and subordinate roles are established within the same level of complexity, we usually see signs of friction, unclarity, and micromanagement because they both require the same type of thinking. The manager feels more like a peer than a value-adding, accountable manager. When manager and subordinate roles are separated by more than one level, on the other hand, we see disconnects where the manager's way of thinking is too far removed from his subordinates' thinking. Consequently, the manager is unable to add the necessary level of clarity and degree of value and to hold subordinates accountable.

In Chapter 2, I explored the nature of managerial leadership and the role of L.E.A.D. in leveraging the potential of employees. In particular, the "A" stands for managers aligning the judgment and thinking of one's subordinate employees with that of the greater organization and with their peers—setting context. This is the single most valuable leadership practice and productivity multiplier for managers to be able to fully leverage their employees' potential.

The goal of context setting is for managers to translate—for their subordinates—the complexity of the plans and intentions from the managers' level and above into language and concepts that can be best understood and applied by their subordinates below. The more accurately the employees understand the rationale behind their assignments, the more they can keep that ultimate purpose in mind when planning and implementing their own deliverables. As a result, the final deliverables will more likely be optimally "fit for purpose."

Once receiving context from their managers, employees should be held accountable for making whatever nuanced adjustments necessary to best align the way they deliver on their QQT/Rs with the organization's (and their managers') reasons for assigning them. When evaluating employees' effectiveness in role, this requirement should weigh heavily in the overall assessment. Managers, too, should be held accountable for setting sufficiently clear context to enable their subordinates to do so. This further explains why manager roles need to be established precisely one level of complexity greater than their subordinate roles.

Different People Think Differently

The science—and it is a science—underlying different patterns of thinking and decision-making has evolved over the past 60 years, culminating in a definitive study during the 1980s. Dr. Elliott Jaques, working with the U.S. Army Social Research Institute, conducted a carefully designed and controlled study correlating the assessments by managers of their employees "current potential" with the actual way those employees structured their arguments when expressing a point of view.[1]

There was nearly a one-to-one correlation between how their potential had been assessed and the type of logical connectors they revealed in transcripts of their interviews.

During the 1980s, Dr. Jaques went on to demonstrate in adults repeating patterns of four types of mental processes within each of three different levels of information complexity. Most adults use everyday symbolic language in conversation. Fewer adults demonstrate abstract-conceptual reasoning abilities. And the few adult geniuses reveal the ability to imagine and create entirely new bodies of knowledge.

Individuals who think with adult symbolic language and with adult abstract-conceptual abilities inhabit the world of work. Within each level of information complexity, there is an additional hierarchy of more and more complex patterns of reasoning. The types of judgments required at each higher pattern reveal one greater "complexity link" than the level below.

Discrete Patterns of Thinking Required by Each Level of Complexity

A more comprehensive description of the types of thinking required at each level in order to make these kinds of decisions is summarized below.

Levels 1 through 4 require normal adult symbolic thinking. A pencil is a writing instrument for capturing one's thoughts on paper.

- Level 1 work requires applying learned procedures to standard operating conditions, identifying discrepancies, and applying troubleshooting steps to resolve them. The decisions are essentially binary (defined by procedures) and usually oriented toward maintaining control.

    The logic used when presenting a point of view: "Look at this *or* that *or* this other thing . . . "

- Level 2 work requires collecting and analyzing data, diagnosing root causes, and initiating actions based on the hypotheses. The decisions require accumulating and analyzing data in order for employees to be able to "connect the dots" on their own.

    The logic used when presenting a point of view: "If you look at this *and* that *and* this other thing, *then* you should conclude XYZ."

Type of Work Required at Each Level of Complexity

Different types of decisions are required for each naturally occurring, discrete level of complexity.

- Level 3 work requires generating multiple potential pathways for achieving complex tactical outputs over time, adjusting, as necessary, in order to achieve the optimal trade-offs among such issues as risk, cost, and sustainability. The type of thinking required is essentially serial or algorithmic, creating decision-tree logic and contingency plans.

    The logic used when presenting a point of view: "*If* this happens, *then* X or Y might occur, and *if* X occurs *then* D may happen, but *if* Y occurs *then* E may happen . . ."

- Level 4 work requires generating future-state hypothetical scenarios, identifying new capabilities that may be required several years hence, as well as integrating and orchestrating multiple tactical streams already underway over the next two years. The decisions require critical path analysis and creating and optimizing causal loops. This type of thinking requires assessing and integrating multiple options in parallel.

    The logic used when presenting a point of view: "If you look at this logical thread-X *and* this other thread-Y *and* this third thread-Z, *then* you can understand why combining elements from X and Y will have the greatest chance of succeeding . . ."

Levels 5 through 8 require abstract conceptual thinking. A pencil is one of several means for communicating ideas to many people.

- Level 5 work requires integrating multiple complex streams of information, both internal and external, in order to create new models of operation over a five-to-10-year period. The thinking required is the first level of truly abstract conceptual reasoning.

    The logic used when presenting a point of view: "We could consider this model *or* that model *or* this other model . . ."

- Level 6 work should no longer be involved in conducting business, but rather should focus on growing asset value by aligning and reconfiguring business entities in relation to a 10- to 20-year strategy. The thinking required is abstract conceptual but also involves creating different configurations of models and entities in relation to alternate envisioned future states. Like Level 2 work, it also involves "connecting the dots," but at an abstract conceptual level.

The logic used when presenting a point of view: "If you look at model X *and* model Y *and* this other model Z, *then* when you compare the underlying patterns present in all three, you can begin to see what principles are really critical."

- Level 7 work is similar to that of Level 3 in that it requires algorithmic reasoning, but at an abstract conceptual level, anticipating and preparing for future states beyond 20 years.

   The logic used when presenting a point of view: "*If* we build our strategy over the next decade on this model, *then* based on our success and the evolution of the industry we could expand that model in one of these three ways *or* we may need to replace our model with a different set of assumptions . . ."

- Level 8 work is similar to that of Level 4 in that it requires critical path analysis and creating and optimizing causal loops of asset and ecosystem models, but at an abstract conceptual level with a multiple-generation time horizon.

   The logic used when presenting a point of view: "*If* you look at our existing models for industries X, Y, *and* Z *and* the trends for each of them, *then* we need to develop a different long-term strategy for allocating our assets, which *may mean* venturing into industries A and B *while* we fortify our investments in industry Z."

Profound Implications of These Discoveries

This represents one of the truly amazing symmetries of nature: complex human managerial work organizations—where work is accomplished in part by delegating pieces of managers' plans to subordinate employees—will always naturally stratify into layers. The person at the top of the organization (e.g., CEO, four-star general, president, etc.) should possess the greatest capacity for managing complexity in order to set the overall strategic objectives and course of action for the entity. That role requires subordinate executives functioning with complexity-capacities one level down to whom she can delegate smaller components of enterprise-wide plans. This pattern must then cascade down throughout the entire organization, with each subordinate layer requiring complexity-capacities one level below its manager layer.

When designing an organization's levels and structure, top management needs to be able to translate the required mental complexities into the corresponding role complexity levels. This enables a straightforward engineering approach to ensure each layer adds the optimal value to the layers above and below.

The profound value of this knowledge is that employees who demonstrate the specific types of judgments and thought processes required by roles at every level of complexity can now be reliably identified.

This represents a quantum leap forward in selection processes, ensuring optimal fit of person to role. As I discuss later in this chapter, it also significantly enhances the accuracy and strategic power of an organization's succession-planning processes.

This is why I stated that there is a third fundamental property of all managerial systems. They are also judgment hierarchies.

The Search for Core Capabilities

The next challenge is to ensure that the selection of employees into roles yields the greatest chance for success. Having the requisite cognitive "thinking and problem-solving capacity" is obviously the first criterion for identifying a pool of potential candidates for any particular role. While this is a necessary criterion for success, it is not in and of itself sufficient. What other types of capabilities must also be present and robust enough to warrant selecting an individual for a role?

What part does experience or training play in ensuring optimal fit of person to role? How important is an employee's degree of commitment to do the types and nature of work in a particular role? How much is dependent on an employee's ambition to be promoted to the next level up? What aspects of an employee's personality predict for success in certain roles?

To answer these questions, it is useful to step back and ask a more general question: What are the minimum necessary capabilities for an employee to be successful in any particular role?

I have asked this question of over 20,000 managers during training sessions and leadership seminars over the past 30 years. Below are samples of answers I routinely receive and the way I have chosen to group them.

Category #1: Strategic thinking, agile thinking, comfort with ambiguity, creative, visionary, ability to learn quickly, innate or raw capability, highly adaptable, quick study, analytic.

Category #2: Experience, expertise, highly knowledgeable and skilled in interpersonal, teambuilding, technical, physical, communication, sales, and other techniques.

Category #3: Adaptability, flexibility, resiliency, empathy, innate aptitudes or talents in spotting trends, thinking in three dimensions, discerning subtle nuances in many areas (e.g., patterns, shapes, colors, musical
tones, etc.).

Category #4: Ambitious, strong work ethic, motivated, self-starter, dedicated, positive attitude, collaborative, friendly, open-minded, curious,
values leadership, teamworking, accountability, etc.

Category #5: Honest, trustworthy, respectful, fair-minded, unselfish, cou-
rageous, risk tolerant, independent, self-aware, balanced.

Category #6: Social acumen, ability to prioritize, team builder, transfor-
mative, life learner, effective collaborator, communicator, leader, influ-
encer, etc.

When I then ask managers to infer the core capabilities underlying each of
these broad categories, I always get the following kinds of answers:

Category #1: Raw intelligence seems to be the common factor in these
descriptors.

Category #2: Skilled knowledge is acquired by training or years of
experience.

Category #3: Innate talents and perspective are at the root of these seemingly instinctual characteristics.

Category #4: Motivation and nature of work valued seem to underpin the
level of commitment shown.

Category #5: A person's character and values are the common themes
here.

Equally consistent are people's conclusions that the descriptors in Category
#6 (social acumen, etc.) are not in themselves core capabilities. Instead, they
represent various combinations and permutations of several core capabilities
found in Categories #1 through #5. For example, good teamworking requires
a combination of skilled knowledge, empathy, valuing collaboration, mature
interactions, as well as the appropriate level of raw intelligence to be able to
contribute meaningfully.

It is extremely useful and certainly no surprise that these core capabilities
line up with the core characteristics that can be used to define multiple properties of a work role.

ALIGNING PERSON TO ROLE

Populating Roles with Capable, Motivated Talent with the:

- **Potential** to Handle the Complexity of Work of the Role
- **Skilled Knowledge** to Master the Types of Work of the Role
- **Commitment to** and **Valuing of** the Nature of Work of the Role
- **Natural Aptitudes** for the Types and Nature of Work of the Role
- **Maturity** to Effectively Manage the Role's Working Relationships

Achieving optimal fit of person to role requires precisely matching role requirements with the corresponding human capabilities.

A Concise Model of Core Capabilities

One of the remarkable findings by Dr. Jaques shortly after he discovered how to measure degrees of role complexity and then identified distinct levels of role complexity was that managers were remarkably accurate in "judging" their employees' current innate mental capacity (i.e., potential) to handle work complexity.

As we will see, good leaders can learn to accurately judge both employee effectiveness and potential in a process that helps to eliminate personal bias. An employee's effectiveness in a role is a function of five criteria: the individual's current potential, knowledge and skills, commitment to and valuing of the job, aptitudes, and maturity.

Current Potential (Innate "Brain Power")

I have already described the levels of complexity of work required for different roles, which obviously must be matched by employees who possess the innate intelligence to work at those levels. A way of framing the question about an employee's innate problem-solving capability is by asking the following question: Does this person have the raw potential today to work in some role at this level or even a level higher or only at a level lower?

This, however, is a hypothetical question. To answer this question, a manager needs to imagine that the individual would also have acquired all of the skilled knowledge required of a different role, was highly motivated and committed, had any unique talents that might also be required, and possessed sufficient maturity to handle the stresses and strains that occur at different levels. Practically speaking, if the employee is not enthusiastically committed to applying his potential and skilled knowledge to solve the problems necessary to create value and deliver on assignment, it does not matter how bright he is. Nevertheless, it is possible to imagine what level of challenge an individual— who does not currently engage his considerable brainpower—could master if he were highly motivated.

In this sense, potential refers to the value one is capable of demonstrating, i.e., what she could do if she were fully developed and under ideal circumstances. Effectiveness refers to the degree of value one is actually demonstrating in his role, i.e., what he is currently doing or what value he is currently contributing relative to the range of value expected of his role.

In this narrow sense, potential reflects only one's innate abilities, while effectiveness is one's applied potential. Effectiveness is a byproduct of not only her current potential, but also the individual's level of maturity, degree of commitment to getting the job done, unique relevant aptitudes, and level of acquired skilled knowledge required for that specific role.

Current potential is what we need to identify for making selection decisions today. Effectiveness is what we should pay for today.

Future Potential (Predictable Maturation of Potential)

Another remarkable finding by Dr. Jaques emerged from his returning regularly to the companies he researched over a 40-year period and having their managers reassess the current potential of the same employees every five to 10 years. As he mapped the progression of each employee's ratings, he realized that their level of innate potential matured (i.e., increased) at predictable rates just as a pediatric growth chart curve predicts the rate of growth of an infant's height, weight, and head circumference. The difference was that infants

Assessing Current and Future Potential

Applying the science behind the maturation of potential, managers can accurately assess how much "headroom" (capacity greater than current role complexity) employees have today and how much career "runway" (likely maturation of raw potential) to plan for in the future.

achieve their full adult height in 15 to 20 years, but adults do not achieve their maximum cognitive potential until well after 60 years of age.

As I will discuss in Chapter 10, this finding enables companies to map their employees' "pipelines of potential," which becomes the basis for the most accurate and proactive succession-planning process found anywhere.

Future potential is what we need to forecast in order to enable appropriate career planning and mentoring and to develop comprehensive succession plans that ensure having the talent necessary to meet the company's near-, mid-, and long-term strategies.

Skilled Knowledge and Experience

Consider the difference between how an experienced mechanic might go about adjusting the flow rate of a pump by a specified amount and how a recent mechanical engineering graduate would approach the same task. The mechanic, having made similar adjustments hundreds of times over the decades, will draw upon the lessons learned from previous trial-and-error experiments. The mechanic will first attempt two or three proven solutions that seem closest to the current circumstances and then adjust them incrementally to get the desired result. The mechanical engineer, on the other hand, will obtain measurements of the diameter of the hole in the pipe and height of the surface of the fluid above the hole, calculate the cross-sectional area of the hole, use the Bernoulli equation formula to find the fluid velocity, and then adjust the pressure and temperature to achieve the desired result.

The mechanic, using trial-and-error approaches developed over a long period, will acquire a wide range of potential solutions to a wide range of circumstances and then refine those that seem to best apply to a new circumstance, also using trial and error.

The engineer, armed with engineering principles, knowledge, and tools, will gather the data required for calculations, use formulas that have been scientifically verified over many decades, and calculate a novel solution, tailored precisely to a particular circumstance.

Knowledge, of course, can be acquired from both training and experience. Repeated application of that knowledge leads to skilled knowledge: the ability to apply knowledge without having to give it much conscious thought. The mechanic and engineer both have acquired skilled knowledge. However, they have achieved it in markedly disparate ways and must apply their knowledge in different ways, as well.

Skilled knowledge of any kind is a means for leveraging one's potential or innate problem-solving ability. All knowledge originally was created when people used their innate problem-solving abilities (i.e., mental capability) to get something done. Once an unknown method for getting something done becomes known, the new knowledge is added to existing knowledge and can then be applied to similar tasks without having to repeat the original discovery process.

Knowledge is captured or encapsulated problem solving from the past. It becomes a shortcut for how to do some known things. Knowledge frees up someone's problem-solving ability to skip that step and apply it to something new that must be figured out for the first time.

So, what aspects of a role require skilled knowledge?

Every role in an organization is accountable for a set of functions. Functions are broad categories of accountabilities and may consist of many sub-functions, most of which have further sub-sub-functions. I will explore a variety of architectural models for aligning and structuring functions in relation to strategy in

Chapter 7. Every function carries with it sets of tasks that require wide ranges of skilled knowledge.

Sales is an example of a high-level mainstream business function that is often described as having four primary sub-functions:

1. Setting goals for a sales force;

2. Planning, budgeting, and organizing a program to achieve those goals;

3. Implementing the program; and

4. Controlling and evaluating the results.

However, these can be further broken down into long lists of sub-sub-functions and eventually procedures, each of which require a baseline level of skilled knowledge that can be taught and improved upon subsequently with experience. Many of these more granular accountabilities are subsumed in the higher-level processes "owned" by more-senior managers but will also show up as the primary accountabilities for roles further down the hierarchy. For example,

- Develop sales plan and strategies for developing business.

- Provide detailed and accurate sales forecasting and track the same.

- Compile information and data related to customer and prospect interactions.

- Monitor customer, market, and competitor activity and provide feedback to company.

- Achieve desired market share in defined areas.

- Keep team members highly motivated and support them to accomplish desired results.

- Work closely with marketing functions to establish channel and partner program.

- Look after national sales set for products in terms of all aspects, including achieving sales through distribution network.

- Establish strong customer base, creating and managing list of prospects across various target client segments. Create awareness and branding of services.

- Manage key customer relations and participate in closing strategic opportunities.

- Contact client prospects across target client segments/markets and systematically follow up with each prospect.

- Grow and manage the sales teams, operations, and resources to deliver profitable growth.

- Control receivable management.

- Proactively support each of the team members to achieve their target.

- Define and oversee incentive programs that motivate the sales team to achieve their sales.

- Define and coordinate sales training programs that enable staff to achieve their potential growth.

- Manage, motivate, and direct the team in achieving their targets.

- Achieve sales target in terms of value and units.

- Exceed customer expectations and contribute to a high level of customer satisfaction.

- Develop a strong key opinion leaders' base.

- Build relationships with customers and develop business in a district/territory/region as per company policy and goals.

- Develop new territories and establish new dealer network.

- Develop and implement sales strategies and objectives.

- Through effective leadership, inspiration, and L.E.A.D., develop sales team to achieve/exceed sales targets, due to in-depth knowledge of customer needs and sharpen competitive knowledge and market trends.

- Work with all levels of customer management, developing long relationships; increase customer self-satisfaction and build loyalty and confidence.

- Hire and develop sales staff; have excellent people management, communication, and analytical skills.

- Work with operations and other teams for developing new service offerings.

- Put in place infrastructure and systems to support the success of sales function to increase market share at sectors level.

- Develop ethical work culture, process, and desire to achieve success among team members.

- Travel for in-person meetings with customers.

The amount of detailed knowledge required for any role depends in part on the level of complexity of the role. Machine operators in Level 1 roles need precise skilled knowledge of all aspects of their machine and immediate manufacturing environment. They need to be quite skilled in all quality, safety, and environmental policies and practices. They need to know enough about how their work directly affects, and is affected by, other roles in the same process stream. They also need to know who is accountable for what in relationship to whom.

Their immediate Level 2 first-line managers need to possess all of the same detailed knowledge (but do not need to be as skilled in each), because they are accountable for ensuring their subordinates apply that knowledge effectively. However, the supervisors need additional managerial leadership knowledge, knowledge about driving quality initiatives, tracking metrics, and the impact of their areas on other functions beyond manufacturing.

There is even less need for Level 1 types of detailed knowledge for Level 3 production managers, but they need to be able to assess how knowledgeable their Level 2 supervisors are in overseeing the work on the shop floor. The production managers need quite a bit more knowledge than their first-line managers do about leadership, the overall manufacturing, supply chain, product development, technical customer support processes, cost and trend analysis, and process improvement processes.

The general principle here is that granular, detailed procedural skills are required at Level 1. Whereas, detailed knowledge about those procedures (vs. skills) is critical at Level 2, in part, because first-line managers are accountable for continually improving those procedures. The first-line managers need to be skilled in running the processes (consisting of multiple procedures), which exist at their level. However, it is their Level 3 production managers who must have deeper knowledge about the interconnectivity of those processes, because they are accountable for continuous process improvement. The Level 3 production managers need to be knowledgeable about the end-to-end value streams, which include their units, in order to improve their section of the value stream relative to the other Level 3 units lateral to them.

The higher a role is in the hierarchy, the more its incumbents need to know about the other functions and processes (inside and outside the organization) and the less they need to know about the detailed skilled knowledge required in levels below them.

These include the business's go-to-market model; their suppliers; their customers; the industry's technologies and competitors; and financial, human resource, safety, and quality systems and policies. The detailed knowledge required by roles at Levels 1 and 2 becomes less and less important the more complex the roles are.

As one would expect, every role also has accountabilities for a group of processes or process steps. Some of these represent direct accountabilities for making and implementing specific decisions. Others represent indirect accountabilities for affecting the decisions of others. In Chapter 8, I will present a model for clarifying in every process which roles are singly accountable for making what decisions and which other roles have specific indirect authorities and accountabilities to affect those decisions.

Innate Talents and Aptitudes

The capabilities that I call *aptitudes* refer to a person's natural talents or inclinations for performing selected types of work without having first acquired skills through learning or practicing. Some roles benefit from employees possessing unique talents that might give one person a distinct advantage over another. If you want to be an architect and you have no innate sense of spatial design, then it does not matter how smart you are; it is probably not going to work. If you want to become a psychologist and lack a basic capacity for empathy, it also is probably not going to work.

Many of these talents can be learned. With sufficient practice, one can overcome a relative lack of innate aptitude. However, there are roles that clearly benefit incrementally from a more nuanced and natural command of these senses and actions.

Furthermore, I find it useful to differentiate these types of *innate aptitudes* from a person's *innate cognitive potential* to unravel complexity—similar to the difference between a computer's CPU and GPU. The CPU delivers generic processing speed, whereas a GPU is coded to facilitate specific applications. I believe both of these are fundamentally different aspects of the brain's "wiring."

It is also difficult at times to differentiate aptitudes from one's innate personality characteristics, such as integrity, respect, and fairness. Talents and natural inclinations like empathy and resilience may enhance these positive personality traits, just as one's innate abilities to learn foreign languages or to apply a perfect musical pitch may facilitate the ease and speed of acquiring more enhanced skills.

Finding it relatively easy to learn specific skills will often increase the degree to which one values those capabilities and will result in greater commitment to apply them in role. We know that becoming expert in certain professions is achieved not only by acquiring deep skilled knowledge, but also by possessing innate traits. These include fine motor skills (diamond cutter), spatial visualization (neurosurgeon), and hyperosmia or heightened sense of smell (perfumers). Outcomes research among neurosurgeons shows that the most successful surgeons are not the most "intelligent," but the ones who have an extraordinary ability to visualize and rotate objects in three dimensions in their "mind's eye." This multiplier aptitude enables them to surgically approach brain lesions from directions that will cause the least residual damage.

When making selection decisions, aptitudes and talents are rarely the final make-or-break criteria. Nevertheless, one should always be cognizant of roles that require an unusually high degree of nuanced perceptions and actions and consider assessing candidates' innate aptitudes for them.

Commitment and Valuing the Nature of Work

There currently exists a billion-dollar assessment industry consisting of personality testing purporting to predict which personality types are best suited for particular types of roles in work organizations. These tests are often required before even being interviewed as a candidate. Sadly, every serious scientific review of the published personality assessment profiles has failed to demonstrate any statistical significance for these profiles in predicting success in a specific type of role. Even more troublesome is that many of them are based on stereotypes that have been perpetuated for generations without serious examination and only reinforce them.

For example, a common perception is that to be an effective salesperson one must be an outgoing extravert who loves talking with people and gaining their friendship. However, if you examine the list of sales sub-functions itemized in the earlier section on skilled knowledge, you will see many of the function's accountabilities have little to do with this personality stereotype.

What is important in determining whether employees will be highly committed, however, is the degree to which they value the nature of work of their roles. Employees with many different personality profiles may value very different aspects of the sales role and be equally committed to their roles, but for different reasons.

How can we assess an employee's level of commitment and dedication to be successful in his current role? Commitment to and valuing the work of a role is often revealed in the employee's level of enthusiasm and the amount of effort that she willingly puts into the work of her role to add the greatest amount of value possible. When people are given work for which they are qualified and that they value highly, they experience "being in flow" or in a mental state where they are fully immersed in a feeling of energized focus, full involvement, and enjoyment in the process of the activity.

Is the person genuinely interested in the role itself? Does he really value the nature of work of the role? Some people love being managers and others do not. Some people love detailed work and others are drawn toward being "big picture" generalists. Some people have acquired a strong work ethic and are self-starters irrespective of the nature of work of a role.

The following attributes of different roles can be useful in understanding the specific aspects of work that candidates might be seeking in a role. They also provide clues to understanding why some employees excel in certain aspects of their roles, while ignoring other aspects.

- Role relationships: managerial, individual contributor, teamworking, project management
- Types of work: analytical, executing and implementing, servicing, resourcing, controlling
- Types of process accountabilities: direct decisions, indirect influencing, stewardship
- Primary focus: internal, external, supplier, customer, market, regulatory, technical, relationship

The better a manager understands the nature of work of a vacant role, the more confidently she can interview candidates about past roles they valued more strongly than others. The manager can also decide how closely the nature of work of the vacant role is aligned with what a candidate valued in previous roles. Similarly, when providing feedback to one's subordinate employees who may not be applying themselves fully in certain aspects of their roles, it is often useful to engage them in discussions about the nature of work they do and do not value.

Maturity, Balance, and the Ability to Self-Regulate

As I discussed in the previous section, what is important in determining whether employees will be highly committed is the degree to which they value the nature of work of their roles, not whether their particular personality profile conforms to some old assumptions.

An important aspect of employees' character or personality, which can have a profound effect on their effectiveness, is the degree to which they can "self-regulate" and respond to stressors in an appropriate and constructive manner.

From time to time, in often memorable and sometimes uncomfortable incidents, we have all experienced otherwise-qualified employees demonstrating extremes of behavior that detract from and undermine the value they would otherwise contribute to the organization.

Maturity, or the absence of disruptive extremes of behaviors (X-factor) that interfere with performance, is the final criterion here. Does the employee have negative behavioral traits that, with or without significant pressures, detract from her overall effectiveness? Put another way, does the person have the maturity and balance to "self-regulate" under conditions of stress and ambiguity? Is the employee well grounded and will she work well with others under difficult circumstances? An important negative predictor of effectiveness is the presence of disruptive extremes of behaviors.

In well-run and well-led organizations, there will be both oral and written records of employees who exhibit such disruptive behaviors. A significant portion of managerial coaching (which we will discuss in Chapter 10) should focus on how adaptive and appropriate one's subordinates' behaviors are in general and particularly in stressful situations. In mentoring and career planning conversations, it should be made clear to employees that disruptive behaviors may represent a barrier to promotion and, if extreme enough, may result in termination for cause.

The problem with assessing an external candidate's ability to "self-regulate" is that it is easy to mask episodic—even chronic—disruptive behaviors during interviews. Previous employers and references are reluctant to communicate a history of these behaviors. This should be far less a problem for internal candidates if their previous effectiveness appraisals have been done accurately and are well documented.

I characterize this capability as the absence of disruptive behaviors, because ironically, I find it difficult to describe what greater maturity looks like. This is different from what we find in employees who demonstrate greater potential than required for their roles, deeper skilled knowledge, uniquely valuable talents, and exceptional commitment. In these instances, more usually generates greater effectiveness.

In the late 1990s, we helped a multinational company reorganize and separate out a quarter of its 280,000 employees in order to create a new company with 80,000 employees. After four solid months of gathering data and high-level analysis, every day for the next six weeks we met with the CEO and his executive team and walked through the options and logic for designing the new organization. In parallel, we facilitated their assessment of effectiveness and potential of the top 1,500 managers in the new company.

Once the high-level structure, including the top 400 roles, was finalized, we conducted a two-day NFL-style draft-selection process with the top 10 executives and each of their HR heads. There were 24 Level-5 business roles we had to fill and six advanced engineering roles we had to fill, all at Level 5. They had 40 managers who had Level 5 capability or greater and three quarters of them had significant disruptive behaviors (X-factor). The CEO of the new company

DISRUPTIVE BEHAVIORS: "PULLING THE ROLE DOWN"

EXTREMES OF BEHAVIOR that undermine one's effectiveness in role and/or the effectiveness of one's ability to interact "appropriately" with others: clients, suppliers, peers, managers, and/or reports.

| TOO EXTREME | BALANCED BEHAVIORS | TOO EXTREME |

Underlying EXTREME personal characteristics that may result in disruptive behaviors.

TOO EXTREME	BALANCED BEHAVIORS	TOO EXTREME
Too Flexible	Mature responses to a variety of challenging conditions	Too Rigid
Too Passive		Too Aggressive
Too Risk Averse	Ability to "self-regulate" one's reactions under stress	Too Reckless
Too Insecure		Too Confident
Too Negative	Reasonable and reasoning responses to pressure	Too Positive
Too Conflict Averse		Too Hostile
Too Self-Effacing	Ability to maintain perspective under difficult circumstances	Too Boastful
Too Agreeable		Too Argumentative
Too Deceptive	**WORKS WELL WITH OTHERS**	Too Candid
Too Cautious		Too Impulsive

Otherwise qualified employees may pull their roles down by exhibiting extreme behaviors, which detract from their contributions.

who had joined the company about five years earlier turned toward his team who were all long-term veterans and asked, "How did we allow our most valuable resources to get through 20-to-25-year careers and be so dysfunctional?" And they responded in unison, "You had to be dysfunctional to get anything done in this heavily matrixed organization."

The CEO responded that a major focus for the new company would be to implement a transparent accountability culture in which disruptive behavior would no longer be tolerated.

The Foundation for Development: Understanding and Assessing Capabilities

Rarely does any individual function at his full potential effectiveness, except perhaps certain professional or Olympian athletes.

There is nearly always latent potential for an individual to enhance her effectiveness in role.

An individual realizes and delivers more of his full potential by:

- Acquiring and applying more skilled knowledge;
- Applying oneself more diligently, consistently, and with greater focus and attention;
- Utilizing one's innate talents; and
- Learning how to better self-regulate one's behaviors in response to internal or external stressors.

This is where coaching, mentoring, and other forms of development are critical for the employee, the manager, and ultimately, the company.

An organization is only able to realize and deliver on its full potential value when it organizes and develops employees in such a way that they can all deliver on their full potential value.

In Chapter 10, I present a systematic approach to talent assessment and development that walks managers through the process of assessing their subordinates' potential (current and future) and demonstrated effectiveness in role. This will lead managers logically through an analysis of employees' strengths and effectiveness gaps. The chapter also lays out systematic coaching plans that address skilled knowledge, commitment gaps, and disruptive behaviors.

CHAPTER 5

Principles of Organization Design: How the Multipliers Are Integrated

WHEN EXPLAINING HOW complex organizations operate, it is always a challenge to decide where to begin a systematic and sequential analysis of each of their components. As we continue to explore the productivity multipliers themselves, we first need to identify a logical starting point.

Should it be strategy, structure, processes, systems, or people? Should it be leadership or accountability? Or should it really begin with "the work"?

I find it useful when developing strategy to start with one's existing capabilities. "Given the kinds of things we know how to do, what and where are there markets that would benefit from purchasing our associated products and services?" *Processes* are the articulation of what we know how to do. Processes consist of work steps that—implemented properly—will produce outputs. Processes are how we document "the work" of an organization.

Processes define the steps that need to be completed, each of which requires a decision, either in real time by an actual person or programmed in advance by people and then automated. Structure is how we create roles into which we hire people to make those decisions. People in roles need to have authority to make those decisions, so structure is the means by which authority is delegated from managerial roles to subordinate roles. Since managers are accountable for the work conducted in their units, they must hold each of their subordinates accountable for their work: their effectiveness, outputs, and adherence to process.

Here is a useful analogy. Think about the human musculoskeletal system. Over the past million years, human anatomy has evolved to yield a skeletal structure to which muscles can be attached in such a way as to create the optimal leverage for walking and running rapidly in an upright position. In contrast, the corresponding anatomy of great apes is different to accommodate a different set of functional requirements. For apes, climbing is much more important than running.

The purpose of physiology (e.g., contracting muscles) is to support good functioning (e.g., running fast). However, without good, aligned structures—a sturdy, upright skeleton—to support the physiology, you will not get good functioning.

Design Organizations around the Work

Designing work organizations is not that different. Business leaders need to start by creating processes and structures which—together—optimally and accountably support the work (i.e., the physiology) necessary to achieve maximum productivity.

- The goal of process design is to achieve the optimal balance between capability (reliably and repeatedly getting the desired outputs) and efficiency (at the lowest cost and in the shortest time);

- The goal of structural design is to ensure that roles with direct accountability for making process decisions and roles with indirect accountability for optimizing and controlling processes have the requisite authorities and can be readily held accountable for their work; and

- The ultimate design must then reconcile the trade-offs between efficiency (fewest number of roles required to do the work) and accountability (the most seamless and unambiguous structures for accountably integrating and optimizing the overall work) while maintaining the requisite process capability.

In Chapter 1, I discussed the root causes of the management-fad pendulum. I described the importance of reconciling an organization's need for employees to exercise creative initiative while simultaneously maintaining process control.

These structures and processes are then embedded in an enterprise-wide management operating system. The purpose of this system is to define and ensure the effective implementation of the rules of engagement across all roles and role relationships (e.g., manager-subordinate, manager-once-removed-subordinate, project leader-members, teammates, cross-functional peers, etc.). It is also to clarify the limits within which people in roles can take initiative when not explicitly specified.

We need to apply the tenets of organizational science to design strategically aligned optimal processes, structures, and management operating systems that—if properly implemented by employees—will achieve process control. These designs enable process control. However, to achieve it, each employee in every role still must be held accountable by her manager for keeping her word, no surprises!

Keep in mind that the designs permit—but do not ensure—process control.

Creativity and control are not only compatible; they are essential to leveraging the full potential of a company. Aligning them properly is the key to maximum productivity.

Four Multipliers Required for Strategic Organizational Engineering

Just as there are many ways to design a building to meet different customer requirements, every blueprint must nevertheless adhere to proven engineering and material science principles, along with regulatory requirements.

I have found that there are properties of organizational engineering that need to be systematically applied to diagnosing an organization's current state but also to designing the optimal strategically aligned organization going forward. I call these four multipliers the multipliers of organizational engineering.

1. **Levels of role complexity**. The total number of requisite value-adding managerial levels in every organization is defined by the complexity of the top executive's long-term strategy. It then requires establishing subordinate roles precisely one level below each manager's role. This way, employees can add optimal value at every level and increase overall productivity.

   Too many levels create bureaucratic delays due to confusion about who has the "real authority" to make decisions. Too few levels create "disconnects" because managers have extremely large spans of control and are too busy and too far removed from their subordinates to add value and hold them accountable.

2. **Functions and functional alignment.** A business unit must establish and organize roles in such a way as to ensure clear accountability for each of the functions required for "doing business." There are optimal architectural principles for establishing functional roles at the right levels to support business heads to have the authority to be held accountable for the overall success of a business in a defined market. An organization's structure must always reflect and accountably support its strategic intentions.

   It is useful to differentiate between mainstream business functions, resourcing and control functions, and ancillary services.

3. **Cross-functional processes.** Once processes have been engineered for optimal capability and efficiency, they need to be "structured" in such a way that accountabilities for an entire process, each of its sub-processes, and each work step are unambiguous and aligned with the requisite authorities. The cross-functional accountabilities and authorities for each role must be established by the manager accountable for the entire process (i.e., the crossover-point manager one, two, or even three levels up).

4. **System stewardship.** Every manager is accountable for the optimal and proper use of every resource under his control. Higher-level managerial roles—that are accountable for entire processes—may need subordinate "system stewardship" roles to assist in continuously improving their units' policies and processes, supporting their effective implementation, and influencing or preventing actions that may threaten to undermine those processes.

   System stewardship is a critical concept for maintaining the integrity of company-wide systems, without blurring accountabilities and without resorting to dotted-line managerial relationships.

These four productivity multipliers *(levels, functions, cross-functional processes, and system stewardship) each need to be applied independently in order to interpret strategy into organizational requirements. Then they need to be carefully integrated with each other to create the optimal balance between capability, efficiency, and accountability.*

Keep in mind that there is no perfect design for any one organization. Companies will vary as to how they use, coordinate, and integrate the various multipliers. That said, an organization and its leaders must endeavor to model options that represent the best trade-offs for each multiplier. In doing so, they will create an accountable work system that will deliver most fully on its enterprise value.

Digging deeper, I now want to illustrate the critical importance of integrating these productivity multipliers.

- *Organizational multipliers* consist of capable, efficient, and accountable cross-functional processes that connect fully authorized business, resourcing, and control functions at the appropriate levels of complexity for an organization's strategically defined market, operating within management accountability systems.

- *Managerial leadership and integration multipliers* require:

  - Setting context by managers at every level, including decision-making frameworks;

  - Delegating unambiguous assignments (QQT/Rs);

  - Clarifying which roles are accountable for what in relation to which other roles; and

  - Holding people accountable for both their own outputs and collaborating laterally to support their common context.

It is not enough for a business-unit head to hire qualified heads of marketing, development, provisioning, and sales and then delegate to each of them separate accountabilities and authorities to pursue independently.

Extracting the maximum value from a marketplace requires the dynamic interaction among these functions in relation to the changing conditions and requirements of marketplace forces.

Organizational Multipliers

It is the integration of the tactical business functions at Level 3 (in the one-to two-year horizon) that is central to delivering annual results and queuing up results for the following year. Since the forward-looking heads of these functions need to operate at Level 4 (in the two- to five-year horizon), their common manager, the business-unit-head role, needs to operate at Level 5 (in the five- to 10-year horizon).

As the illustrations below indicate, effective organizational design of business-unit functions requires reconciling levels, functions, and processes accountably.

ALIGNING ORGANIZATION TO STRATEGY

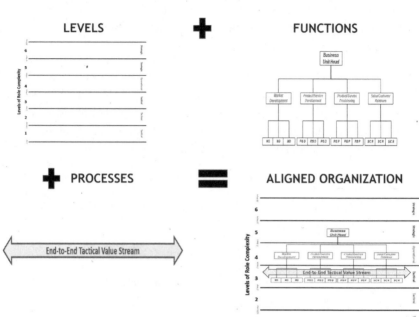

The art of organizational design requires aligning levels, functions, and processes to ensure unambiguous accountabilities aligned with authorities.

By systematically integrating these organizational design multipliers, organizational leaders can model structures and processes that optimally align with strategy and ensure unambiguous accountabilities, aligned with the requisite authorities. In the illustration above, the business-unit head has the authority to hold each of the functional units accountable for their own targets and to, simultaneously and dynamically, integrate the work of each function, as his context requires.

Managerial Leadership and Integration Multipliers

Effective managerial leadership requires three-level context setting (upward, teamworking, and cross-functional) to ensure that roles with accountabilities in common thoroughly understand the overarching critical objectives.

This enables them to ensure those common goals are central in the planning and executing of their subordinates' own assignments and drives effective collaboration among them laterally to ensure the optimal overall results.

In this way, business-unit heads (at Level 5) can ensure that their teams of subordinate mainstream business functional heads understand the overall business strategy. They can then—in concert—model and agree upon the dynamic interactions and adjustments necessary to deal with changing conditions and challenges in the marketplace.

By constructing—with their subordinate functional heads—decision-making frameworks (defined below), they can also increase the effectiveness of collaboration among the Level 3 functional tactical heads.

A decision-making framework is a set of guidelines (perspectives, principles, and priorities), established by a manager accountable for cross-functional processes.

Upward—Vertical Context

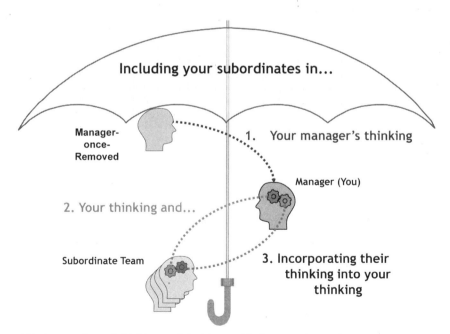

Aligning employees' thinking and decisions with the organization's intentions requires that managers communicate upward context.

Teamworking—Lateral Context

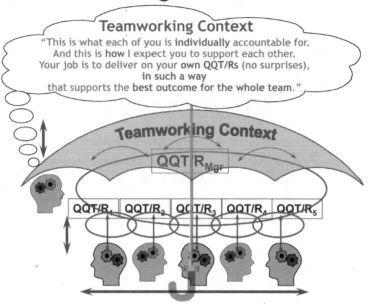

Aligning employees' thinking and lateral collaboration requires that managers communicate teamworking context.

THREE-LEVEL CASCADING CONTEXT TO ALIGN CROSS-FUNCTIONAL EMPLOYEES

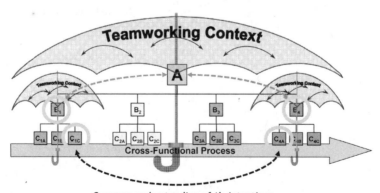

Ensuring optimal collaboration among cross-functional employees working on a common process requires cascading upward and teamworking managerial context across three levels.

The decision-making framework governs the trade-off decisions that subordinate employees (one, two, or even three levels below the manager) must make together in relation to common resources and common outputs.

All subordinate employees working within those cross-functional processes are accountable for working together to develop and reach consensus on the optimal enterprise-wide solutions that best reflect the decision-making framework criteria and still allow each subordinate to meet his own individual accountabilities.

Clear Delegation of Assignments (QQT/Rs)

Effective managerial leadership then requires clear and unambiguous assignment delegation, using the QQT/R formula and accurately assessing whether subordinate employees are both keeping their word, no surprises, and earning their keep.

1. Accountabilities must be clearly defined and understood.

2. Authorities and resources (necessary to make and implement decisions) must be sufficient to meet the accountabilities.

3. Outputs and throughputs must be accurately measured, and effectiveness in role fairly assessed.

4. Consequences must accurately reflect the degree to which accountabilities are met, i.e., positive consequences for meeting accountabilities and negative consequences for failing to meet accountabilities.

Aligning accountabilities with authorities goes beyond managers delegating ambitious, yet achievable, QQT/Rs.

Process-accountable managers are directly accountable for a cross-functional process. They require having positional authority over all of the roles that have some accountabilities for steps in the process.

Direct accountabilities for any role are the key functions and processes a role "owns" and is, therefore, fully accountable for their outputs. With a direct accountability, the role incumbent has the authority to make decisions and implement her own decisions.

I cannot overemphasize the importance of positional authority. Being directly accountable for a work step within a process requires having the positional authority to make those decisions, but always within defined limits and managerial context.

In these situations, it is the manager who holds her subordinates accountable for the outputs, for the adherence, and for working effectively within the role's requirements.

Working across Functions: More Integration Multipliers

There are countless circumstances, however, where employees with direct accountabilities may not be in a position to be informed fully about all of the relevant factors necessary to make optimal decisions. In addition, they may not be fully aware of the potential second- and third-order adverse consequences of their decisions or may not even realize some decisions are clearly outside of limits.

To address these situations, managers may need to establish other roles with *indirect* accountabilities and authorities to take the initiative to inform, persuade, or instruct other roles with direct accountabilities. Indirect accountabilities are the key actions in which a role affects the decisions of others, generally (but not always) at the same level of work. The role is not accountable for the other role's direct output. However, this role must collaborate with another role, which is accountable for the direct output. Indirect accountabilities describe non-managerial role authorities and ensure the cross-organizational effectiveness of a system or process.

Managers must be mindful of the fact that most processes have many people acting on them and making decisions that could affect their employees. Disconnects, conflicts, unintended consequences, and even outright hostility often arise because it is usually not clear as to "who is accountable for what in relationship to whom."

A framework, a language, and a methodology are required for clarifying who needs direct, decisional authority around which steps and who needs indirect, influencing-or-regulating authority in relationship to whom. And it reinforces the requirements for overarching decision-making frameworks necessary to ensure that people will construct solutions together that optimally support the total goal—not just one unit's objectives at the expense of others.

Clarifying Accountabilities and Authorities in Different Types of Teams

Managerial systems are complex, interconnected structures and processes populated by employees who are held accountable by their managers. By giving teams or team leaders the authority to make decisions that must be carried out by people in other functions, disconnects are created and productivity is derailed. As we shall see, the nature of accountability for different types of teams—specifically, manager-subordinate teams, collegial teams, improvement teams, and project teams—must be consistent with the facts of authorities in managerial hierarchies. We will elaborate on this in Chapter 6.

What Comes Next

These multipliers are extremely important. Used prudently, they ensure the dynamic balance between process control and creative initiative. Just as I investigated levels of role complexity in Chapter 3, in the next four chapters, I explore additional productivity multipliers in detail—highlighting teams, functional alignment, cross-functional working relationships, and system stewardship.

Here is a preview:

- Business units (usually at Level 5) must be aligned so that the business-unit head has sufficient authority to deliver on all of the unit's objectives. Mainstream business functions, "resourcing" functions, and control functions need to be clearly delineated and strategically aligned in relation to the markets identified by the business unit's strategy.

- Processes must be structured in such a way that they are accountable, capable, and efficient in order for managers to achieve a common goal. This means using functional alignment to limit the degree to which people have to work across functional lines in order to meet their own direct accountabilities. However, indirect lateral accountabilities (often neglected and, therefore, unclear in many companies) need to be defined when value can be added or when value can be enhanced.

- The distinction between *owning* a process (i.e., being managerially accountable) and *stewarding* it on behalf of the process owner or system owner must be clearly and universally understood. Establishing stewardship functions, with service-giving, influencing-and-regulating, and process-improvement support accountabilities, can help to avoid the quagmire of ambiguous, matrixed, straight-and-dotted-line relationships.

By adhering to these multipliers, organizational leaders will be well on their way to achieving greater productivity and greater success.

CHAPTER 6

Accountability and Types of Teams

THERE ARE PROBABLY more books and articles written about leading teams than any other aspect of leadership and management. Unfortunately, the majority of them are based on erroneous assumptions that result in undermining productivity and accountability. Simply stated, the concept of "team accountability" is a fiction in managerial systems 99 percent of the time. The one exception is a board of directors, where the directors can be held collectively accountable by the company's shareholders.

In light of that, why do so many companies try to function by holding their teams collectively accountable? Why are there bonuses for successful teams? And why are failed teams sent to the doghouse?

More importantly, have you ever been on a team, where you personally worked diligently for long hours and with tremendous enthusiasm, but because of the ineffectiveness of a few of your teammates, the team failed to achieve its goals? Consequently, your reputation, employment record, and career aspirations may have suffered. How did that feel? Did it feel fair? Or did you feel betrayed?

As I pointed out in Chapter 1, the "magic sauce" of employee engagement, commitment, and loyalty is a healthy psychological contract, i.e., a consistently and mutually earned culture of trust and fairness. When employees experience their managers' actions as evidence of their commitment to support them to be successful both in role and in career, employees will want to reciprocate and do whatever they can to help their managers and companies be successful. Yet, sometimes employees are assigned to teams where they feel they are being set up to fail. They feel that they have no authority over the working effectiveness of other team members and a sense of distrust and unfairness sets in. The psychological contract gets broken!

This reality is a principal contributor to the breakdown of the integrity of the accountability hierarchy in many managerial systems. Remember, accountability without authority is fantasy and stress.

The misguided practice of team accountability is a failing attempt to compensate when companies are not holding their managers accountable for holding each member of their subordinate teams individually accountable:

- For working effectively to achieve their own outputs, no surprises; and

- For effectively collaborating with their teammates to develop optimal solutions in common that best support the manager's teamworking context.

Manager-Subordinate Teams

Managers of manager-subordinate teams have all the authorities necessary to be held individually accountable for the effectiveness of their teams, the teams' outputs, and the teams' adherence to defined limits.

It only confuses matters to attempt to hold the entire team collectively accountable. (We will come to cross-functional team "leaders" later.)

This raises a fundamental question. What authorities do accountable managers have relative to their teams? These undisputable authorities are:

- To define the accountabilities and role requirements for each subordinate position;

- To select from candidates for a vacant position (and veto, if necessary, unqualified candidates);

- To develop plans to achieve targets that require delegation of related assignments (QQT/Rs) to multiple members of a subordinate team;

- To set context (upward, teamworking, and three-level) for each subordinate team member around the team initiatives;

- To define ambitious, yet achievable, QQT/Rs for each subordinate team member;

- To evaluate each subordinate's effectiveness in role, including her teamworking collaboration within the manager's context;

- To provide feedback, coaching, and additional development to enhance subordinate effectiveness in role;

- To call subordinate team members individually to account when they are not effective or if they fail to keep their word, no surprises; and

- To initiate removal of ineffective subordinates from role.

The accountable manager of a team has the authority to set the entire team up for success. He must also address the barriers that prevent the team from successfully executing on its objectives. If there are ineffective subordinates bringing the team down, the manager—not their teammates—has the authority and therefore is accountable for addressing the problematic team members.

With this concept in mind, I want to explore a more general issue with accountability hierarchies. Up until now, I have addressed the vertical nature of accountability. Manager "A" delegates to subordinate manager "B" a subordinate resource "C" to whom B can delegate work. However, A still holds B accountable for C's outputs, adherence, and effectiveness in role. B is not "off the hook" with A, if C fails to get the job done.

TRANSFORMING ACCOUNTABILITY FROM VERTICAL TO LATERAL DIRECTION

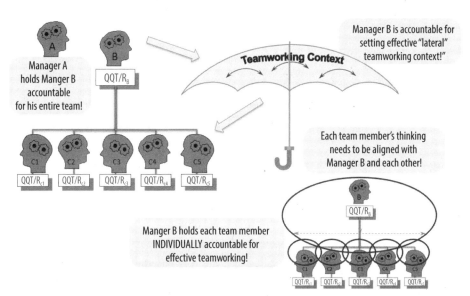

For managers to be accountable for their teams' outputs and effectiveness, they must set clear lateral context and hold each subordinate individually accountable for effective teamworking in support of that lateral context.

Manager A can also hold subordinate manager B accountable for the effectiveness with which each of his subordinates collaborate with each other and for delivering to A the overall team's outputs, no surprises! One can now think of a manager-subordinate team as a "universal joint" which converts vertical accountability (A-B-C) into lateral (i.e., teamworking B_1, B_2, B_3, B_4, B_5) accountability. I view Manager B to be the teamwork process owner because B has all of the authority necessary to "own" the team's outcome.

For this reason, cascading manager-subordinate teams are the backbone necessary to ensure the integrity of both the vertical and lateral accountability "chains." Later, I will extend the notion from a manager being teamwork process owner to a manager with two or more subordinate levels becoming a cross-functional process owner.

Just as every manager is accountable for continuously enhancing the effectiveness of his immediate team, every manager-once-removed (i.e., managers that have two levels below) is similarly accountable for continuously enhancing the effectiveness of that three-level unit.

The lack of clarity about the nature of accountability dealing with non-permanent cross-functional teams becomes even more problematic. To address that fact, I want to differentiate between two broad categories of cross-functional, time-limited team multipliers.

These are:

- Those created to support process improvement initiatives; and

- Those that are project-based and created to deliver outputs and that require employees from different teams to work in concert for periods of time.

Cross-Functional Process Improvement Teams

In many companies, the notion of a process owner is a role that has matrixed relationships with roles in different functions or silos.

For example, the senior HR executive in a company is often referred to as owning the HR system. This implies that the role has the authority to decide to make changes in HR processes. It also implies that the role has the authority to implement them even when it could require significant changes in the way managers and employees in other functions work. However, some of these changes might prevent employees from meeting the accountabilities that their managers had already assigned and committed to delivering to their own managers. This creates inevitable short circuits resulting in conflicts, delays, politics, and countless other productivity demolishers. (Chapter 9 will explain the proper accountability of these types of roles as system stewardship.)

However, the problem remains. How does a senior manager with three or more levels subordinate to her role organize a process improvement initiative to either fix or improve a workflow several levels down?

Here is a case of how sloppy thinking can get executives into trouble.

- A business unit executive within a major electric utility was tasked with making significant improvements in several areas. He was under considerable corporate pressure to streamline processes, reduce headcount, and reduce other operating and maintenance expenses.

- The executive established five "key lead teams," one each to address cost, employee development, safety, reliability, and new business development. He populated each team with members from each of his four operational units and his six other subordinate "staff" functions. He established five sponsors and five cosponsors from his 10 immediate subordinates, trying to match their functional expertise with the teams' focus. Each team was encouraged to appoint its own team leader and its own agenda. As problems or opportunities surfaced within the business unit, the appropriate key lead team was identified, and the issue was sent to the team for inspection.

- These teams were told that they were accountable for (1) studying, collecting, and analyzing data; and then for (2) designing, deciding on, and implementing changes in processes, standards, and policies. In effect, they were told that they were accountable for business-unit-wide improvements in their areas of focus.

- Most of the key lead team members (who were selected from the business unit's "high-potential" talent pool) were at the level immediately subordinate to the sponsors (i.e., subordinate to executive's immediate subordinates), though some were down an additional level.

- During an initial data-gathering phase, several issues were consistently identified by team members and leaders as interfering with their own team's effectiveness and their personal comfort. Nevertheless, there was initially a high degree of enthusiasm about being

on these teams. Key lead team members expressed hopeful antici-
pation about the positive impact their conclusions would have on
the business unit's productivity and on their own careers.

- Unfortunately, things did not turn out as expected. What happened instead was that the team leaders felt paralyzed when trying
to make decisions. In part, this occurred because members of the
teams could not reach consensus and the sponsors and cosponsors
often vetoed their decisions. Team members felt strong pressures
from their "line managers" to dig in their heels and "not give up an
inch" of their managers' authorities.

After several months, when the program of initiatives ground to an uncer-
emonious halt, my firm was called in to sort out the problem.

The diagnosis was simple: The business unit executive was the only role
that had full authority (within corporate constraints, of course) to decide on
changes in any of the business unit's processes because those changes could
conflict or interfere with other things he needed to hold each of his immediate
subordinates accountable for.

As I have pointed out several times, managerial systems consist of complex
interconnected structures and processes activated by employees who are held
accountable by their managers. The structure (i.e., accountability hierarchy)
requires that each employee have only one manager with the authority to hold
him accountable for his effectiveness, outputs, and process adherence.

By giving the entire team, its team leader, or even the sponsor the authority
to decide on and implement changes that will require implementation within
other functions, the business unit head "short-circuited" his own authority.

*A manager cannot delegate the authority to one subordinate to change a
process if it could undermine that manager's ability to hold his other subordinates accountable.*

Study-Recommendation Process Improvement Teams

Nevertheless, a "process owner A" can delegate the authority to a subordinate
manager "B_1" to study a cross-functional process and make recommendations
about improvements, which the owner must then decide upon. To support her in
this initiative, A would need to authorize B_1 to negotiate for temporary resources
from his (B-level) peers' organizations and "attach" them (C_2, C_3, C_4) to her own
subordinate C_1 who will serve as a study-recommendation team leader.

The study-recommendation team leader, C_1, would be given the authority to delegate *only* direct output support (DOS) QQT/Rs to the attached cross-functional team members (C_2, C_3, C_4). Direct output support is where the output of the assignments is designed to support the team leader C_1 in understanding the issues and formulating options.

These assignments may involve gathering and assessing data, brainstorming potential solutions with C_1 and other members of the team, taking emerging recommendations back to their line managers to "pressure test" them to identify possible second- and third-order negative consequences.

The members of the team do not vote based on the feedback they encounter and C_1 is not required to get a consensus from everyone on the team. Instead, C_1 must decide on what to recommend to B_1, who likely will further pressure test and adjust that recommendation, based on feedback he receives from B-level peers. B_1 must then decide on what to recommend to A for making the final decision.

The principle is straightforward.

Only the true process owner (i.e., the crossover-point manager who has authority over the process's structure, employees, policies, methods, limits, resources, and frameworks for subordinate decision-making) can decide on process changes that could undermine existing aspects of the accountability system.

This does not mean the process owner must personally collect and analyze data and come up with strategies for change on his own. However, it does mean that only he can decide on the changes.

Implementation-Coordination Process Improvement Teams

The next dilemma that the "process owner A" faces is how to implement a process redesign—across multiple functions—in such a way as to optimize the process implementation while minimizing the degree to which it might disrupt the "vertical" accountability by giving one subordinate authority to direct another subordinate in a different function. Once again, A cannot delegate to B_1 the authority to hold his B-level peers accountable for their implementations because that would once again short-circuit the accountability hierarchy.

A manager cannot be released from accountability for all of her subordinates by delegating authority to one subordinate over the others.

However, process owner manager A can delegate the authority to his subordinate manager B_1 to coordinate the implementation of the process improvements with each of his B-level managerial peers to achieve the gains while minimally disrupting them from running their own functions accountably. Therefore, it is manager A who must delegate directly to each of his subordinates the accountability for implementing the required changes in each of their functions and who holds them accountable for collaborating effectively with B_1 to ensure the entire cross-functional process is optimized and productive.

Once again, B_1 may decide to establish his own subordinate C_1 to serve as an implementation-coordination team leader in relation to his cross-functional colleagues, C_2, C_3, C_4. . . , who are accountable for implementing the process changes in their own units. In this instance, C_1 would not require any delegation authority (including DOS), but rather the lesser authority to be kept informed about how each unit is implementing the process changes. If C_1 concludes that, in aggregate, the implementations are not aligned or synchronized, he has the authority to convene them and attempt to persuade them to agree on a common path forward consistent with the rationale and intent of the newly designed process. If unable to get such consensus, C_1 has the authority to elevate the concern to his manager, who then must decide whether to address it with his B-level peers or further elevate it to A.

While this two-phased approach to accountably designing and implementing cross-functional process improvements may seem elaborate, it is the most efficient way to minimize the games and politics that often accompany such initiatives and to display a transparent process that employees will agree is fair.

Always align authorities with accountabilities at the appropriate levels of decision-making.

Project Teams

The other appropriate use of cross-functional teams is when there is a need for close coordination of employees in different functions when delivering outputs in common. The problem here is that, unlike the manager of manager-subordinate teams, a cross-functional team leader does not have managerial authorities over the members of the team. Therefore, in most cases, it is not possible to hold the team leader singly accountable for the team's outputs or the team's effectiveness.

When creating cross-functional project teams, it is critical to select the proper type of team and team leader authorities and accountabilities. Deciding which type to use is dependent on many variables, such as cost, time, and criticality.

Project-coordinated team leaders are useful roles for coordinating and sequencing routine and relatively short-term initiatives that have well-established processes. A scheduled two-week, plant-wide preventative maintenance pro-gram that involves engineers, tradesmen, operators, and contractors—all from different manager-subordinate teams—often requires a role with the discretion to synchronize, adjust, and troubleshoot work efforts in relation to a pre-defined Gantt chart.

Such a team-leader role has the authority to "call an audible" (i.e., rearrange the order of work at the last minute) when the work of one section is delayed because the materials were not yet available, or the work was more compli-cated than anticipated. This means the team leader can adjust sequences of work to ensure the entire initiative is completed according to plan. However, the team leader does not have the authority to change procedures or to direct team members to do work other than what they were assigned by their own accountable managers.

The project-coordinated team leader's authority is simply to be kept informed about each team member's progress and then to persuade or coordinate them to stay on track. For this reason, project-coordination team leaders can be in roles at the same level of complexity as the other members of the team.

When such a leader is unable to persuade a peer-level member on the team to adjust the timing of her work or if the problems encountered cannot be resolved by rearranging the schedule, she may need to elevate the problem to her own manager. That manager must then decide whether it is important enough to take up with his peer-level managers of the team members and push for consensus as to how to resolve the issues. Those peer-level managers are the ones accountable for the working effectiveness of their subordinates on the team. If that also fails to resolve the issues, then the manager would need to elevate the problem one level higher.

Project-managed teams often require the more common project-manager type role that is at least one level of complexity higher than that of the team members. This more authoritative role is required when the project is less rou-tine, when there are numerous trade-offs that need to be decided along the way, and with projects of longer duration (occasionally, up to a year).

Project-managed team leaders have not only coordinating authorities, but also the authority to set and reset context for the team members as boundary conditions vary.

Additionally, based on their higher-level role and capabilities, project manag-ers may exercise their implied authority to persuade team members to incremen-tally adjust their QQT/Rs and work methods—beyond their usual boundaries—to meet the challenges of keeping the entire project on time and on budget. These implied authorities derive both from their higher level in the hierarchy and from their serving as the "keepers of the context" set by the next higher-level manager who often has overall accountability and authority for the project.

Given that the project manager is at a higher level of complexity, he is more capable of anticipating the second- and third-order consequences of making small adjustments in the project plan and team members' accountabilities. This requires more discretion and confers a greater level of accountability for the effectiveness of both his judgment and his ability to persuade his team members. Moreover, if he is unable to convince some team members to adjust their work and he needs to consult with their accountable managers, he does not need to elevate because they are his cross-functional peers. The team members' accountable managers are the ones who ultimately must call them individually to account. Only if that fails does the project manager need to elevate the issue for resolution.

The crossover-point manager is the only role that can be held individually accountable for the success of the overall project.

Program-directed teams may require program directors to act as though they are the accountable managers of the team members seconded (i.e., temporarily assigned) to their teams for periods beyond a year. With high-impact, long-term (greater than a year) projects (hence, programs) with far from certain outcomes that require employees from multiple functional areas to work closely together, simple coordination and context-setting authority is not sufficient to ensure the desired outcome.

When team members are expected to exercise high levels of judgment and discretion in relation to their individual QQT/Rs and in relation to each other, their "homeroom" or functional managers (the ones who are their regular managers on the organization charts) are not close enough to observe their progress and adjust their assignments.

Program directors are given the authority to both delegate QQT/Rs for the program and assess their team members' effectiveness in the program in keeping their word, no surprises, and earning their keep. They have the authority and accountability to provide feedback and coaching and to call team members to account.

They are not, however, the team members' ongoing accountable managers. These temporarily assigned employees will return to their homeroom managers at the end of their tour of duty on the program. These homeroom or functional managers are accountable for their continued development beyond what is required for any specific program they may be assigned to. The homeroom managers are, more importantly, accountable for developing a large enough group of high-functioning employees with the required functional domain knowledge to resource major programs, when needed.

The program director is directly accountable for the team members' outputs and adherence. They share accountability for their effectiveness with their homeroom managers.

Don't Fail to Prepare (or You'll Prepare to Fail)

Cross-functional teams are critical mechanisms for getting work done accountably in managerial hierarchies. However, they will be successful only if the right type of team is deployed with the right authorities and accountabilities for the nature of the task in question. By not spending the time upfront to think through the most efficient and accountable type of team to deploy, the chances of success are radically reduced.

TYPES OF TEAMS NECESSARY TO MAINTAIN ACCOUNTABILITY IN A MANAGERIAL SYSTEM

Core Teams Manager-subordinate (two-level) teams
Collegial (one-level) teams

Improvement Teams Study-recommendation (two- or three-level)
Implementation-coordination (one- or two-level)

Project Teams Project-coordinated teams
Project-managed teams, with part-time members (often less than one year)
Program-directed teams, with full-time "secondment" (greater than one year)

Accountability for the outputs of teams varies and depends entirely on the purpose and type of team.

CHAPTER 7

Functions and Functional Alignment

SOME OF THE MOST IMPORTANT productivity multipliers derive from understanding the fundamental nature of, and the requisite functions required for, "doing business." Simply stated, *doing business* means trading successfully in a marketplace by identifying, designing, producing, and selling high-value products and services resulting in maximum net profit and free cash flow. Doing business effectively should capture significant market share and customer satisfaction to secure its position over the next few years. Investments in the development of new types of products and services is simultaneously underway to secure the longer-term market position. All of this is in the service of supporting the desired return on assets invested and enhancing the net present value of the business.

The Functional Structure of a Level 5 Strategic Business Unit (SBU)

While there is no single optimal structure for every business, there do exist clear architectural design principles that enable the optimal, accountable alignment of each organization with its strategy.[1] To conduct business successfully, a business leader first needs to understand the business environment that determines the universe of opportunities and constraints for the organization. A business-unit head needs reliable information about her environment's macroeconomics, dynamics, and trends; its political, technological, and social forces; and its channels, products, services, prices, and competitors.

To collect, assess, and interpret information about these forces, it needs a variety of business, resourcing, and control functions—all working in concert—to help the business-unit head identify the commercial niche that offers the greatest leverage. The business leader needs to deploy all of the requisite leadership practices (i.e., L.E.A.D.) in working with his team, especially context setting, to ensure each piece of information is examined through multiple functional lenses to make comprehensive and internally consistent sense of the marketplace.

It is through this process that the business-unit head will decide which among the many types of internal capabilities should be its driving force for creating its identity when approaching the marketplace (e.g., technology, unique products or services, channels, supply chain, production or industry expertise, scale, etc.). The business model is then constructed and aligned around this identity.

A sustainable business model should be segmented into three separate time horizons, each with a different focus.

- Long-term strategy (five to 10 years) should project what new types of capabilities the business will need to invest in, develop, and master in order to dominate and expand its defined marketplace with its chosen identity in the future.

- Mid-term operational plans (two to five years) need to focus on and invest in developing new products, services, and technologies that do not currently exist but will be required to sustain growth, expand market share, and increase profitability over the next several years.

- Near-term tactical plans (present to two years) must focus on profitably providing and selling existing products and services to current customers and developing new customers.

To be fully accountable for a business's overall results (including profit and loss), an SBU head needs to have sufficient authority over those functions directly involved in conducting business (mainstream functions), resourcing, and controlling (stewarding) the business.

Sales and Product-Service Provisioning

Sales and product-service provisioning are often the largest functions by number of employees in a business unit. These functions are accountable for selling and providing products and services that were decided upon in the business model in the previous one to two years. The nature of work of both functions involves the disciplined execution of plans. Many of the outputs from both functions are delegated to lower levels, where multiple employees are working on common processes delivering outputs directly to customers. This is referred to as delegated direct output (DDO).[2]

The primary accountability of sales is to get current customers to purchase greater volumes of existing products and services to satisfy their known but unmet needs. A second accountability is to form relationships with new potential customers to understand their unmet needs and convince them that the business's existing products and services will best meet those needs.

Here is a high-level breakdown of the processes for selling to, and managing the sales relationship with, customers:

■ Finding customers

■ Understanding the needs—and developing the trust—of individual customers

■ Influencing those customers' purchasing decisions

■ Supporting customer credit status

■ Taking orders

■ Ensuring delivery

■ Doing follow-up work to ensure continued customer satisfaction

A third sales accountability in dealing with customers is to explore with them their current unmet needs for which the business, and perhaps even the competition, lack appropriate products and services. This reconnaissance is especially important input from sales to the business's market-development function (which I will discuss shortly).

The primary accountability of product-service provisioning is to produce and deliver, in a safe and environmentally sound manner, purchased products and services to the customer with the required quality and reliability at the lowest possible cost.

Here is a high-level breakdown of the main processes utilized by product and service provisioning.

■ Procuring: obtaining and maintaining the required level of raw materials and component parts, balancing quality against cost, minimizing inventory, and maximizing just-in-time working

- Transforming: creating the products and service capabilities as specified at the lowest possible cost, in a safe and environmentally sound manner
- Delivering: distributing products and delivering services to the customer

A frequent, albeit short-sighted, approach to maximizing business profitability during the tactical (one to two year) timeframe is for sales to narrowly focus on maximizing product margin and for product-service provisioning to primarily focus only on minimizing cost. The assumption is that the largest "delta" (i.e., difference between margin and operating costs) will yield the greatest profit. The problem is that in most cases there is a fixed or "sunk" cost in the resources and assets required for provisioning. In the narrow focus by sales to maximize margin revenue, sales often loses sight of unused provisioning capacity. This often results in reducing true net profitability as well as significant increased costs of production when high margin–low volume products require frequent changeovers.

Even when companies implement sales and operating plan (S&OP) processes to ensure timely delivery of sold products, they often fail to understand the need to drive customer choices in products and volumes in order to fully utilize the fixed provisioning resource, while simultaneously maximizing revenue. Maximizing "real" profitability requires optimizing the trade-off of achieving the maximum possible revenue, while fully and economically utilizing the provisioning asset to achieve the lowest possible aggregate cost.

To achieve this ambitious goal, the business needs to utilize pricing to drive customer behavior to ensure the optimal product-service mix. Pricing strategy is one of the key business-unit head multipliers for achieving this optimal balance. To realize the benefits, of course, there must be close collaboration between sales, provisioning, pricing, and finance functions to make whatever adjustments are necessary to achieve the best overall result for the business.

However, when salespeople are compensated with commissions based on volumes, revenues, and margins, they have a disincentive to collaborate with the other functions to achieve the company's overall "sweet spot." Their incentive is to maximize their own take-home pay to the detriment of the business's overall value creation. For this reason, the business-unit head must be actively involved, not only in developing the long-term strategy and mid-term investments, but also in ensuring all of her subordinate functional heads understand and apply her context for optimizing tactical business results. This is why compensation should be tied to employees' effectiveness in delivering the greatest possible value to the organization, and not, as is often the case, to maximizing their own outputs.

Market Development and Product-Service Development

While sales and product-service provisioning are primarily engaged in profitable penetrating of the current marketplace, market development and product-service development are most actively engaged in preparing for the future marketplace.

Market development is accountable for providing the business with advice, analysis, support, and some direct accountabilities for positioning the organization in the current and future marketplace. The primary accountability of market development is to support a growth strategy that identifies and develops new market segments for current products and modest extensions. A market-development strategy targets non-buying customers in currently targeted segments. It also targets new customers in new segments.

A second accountability of market development is to develop strategies that expand the potential market through new users or new uses. New users can be defined as new geographic segments, new demographic segments, new institutional segments, or new psychographic segments. Another way is to expand sales by promoting new uses for an existing product.

A third accountability of market development is to collect information from a variety of sources about unmet customer needs for which no products and services currently exist. Market-development managers must analyze the value proposition for new products and services that could address these needs and provide their level of potential value creation as input into the product-service development function and the business-unit head's business model.

A marketing manager should always ask the following questions before implementing a market-development strategy: Is it profitable? Will it require the introduction of new or modified products? Are the customer and channel thoroughly researched and understood?

The marketing manager must understand the aggregate marketplace and develop intelligence with respect to the customer, the competition, and the particular industry. He then has to translate knowledge of the marketplace into specifications for products and services, product-service mix, and pricing frameworks. Ultimately, the manager has to prepare the marketplace for the business's current and future products and services and to develop related promotional materials and media campaigns.

In order to understand markets, customers, and capabilities, market development must perform customer and market intelligence analysis by conducting customer and market research. The function needs to understand consumer needs and predict customer-purchasing behavior. The function also needs to identify market segments; determine market share; analyze market and industry trends and competing organizations, products, and services; and evaluate existing products, brands, and services.

Market development also needs to assess the internal and external business environment by evaluating, prioritizing, and quantifying market opportunities; determining target segments; and identifying underserved and saturated market segments. This leads to prioritizing opportunities consistent with capabilities and overall business strategy and then validating opportunities, testing with consumers, and confirming internal capabilities.

The outcome is the development of a cohesive marketing strategy. This includes defining and developing the value proposition, and then validating the value proposition with targeted segments. It also requires developing new branding; conducting pricing analysis; and establishing and approving pricing strategies, policies, and targets.

Product-service development is accountable for identifying new types of products and services that could add specific and significant incremental value to customers. These innovations may be recognized as known, unmet needs in the current marketplace or may require deeper and, often more technical, investigation of customers' ways of working to discover their unknown, unmet needs. The goal is to enhance the functioning of the business's current and potential customers by applying the business's technologies in new and novel ways to create innovative products and services.

There are three high-level phases in this process:

- Understanding the customer's working methods (using the business's technology expertise) in order to conceive of new-and-improved products and services that could be developed that would increase the customer's working effectiveness.

- Determining the strategic alignment and business rationale for investing in developing and producing these product improvements.

- Designing new-and-improved products and services that are both technologically and economically feasible and that support the business's long-term strategy.

The market-development function, information about industry and technology advances, and customers often provide ideas and insights about new uses for existing or new types of technologies. The purpose of a market-facing or ideation aspect of the product-service development function is to conceive of new creations and innovations that would add significant value to the customer. These concepts then need to be screened both internally and with customers to test their potential commercial merit.

These ideas then need to be background checked with market development and finance to establish the potential economic value of such improvements and the likely investment required for their development and production. They need to be vetted with manufacturing and engineering to determine the viability of producing them; they also need to be vetted with sales to understand the impact on their existing sales strategy. Ultimately, these ideas need to be approved by the business-unit head and his entire team to assess their congruence with the existing long-term strategy.

Designing new-and-improved products and services begins with developing prototypes—iteratively testing them against customers' needs, assumptions of the value proposition, manufacturability in scale, and economic feasibility. Regardless of how innovative they are, all new product ideas must meet certain rigorous criteria for the business. They must fit the company's expertise, fit the interest of the company, be scalable, solve a problem for someone, and ultimately, be something that someone will buy.

Profit and Loss: Accountabilities for an SBU in the Near-Term and Mid-Term

Up until this point, I have been describing the mainstream business functions of a Level 5 business with a five-to-10-year strategic horizon. If this were a business unit within a larger corporation, it is important to understand the context within which the business-unit head must operate. The parent corporation must always define each of its strategic business units' (SBUs') scope by their:

- Markets and market logic (i.e., geography, product, industry, major customers, etc.);
- Scope of products and services;
- Range of technological capabilities;

- Business strategies (i.e., business mission, profit, market share, asset-worth requirements, economic value added, etc.); and

- Budgetary and other organizational conditions and limits.

Once established, it needs to be clear that the strategic business unit (SBU) head is accountable for "doing business" by effectively trading goods and services in its agreed-upon marketplace while enhancing the value and position of the total business entity. This requires balancing the efforts and resources necessary to define marketplace need, develop improvements in existing products and services, efficiently provide products and services, and sell those products and services.

The goal is to achieve mission and financial objectives by ensuring that total revenues (from a strong value chain) optimally exceed total expenses (from a lean supply chain) and that every other element of the business strategy is achieved.

A frequent source of confusion, conflict, and ultimately loss of productivity occurs when an SBU head delegates portions of his own profit-and-loss accountability to his subordinate functional heads. In some companies, sales, manufacturing, supply chain, and even marketing are all given a "portion" of the P&L accountability. This inevitably leads to each function working to maximize its own fictional P&L at the expense of the overall business success.

Instead, an SBU head's profit-and-loss results from the interaction of all the mainstream business functions deployed by the SBU head in relation to her strategic goals. She must also have sufficient authority over the resourcing and control functions to be able to integrate them into her teamworking processes.

In order to optimize the return on his overall resources, an SBU head must be held accountable for providing the context and decision-making frameworks for, and integrating the interactions of his subordinate functional heads with respect to, product-service mix (value chain), workload optimization (supply chain), and pricing.

Instead of having portions of the SBU P&L, each of the subordinates of a business-unit head must be held accountable for contributing to the SBU head's profitable success by developing and implementing their own effective plans for meeting their assigned outputs that are consistent with, and reinforce, their manager's logic and plans. They must be held accountable for effectively recommending adjustments to their manager and immediate colleagues that would optimize the overall return on the business unit's total resources. And they must be accountable for identifying and implementing, whenever possible, integrative solutions (to conflicts or obstacles between functions) that simultaneously support their own accountabilities, the SBU head's frameworks, and the overall business objectives.

The Functions of "What If . . ."

Napoleon allegedly stated, "An army marches on its stomach. To be effective, an army relies on good and plentiful food." Similarly, one cannot run a business without resources. However, for an SBU head to be held accountable for his business results, he needs sufficient authority over the functions necessary to obtain, deploy, and optimize resources—with emphasis on money, people, processes, and technologies. Not surprisingly, just as an SBU head needs to integrate the actions of his mainstream business functional heads, he also needs to integrate the actions of his resourcing heads.

Every time a major change in a process or piece of equipment is contemplated, the SBU head will require the process or technology function to work with the financial function to explore the economic feasibility of making the change and to evaluate the likely return on investment. He will also require that they interact with the human resources functions to understand the capabilities necessary to operate in the new ways of working, the costs and feasibility of developing those capabilities within the existing talent pool or by recruiting externally, and the time and resources necessary to ramp up once trained. After all, no major change is ever made in a vacuum.

Broadly speaking, there are three categories of resourcing functions that an SBU head requires to staff and run a business.

- **Financial resources.** Obtain resources as economically as possible to support the delivery of business strategy. Allocate financial resources to optimize the delivery of the business strategy. Steward the financial systems required to meet the organization's current and future strategic needs.

- **People.** Establish and structure roles to optimally support current and future business strategies. Recruit and support the development of people with the capabilities to effectively discharge the accountabilities of those roles. Steward the talent assessment, development, and reward systems to ensure the necessary pipelines of talent required to meet the organization's current and future strategic needs.

- **Processes and technologies.** Create and implement technologies and working methods that capably support and continuously improve the processes for all business functions required for current and future business operations.

In addition, resourcing functions usually carry system stewardship accountabilities. Generally, system stewardship contains four primary types of accountabilities. These include supporting the "system- or process-accountable manager" in continuous improvement, providing services to functional units within the organization, exercising the full gamut of indirect accountabilities to ensure the optimal application of the system's processes and procedures, and finally, directly overseeing aspects of the system. I cover these accountabilities in detail in Chapter 9.

Resourcing functions continuously work with the SBU head and the mainstream business functions to model alternative strategies and approaches and then obtain and deploy the resources necessary to implement them. They support the others in model "what if. . ." scenarios.

The Functions of "Yes, But . . ."

Control functions exist to ensure that the deployed resources are utilized as intended, are kept in proper working order, and that the plans that they support unfold as intended. The control functions exist to identify and remediate deviations from any plan.

Resourcing functions are constantly supporting "what if..." scenarios and analyses and proposing adjustments to existing plans to capture greater value in a changing environment. Control functions are supporting "Yes, but. . ." analyses to determine whether deviations from the original plan exist by design or by default. In the pendulum metaphor, resourcing functions support the exercise of creative initiative; control functions support process integrity.

Not surprisingly, control functions exist for the same categories as resource functions: money, people, processes, and technologies.

- **Financial resources.** Ensure the proper control of financial systems and resources. Continuously examine and account for discrepancies between budgeted and actual flow of cash and capital. Periodically audit the integrity with which the financial system is adhered to.

- **People.** Ensure that the systems (structures; policies; procedures; support, influencing, and regulating mechanisms) governing the health and safety of employees and of the environment are effectively stewarded (i.e., maintained in good working order and continuously improved).

- **Processes and technologies.** Ensure that all processes are continuously monitored for adherence and control by implementing and stewarding a quality assurance system.

The operational mission of an SBU head is to develop, produce, market, and sell products and services to customers and to sustain a reasonable rate of profit, business survival, and capital enhancement.

Functional Alignment vs. Structural Alignment

For an SBU head to be held accountable for achieving optimal business results, he must have authority over the mainstream, resourcing, and control functions aligned to his SBU's market. In particular, he requires sufficient authority to

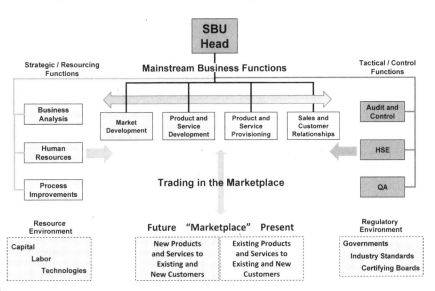

BUSINESS UNIT FUNCTIONS
Alignment of Mainstream, Resourcing, and Control Functions

For a business-unit head role to be fully accountable for its success in a marketplace, it must have managerial authority over the mainstream, resourcing, and control functions.

assign QQT/Rs to each function, to set upward and teamwork context about the business model for all of them, and to hold them individually accountable for keeping their word, no surprises, and earning their keep. Each functional head must be held accountable for collaborating effectively with the other functional heads to make whatever adjustments are necessary to support the overarching business model while still delivering on his own QQT/Rs. As Aristotle said, "The whole is greater than the sum of its parts."

A question frequently emerges in Level 6, 7, and 8 corporations—companies trading in multiple markets. Are there advantages of centralizing functions (to achieve economies of scale, consistent systems and standards, centers of excellence, etc.) vs. providing "local" control over each of those functions by their Level 5 SBU heads who are accountable for a single market? While critical mass can be a limiting factor (i.e., not enough revenue or employees to justify dedicating full-time functions within each business unit), the general principle, once again, is accountability without authority is fantasy and stress.

Achieving an SBU's optimal business results requires sound strategy, operational excellence, and real-time alignment, integration, and collaboration across the four mainstream business functions, three resourcing functions, and three control functions. Absent managerial, or managerial-like, authority over any of these functions inevitably leads to suboptimal decisions by those functions when their accountable managers are outside the SBU, often holding them accountable for a different set of priorities.

The "Business Work" at Levels 5, 4, and 3

Irrespective of the structure, what is most important is that each of these functions collaborates effectively with the others to discuss and agree on how together they can make enterprise-wide optimal decisions.

The SBU head relies on his Level 4 functional heads to bring each of their unique perspectives together to help him construct a vision of their future environment and market (in the five-to-10-year horizon). And from this vision, they explore their strategy for positioning the business to be in a dominant position by that timeframe. This becomes the backbone of the business-unit head's business model against which all subsequent decisions should be referenced.

The Level 4 functional heads then need to operationalize the long-term business strategy into mid-term operational plans and near-term tactical plans. The mid-term plans (two-to-five-year horizons) need to identify what new types of products, services, technologies, resources, talent, and customers need to be developed and acquired to supplant the existing "portfolios" over the next several years. This is critical both to expand their market share and to defend against encroachment by competitors' innovations.

The Level 4 functional heads then must delegate three types of multipliers to their managers at Level 3.

First, it is the fundamental block-and-tackling of effectively and accountably leading their units (Levels 3, 2, and 1) and deploying all of the L.E.A.D. practices. If those units are sub-par in their functioning, the Level 4 managers will be "pulled down into the weeds" to compensate for those gaps and have less time to engage in the higher-level multiplier work required of their own roles.

Second, the Level 4 functional heads must task their Level 3 managers with continuous improvement objectives to enhance productivity, resource capability, and efficiency. These improvements are necessary both to remain competitive and to increase free cash flow to fund new developments.

Third is leading the new development initiatives by their Level 4 managers of products, services, technologies, resources, talent, and customers that will supersede the existing generation of capabilities. This is building the connector between what we currently do (near-term) to what we will need to be able to do in a few years (mid-term) in order to dominate the marketplace over the next decade (long-term).

It is critical that both the improvement and new capability development initiatives be coordinated to achieve seamless cross-functional, end-to-end processes at Level 4 and integrated value streams at Level 3. Once again, the cascading of context from the Level 5 SBU head to Level 4 and then from the Level 4 functional heads to their Level 3 managers is the means for ensuring alignment, integration, and synchronization. Since Level 3 is where near-term tactical plans are developed and implemented, managers in Level 3 roles need to understand completely the business model that ties them together.

Moving Up: Functional Alignment at the Corporate Level

There is considerable evidence that corporations trading in multiple marketplaces—with strategic horizons greater than 10 years—will be more successful in aggregate when they organize around discrete Level 5 SBU markets than by creating business function silos at higher levels (i.e., led by roles at Levels 6, 7, or 8). There are many reasons why this principle seems to apply to all managerial systems and thousands of examples in business and in the military that support its usefulness.

The strategic business unit (SBU) head is accountable for developing and implementing growth strategies for her market in the five-to-10-year horizon. Level 5 is the first of the abstract conceptual work levels and is, therefore, capable of translating higher-level corporate strategic requirements into an SBU's business models. These models, then, set the context for the subordinate Level 4 functional-operational heads to develop and implement the programs necessary to support the SBU strategy. The Level 4 heads then delegate the one-to-two-year tactical implementation to their Level 3 unit heads.

The higher the organizational level where P&L accountability first occurs, the more complex the task of:

- Deciding on functional resource allocations to multiple units, which are conducting business in multiple markets; and
- Keeping functional focus on each business campaign across multiple markets.

The lower the level of initial P&L accountability,

- The more complex the task of integrating each SBU's products and services into the larger "product-service families" desired by the marketplace, which require many SBUs to produce; and
- The more difficult it is to have sufficient critical mass and capability to support "true" product and process development (i.e., in the two-to-five-year horizon), which is necessary for the company to remain competitive.

Consequently, the starting point in designing a corporate structure is to establish self-contained Level 5 business units with the necessary resources and authority to trade successfully in the marketplace. The fundamental building block of all corporations (Levels 6 and above), therefore, is the trading strategic business unit (SBU), optimally a five-level unit, working in the five-to-10-year horizon. Once the SBU markets and marketplace logic and driving forces are defined, the design proceeds down within the SBU (Level-4 functions) and up (Level-6 portfolios of SBUs), and so on.

"Driving Force" as the Cornerstone for Strategic SBU Design

In his 1997 book, *Strategy Pure & Simple II: How Winning Companies Dominate Their Competitors,* management consultant Michel Robert used an American football metaphor that still holds up today.[3] He asserted that "the purpose of a winning strategy is not to play on one's opponent's 40-yard line more often than they are on your 40-yard line; it is to permanently tilt the playing field in your favor!"

To achieve that status, to dominate any particular marketplace, business leaders must first identify which component of their organization is its "driving force." By that, Robert meant of all of a business's capabilities, which one does it excel at? Which capability stands out and would help to define the marketplace by its unique identity? Furthermore, the design of the business's structure should emphasize and optimize this capability (e.g., technology, productive capacity, distribution method, geographic market, etc.) above all others. Robert goes on to say that a company should choose to define its marketplace solely to its advantage and not attempt to compete with others in the way they define their markets.

The challenge is to choose only one capability and build the business model around that capability.

Level 5 Business Units and Level 7 Corporations

The nature and flow of work of the provisioning and sales functions, as mentioned earlier, is a cascading delegation of direct outputs down from the business-unit head at Level 5 to roles at Levels 4 to 3 to 2 and, sometimes, even to Level 1. The work requires disciplined execution on plan and the outputs go

The first step in organizational design is identifying the primary driving force that moves the organization forward. Once identified, each business unit needs to define its markets in a way that will optimize the expression of that force.

out into the marketplace. I refer to this as *delegated direct output (DDO)* work down from the SBU head.

The nature and flow of work of the market and product-service development functions begins in the marketplace, collecting and analyzing information, identifying and testing opportunities, and formulating plans that then become inputs to the Level 5 business unit head's business model. I refer to this as *direct output support (DOS)* from the market up to the SBU head.

Market and product-service development functions prepare the business to be able to conduct business several years in the future. Provisioning and sales functions execute the business model today that was formulated in the past. The resourcing functions provide both direct output support to the SBU head, and provide support services, as *direct output (DO)*, to the business functions. The control functions similarly provide both DOS and DO, but more in the form of risk management work than support services.

If we now look at a Level 7 corporation, consisting of several Level 6 portfolios (of Level 5 SBUs) and a Level 6 corporate business development (CBD) function, we see a similar pattern. The Level 6 CBD function may consist of several Level 5 longer-term development groups (new technologies, markets, types of businesses, raw materials, and joint ventures or acquisitions), each of which require scouring the environment and then making investment DOS recommendations upward to the corporate CEO. The Level 6 portfolios of Level 5 strategically aligned SBUs are more focused on executing on their 10-to-20-year portfolio asset growth plans, which leads to DDO work with their subordinate Level 5 SBU heads.

This gives rise to natural structural symmetries at every organizational level. Accountability for "doing business" always has three components—long-, mid-, and short-term—even though the time horizons for each varies depending on the level of complexity of the accountable role. One should attempt to structure the subordinate units and/or resources to reflect each of these different time-based components in order to provide focus and clarity of authorities and accountabilities.

The Trap of Success

A mid-tiered, Level 5 (five-to-10-year timespan) technology company, Smart-Tech, with products similar to those of much larger multinational companies (Level 7 with 20+ year timespans), competed with them in several different markets, each with different applications for their products.[4] One major market opportunity for all of them, a complex global commercial industry with interdependent players, remained locked into previous generation technologies. The costs for each of the players in that industry to, simultaneously, transition to a new platform was enormous and prohibitive for some. The economics and supply chain mechanics once transitioned, however, would be enormously beneficial to all of them.

After several of the major competitors failed in their attempts to change this complex ecosystem, the SmartTech CEO devised a brilliant collaborative economic model that in less than 10 years changed the entire industry. Because of their early involvement, they captured over a third of the global industry market share for their products. They increased their revenue by a factor of 10 and their margins for these products more than doubled. The size and complexity of the organization expanded accordingly. The CEO role morphed into a Level 6 role (with a 10-to-20-year timespan) while his heads of sales, product marketing, product development, and manufacturing all expanded into Level 5 roles.

In order to meet the enormous production demand for products during these 10 years, they chose to abandon their other market segments. This allowed their large competitors to increase their market share in those channels. Once the global market became nearly saturated, however, the volume of products for this specific industry dropped to less than a quarter of the peak sales. The CEO realized he had to rebuild SmartTech's foothold in the other channels they had walked away from.

It became an impossible challenge for the Level 6 CEO to integrate and coordinate each of the Level 4 business functions corresponding to each of the three or four distinctly different markets. The intervening Level 5 business functional heads tended to focus rigidly on having their Level 4 managers meet their targets set at the beginning of each year, despite the fact that conditions in each market were highly fluid and required frequent readjustments in relation to the other business functions.

I helped SmartTech break up the functional silos and subordinate the appropriate Level 4 functional managers to the newly created, fully P&L accountable Level 5 SBU heads. The company was then able to regain traction in each of its markets.

Levels of Complexity and Functional Alignment

The detailed design principles for Levels 8, 7, and 6 corporations are beyond the scope of this book. However, there are unique, primary sources of value contribution for roles at each level of complexity. Both Levels 6 and 7 transform the industry model. Where Level 6 develops new businesses into new markets within an industry over two decades, Level 7 dominates a particular industry over the course of 30 years or one generation. Level 8 is breathtaking in scope. It transforms whole industries and spearheads and leads in multiple industries over the period of two or more generations.

However, regardless of level, organizational design must always begin with strategy.

Strategy is a roadmap for how an organization can fulfill its mission and achieve a specific vision of the future. This work must begin with the governing body and engage the CEO and the executive team. The board must ultimately decide on the long-term strategy that it will authorize the CEO to pursue and then hold him accountable for aligning the organization, its people, and its leadership accordingly.

The timespan of the CEO and corporate strategy is then translated into the level of complexity of the CEO role and determines the number of subordinate levels to establish. The architectural principle is to design corporations around Level 5 business units, each with subordinate mainstream business, resourcing, and control functions. For a Level 6 corporation, for example, the CEO should structure Level 5 SBUs immediately subordinate. For Level 7 corporations, the CEO should structure subordinate Level 6 portfolios of SBUs and a Level 6 corporate business development function.

Toward a Logical Approach to Integrating Multipliers

I begin every inquiry into a new client's request for support in achieving step-change improvements in productivity the same way.

"What is your strategy and your business model for achieving that strategy? Walk me through your organizational chart and explain to me which roles are accountable for what elements of the strategy. Do each of these roles have the requisite authorities to make and implement the necessary decisions or to affect others who have the authorities to make the required decisions? What percent of their time is spent 'working the system' in order to get their own work done?"

When the barriers creating this noise are identified, what insights can we gain by applying the lenses of levels of complexity and functional alignment (i.e., multipliers) to understand the requisite structures required to eliminate them?

The remaining inquiry, once alternative structures are modeled, requires overlaying the processes onto the structures (i.e., attaching the muscles to the skeleton). Two questions need to be considered. Which roles should be accountable for what process steps? And which other roles should have some accountability in relationship to them? As we shall see, Chapter 8 deals with the productivity multipliers involved in clarifying accountabilities for processes.

CHAPTER 8

Structuring Accountable Cross-Functional Processes

CAPABILITY! EFFICIENCY! ACCOUNTABILITY! This should be the rallying cry for achieving optimally productive processes. Each of these three process attributes is an important multiplier.

It is not enough to design a capable and technologically sound cross-functional process if you want it to operate capably, efficiently, and accountably. Managers must address the fact that processes have many employees acting within them and making decisions in relationship to each other. Disconnects, conflicts, and even hostility often arise because it may not be clear as to "who is accountable for what in relationship to whom."

A framework, a language, and a methodology are required for clarifying who needs direct, decisional authority around which steps and who needs indirect, influencing-or-regulating authority in relationship to whom. And they must define the elements of an overarching decision-making framework necessary to ensure that people will work together to construct integrative solutions that optimally support the total goal—not just one unit's objectives at the expense of others.

There exists an enormous amount of information about, and a glut of global consulting firms providing, process reengineering services. Much of it is useful in enhancing process *capability* (i.e., consistently delivering the desired quality outputs) and in improving *efficiency* (i.e., at the lowest cost in the shortest time). However, there is little guidance about how to structure cross-functional processes to ensure accountability and effective collaboration. As a result, many of these costly, time-consuming initiatives yield disappointing results and often fail to deliver the expected value.

Translating Vertical Accountabilities into Lateral Accountabilities

As I explained in Chapter 6 on teams, it is the manager-subordinate team that converts *"vertical"* accountability (where A holds subordinate manager B_1 accountable for her subordinate C_1) into *"lateral"* accountability (where A holds B_1 accountable for the working effectiveness of his entire subordinate team C_{1A}, C_{1B}, C_{1C}, C_{1D}, C_{1E}, C_{1N}).

Manager A can do that because B_1 has the managerial authority to:

- Select subordinates;
- Set upward and teamworking context for them;
- Delegate ambitious, yet achievable, QQT/Rs;
- Evaluate how well each subordinate engages in effective teamworking collaboration as well as in other aspects of their roles;
- Hold them individually accountable for keeping their word, no surprises, and earning their keep; and
- Provide consequences (both positive and negative) appropriate to their degree of effectiveness in all aspects of their roles, including initiating removal from role for lack of effectiveness.

Setting *upward* context by manager B_1 with his subordinates (C_{1A}, C_{1B}, C_{1C}, C_{1D}, C_{1E}, C_{1N}) begins with explaining what his own manager, A, is planning to accomplish and his rationale for doing so. As a result, each of the Cs on B_1's team should have a common understanding of both A's logic and B_1's logic, which they are required to take into account whenever making decisions about how to implement their own QQT/Rs.

Three-Level Processes Translate Vertical Accountabilities into Cross-Functional Accountabilities

It is often the case that several employees—each on a different team but also working on different sections of the same cross-functional process—will have conflicting points of view about how to proceed with their own QQT/Rs. Not surprisingly, each person's decision could have adverse second- and third-order consequences for the others. The constant challenge is to avoid sub-optimizing the process's overall outputs and effectiveness when each employee wants to maximize his own outputs.

Now, let us extend this "team collaboration model" to include A's other subordinates, B_2, B_3, and B_4. If each of them sets effective context with their C-level subordinates, they, too, should have a common understanding of A's logic. So, in the diagram below, when C_{1C} and C_{3A} are working toward an output in common but have different points of view about how to proceed, they should be expected to ask each other, "What would A decide if we were to ask him?"

For this reason, when structuring cross-functional processes requiring strong collaboration at the C-level, one should always attempt to ensure that their roles' crossover-point manager, A, is no more than two levels above the Cs' roles. In other words, design critical cross-functional processes with only three levels, where the Cs' managers have the same manager.

THREE-LEVEL CASCADING CONTEXT TO ALIGN CROSS-FUNCTIONAL EMPLOYEES

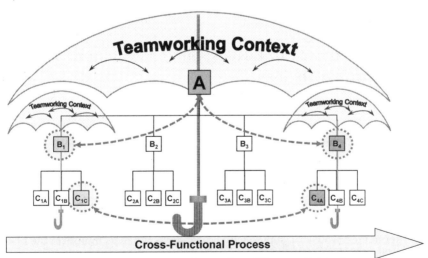

C_{1C} and C_{4A} need a common understanding of Manager A's intentions.

To ensure robust cross-functional collaboration among employees in the service of developing enterprise-wide optimal solutions, three-level context creates alignment about the higher-level primary objectives.

Each of A's subordinate managers (B_1, B_2, B_3, and B_4) are accountable for communicating A's context to their own C-level subordinates. These C-level employees need to collaborate in reference to A's intentions not only with their own teammates, but also with other C-level employees who are on different teams. When these requirements are implemented (i.e., the three-level process structure and the cascading context), each of the Cs can be held accountable for collaborating effectively with their cross-functional counterparts to modify their own QQT/R approaches in such a way that ensures the optimal overall process outcomes (as inferred from manager A's intent).

This cascading A-B-C context—down and across three levels—is the key to achieving dynamic alignment and collaboration across functions and to supporting the goal of optimizing enterprise-wide processes.

This multiplier model of three-level processes and context setting is powerful. It is the antidote to productivity-stifling silos and internal competition. It intentionally places more pressure on employees working within a common process, because it prevents them from simply defaulting to either maximizing their own outputs or selflessly accommodating the requests of others. For any employee to achieve her greatest overall effectiveness requires that she regularly collaborates with her cross-functional peers to craft and agree upon the enterprise-optimal solutions (i.e., "What would 'A' decide if we were to ask him?"), which will still allow each of them to deliver on their own individual accountabilities.

Introducing the Matrix Busters: Direct and Indirect Process Accountabilities

Additional structure-and-process multipliers are required to avoid the problems inevitably created with matrix-management solutions. The usual rationale for establishing matrix managers is that "line" managers will always be so consumed with the need for their subordinates to maximize their outputs that the managers will ignore problems their subordinates encounter with such issues as quality standards, safety, environment, financial controls, and personnel policies. To address this perceived deficit, companies often establish "parallel" hierarchies, which are staffed with dotted-line managers to inform the line employees about each of their function's policies and to hold them accountable for adhering to those defined limits.

The result is that employees end up with multiple managers. Each manager holds them accountable for different agendas. This creates noise, confusion, and conflict, which all undermine productivity. This, however, flies in the face of the basic nature of accountability in managerial hierarchies. Managers are accountable for their subordinates' outputs *and* their effectiveness in dealing with each of the organization's systems *and* for adhering to defined limits.

The "line" manager must be the one to hold each of his subordinates accountable for meeting all of these requirements, including adhering to defined limits. Adding matrix managers merely creates confusion. When two or more managers are accountable for the same employee, then no one is accountable for that employee. "Don't blame me. Blame my other two managers!"

The principles underlying a sound solution here are straightforward. While each employee's manager must hold him directly accountable for his outputs, effectiveness, and adherence, there are many instances in which the immediate manager is neither close enough nor up-to-date enough to ensure that his employee is making fully informed decisions, is fully aware of potential adverse consequences of his decisions, or realizes that a particular decision is outside of limits. So, instead of creating matrix managers and making them partially accountable for the decisions and actions of other managers' employees, it is much more honest to acknowledge that it is the immediate manager who holds his subordinate directly accountable.

To support the immediate manager, however, we should also establish other roles. These roles should be lateral to that employee, with indirect authorities to inform, persuade, or instruct him on decisions and actions.[1] These roles are indirectly accountable for initiating actions to affect other roles. However, they are not accountable for those roles' actions or decisions.

Direct and Indirect Accountabilities: Vive la Différence!

It is essential to differentiate between direct and indirect accountabilities, especially since many roles carry both types of accountabilities.

Roles that are assigned tasks by their managers, which they must work on and deliver to others (either inside or outside the organization), are held *directly* accountable for their own results and for effective lateral working by their immediate managers. They have been delegated the authority to decide on and implement plans to achieve their QQT/Rs. They have received upward and teamworking context from their managers and they understand the limits within which they must work, based on the organization's policies and standards. For the most part, we expect those employees to accumulate sufficient knowledge to make well-informed, creative decisions that adhere to those limits.

However, this is not always the case. Conditions rapidly change—both externally and internally—which employees may be unaware of and often result in uninformed (though well-intentioned) suboptimal decisions. To cover these exceptions, managers should establish other roles, lateral to roles with direct accountabilities, which are given authorities to do work in relation to them. They are *not* accountable for the results of the others. Instead, they are accountable for having an effect on the decisions, actions, and results of others. In other words, they are *indirectly* accountable.

Many of these indirect roles are accountable for initiating some action toward other direct roles. They must either influence or regulate the decisions and actions of others or support the improvement of processes on behalf of their crossover-point managers. Other types of indirect roles are accountable for responding to the requests from others to provide services or support to them.

Although it is convenient to illustrate these lateral role relationships with dotted lines, they are not dotted-line managers!

However, first, I have to offer a word of caution.

INDIRECT ACCOUNTABILITIES: INFORM, PERSUADE, INSTRUCT

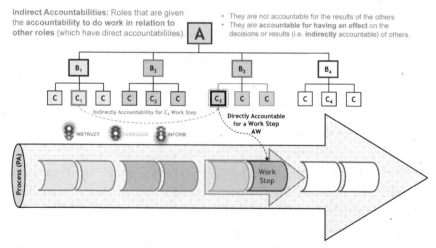

There is a hierarchy of indirect accountabilities that can be assigned to ensure optimally informed decisions, to mitigate potential unintended consequences, and to prevent catastrophic outcomes. The levels of authority to intervene vary, always erring on the side of the least intrusive role relationship necessary.

When structuring three-level processes in such a way that each person in a role with direct accountabilities has the necessary capabilities, authorities, and information to make sound, creative, collaborative decisions, indirect accountabilities often are unnecessary. Everyone working in the same process stream should have a common understanding of and commitment to support the crossover-point manager's high-level goals. By freely communicating both upstream and downstream, they can continuously adjust and fine-tune the cadence and integration of their workflow to achieve optimal overall flow.

However, when decisions could be better informed or be more cognizant of potential risks, then it becomes appropriate to create roles with indirect accountabilities.

As you will see, there are straightforward principles and taxonomies governing the use of indirect accountabilities. The following two paragraphs capture the ground rules.

If you do not need indirect accountabilities, do not use them. Rely instead on managers holding subordinates who have direct accountabilities . . . accountable for their outputs, adherence, and effectiveness.

If you do need indirect accountabilities, begin with the least intrusive, informing. See if it is sufficient to mitigate the risk that you are concerned about. If it is not, then you should move up to persuading. If not, then you move up to instructing.

The Taxonomy of Indirect Accountabilities: Informing

The least intrusive category of indirect accountabilities is *informing*. Informing roles are accountable for communicating with specific roles—which have direct accountabilities—about information that they should consider in order to make fully informed decisions.

For example, a manufacturing plant may choose to require that its tradesmen make at least one visual inspection of all operating machines—that they regularly service—during the course of a shift. Whenever they perceive a potential problem looming (e.g., oil drops on the floor, temperature is approaching the upper limit, unusual sounds, etc.), they must decide whether to advise the machine operator about the risk. "Is it worth distracting the operator from his work?" The machine operator, if informed, would then need to decide whether to adjust the way he is operating the equipment or even request a quick inspection by the tradesman.

Another example would be the business-unit controller, who is accountable for tracking and comparing the rate of expenditures against the operating expenses budgeted for the month. Whenever he identifies a trend that could lead to a budget overrun, he must decide whether it is within the range of usual variability or whether it may be a leading indicator that will only worsen if left unchecked. If he concludes that there is enough potential risk, he may recommend to the operations head that he look into the specific areas that he believes pose the greatest risk.

Both of these indirect accountabilities require the authority to gather information that is pertinent to the roles they may need to inform, analyze the data, and determine whether there are sufficient opportunities to improve a decision or prevent adverse consequences. Both of these indirect accountabilities also require the authority to have access to the role with direct accountabilities to provide advice or recommendations. Once they have informed the other role, their accountabilities for that particular situation end.

The role with the direct accountability must decide whether and how to use new information from an informing role. An adverse outcome resides squarely on the shoulders of the role with direct accountability. If the role with indirect accountability fails to provide relevant information, the absence of which results in an adverse outcome, both parties may carry some degree of accountability.

The Taxonomy of Indirect Accountabilities: Persuading

The next more intrusive category of indirect accountabilities is *persuading*. These roles are similarly accountable for examining the decisions and actions of those with direct accountabilities and have the authority to not only inform, but also to persuade them to adjust their current course of action and decision-making because of likely adverse consequences. This form of indirect accountability is by necessity more intrusive. Its primary goal is to reduce the need for excessively rigid and bureaucratic rules created to prevent possible problems (but that end up constraining creative initiative). Its secondary goal is to ensure the debate about resolving the different points of view occurs at the appropriate level (i.e., within the process stream, without needing to elevate every disagreement).

Building upon the previous example of the mechanic's indirect informing accountabilities relative to the machine operator, we might also consider assigning persuading authorities whenever the visual inspection reveals a more serious or imminent problem threatening (e.g., oil beginning to flow, temperature now at upper limits, etc.).

Having monitoring accountability with which to address impending dangers, the mechanic would have the additional authority to "lean on" the operator and attempt to convince him to let him inspect the equipment either now or at the next break, as long as it is soon. The operator, on the other hand, may be under considerable pressure from his own manager to reach an extremely difficult target that day for a crucial customer and honestly believe that he knows the machine's warning signs better than the tradesman does. This establishes a creative tension in the form of a process that demands constructive solutions. It encourages each party to seriously weigh the other's concerns, to explore and agree upon optimal trade-offs (i.e., optimizing value while minimizing risk), and to develop an integrative solution that both can live with.

For a role with persuading authority to have enough leverage to get the role with direct accountability to seriously engage in discussion and debate, it needs to have authority to delay any further action by that role. This ensures that there will be enough time for the disagreement to be elevated to the next level of management for resolution. If either party can convince the other about his point of view, then the immediate situation is resolved. However, if there is ultimately an adverse outcome that should have been avoided, both parties will share in the blame.

A second category of persuading authority is coordinating accountability. When the success of an undertaking requires that multiple roles, on different teams, working on common processes, seamlessly synchronize and integrate their actions, it is useful for one of those roles to be given coordinating authority in relation to the others.

As with informing and monitoring, this indirect accountability also has the authority to be kept informed about the actions and decisions of the other roles and is accountable for assessing whether or not they are all aligned. If the malalignment is judged problematic, the coordinating role has the authority to convene the other roles and then explain how their separate approaches are not aligned and what the likely adverse consequences would be if they continued to proceed in those different directions. At this point, the coordinating role has the authority to attempt to persuade the others to collectively agree on a common approach going forward that would satisfy the ultimate goals of the initiative. Absent agreement, the role has the authority to delay further action by all parties until the issue is elevated and resolved at the managerial level above them.

A powerful example of the importance of the persuading indirect accountability occurs when a company is trading in global markets, has business units in EMEA (Europe, the Middle East, and Africa), Asia, North America, and South America, and has global customers with business units in those same regions. It is common for its global customers—working centrally—to put pressure separately on each of the regional businesses to lower prices and use the lowest quote to demand concessions from the other regions. Or they may even procure all of the products required for the global organization from the region with the lowest price.

To prevent these corporate machinations from being successful, the company needs to assign a role to coordinate the sales pricing strategies across all of the business units. This is especially important because each of the businesses may have different go-to-market value propositions and getting agreement from each of their business heads on a common corporate pricing strategy may be difficult.

Once again, persuading indirect accountabilities seek to avoid creating rigid bureaucratic rules. They instill a creative tension between many roles to work together to find innovative, common solutions to competing objectives.

The Taxonomy of Indirect Accountabilities: Instructing

The most intrusive indirect accountability, *instructing,* is limited to situations where the individual with direct accountabilities has already begun to operate outside of defined limits or where there is a looming emergency that requires immediate action. This indirect accountability, as with the others, requires the authority to be kept informed about the actions of others and of potentially dangerous situations in the internal and external working environment.

When the instructing role perceives a role with direct accountabilities to be acting *outside* of defined limits, it requires the *auditing* authority to instruct that role to stop further action. Keep in mind that this does *not* supersede the accountability to that role's immediate manager, because it is already accountable for ensuring his subordinate acts within limits.

In most companies, employees have the auditing authority to stop another employee from acting in an unsafe manner. For example, if anyone sees a tradesman working on a piece of equipment without first locking out and tagging out, he is authorized to stop that person from proceeding. In a pharmaceutical manufacturing environment, operating under strict regulatory requirements for good manufacturing practices (GMP), a quality control technician can stop the entire production line if he spots any deviation from the strict protocols in place.

Under extreme conditions, when life, health, physical plant, and environment are at risk of immediate catastrophe, some designated instructing roles may be given *prescribing* authority to initiate emergency action. A safety officer may be given the authority to clear a manufacturing plant when an explosion is imminent, and all employees are required to follow his instructions. A cruise ship physician may have the authority to quarantine a vessel that has an outbreak of a dangerous viral infection.

As with persuading accountabilities, instructing indirect accountabilities do not supersede an employee's immediate manager's authority. The immediate manager is already accountable for ensuring that employee's safety.

INDIRECT ACCOUNTABILITIES: LATERAL WORKING RELATIONSHIPS

Category	Types of Indirect Accountabilities		
(I) Process Support (PS)	Identifying Improvement Opportunities (IO)	Studying & Recommending Improvements (SR)	Coordinating the Implementation of Improvements (CI)
(II) "Resourcing" (RS)	Service Giving (SG)	Contract Servicing (CS)	

(III) Influencing and/or Regulating (IR)

Informing (IF)	Advising (AD)	Recommending (RC)	INFORM
Persuading (PE)	Coordinating (CO)	Monitoring (MO)	PERSUADE
Instructing (IS)	Auditing (AU)	Prescribing (PR)	INSTRUCT

To reduce the need for micromanagement, avoid matrix solutions. To encourage discussions around decision-making "in the line," it can be useful to assign roles—lateral to the decision-makers—with indirect authority and accountability to influence their decisions.

If you do need indirect accountabilities, determine whether:

- *The least intrusive, informing, is sufficient to enhance outcomes or to mitigate the risks that you are concerned about.*

- *If it is not, then you move up to persuading, which is designed to create constructive tension within the process flow.*

- *If still not, then you move up to instructing, which authorizes one to stop others from acting outside of limits.*

The Taxonomy of Indirect Accountabilities: Support for Process Improvement

A basic accountability of all managers is to continuously enhance the effectiveness of their subordinate resources. So far, we have applied this notion to the accountability of every manager to coach and develop immediate subordinates and of every manager-once-removed (MoR) to mentor and develop subordinates-once-removed.

It is equally true that every manager is accountable for the continuous improvement of subordinate processes. We have just examined how managers of three-level cross-functional processes can structure direct and indirect accountabilities and create decision-making frameworks to ensure the optimal and accountable running of their, not his, processes. However, that does not address how to drive continuous improvements in process capabilities and efficiencies.

The need for managers to drive improvements in cross-functional processes that they "own" poses a universal challenge for companies, especially when those processes operate three, four, even five levels below them. I use the term *process owner* to identify the first role up the hierarchy that has managerial authority over all of the roles that have some accountability within the process. Many organizations refer to the stewardship role as the process owner or system owner (e.g., CFO, VP HR, general counsel, etc.). However, it is actually the CEO who "owns" each of the corporate systems. The CEO has the authority to change them and hold immediate subordinates accountable for operating within their requirements.

There are myriad techniques in widespread use (Six Sigma, Kaizen, Theory of Constraints, etc.) that can effectively reduce cost and variance and increase speed and quality. However, the problem that few companies effectively address is how to implement these process analyses, redesigns, and implementations accountably.

In Chapter 6, I described the accountabilities and mechanisms of action of two types of process-improvement teams: study-recommendation and implementation-coordination. The team leaders for these teams can be appointed by the "process owner" managers as a "one-off" or they can establish roles that have the ongoing accountability for supporting process improvement. These are typically described as stewardship roles that are described in more detail in Chapter 9. In addition to having the authority to establish and resource study-recommendation and implementation-coordination teams, they also have the accountability for continually scanning for opportunities to improve processes.

A classic example of this is a manufacturing process engineer who is accountable for taking the initiative to undertake regular and spot analyses to identify trends, compare actual vs. external benchmarking data, and undertake cost-benefit studies for undertaking improvement initiatives and keep a running, prioritized list of opportunities for the process owner (typically the plant or manufacturing manager). The process owner must decide whether to carry out any particular initiative and then turns over the study-recommendation phase to the steward. Once a recommendation is made to the owner, if she decides to implement the changes, she must delegate each piece of the plan to each of her immediate subordinates and, simultaneously, task the steward with coordinating the implementation.

The indirect accountabilities (described thus far) carry with them the requirement to take the initiative to gather information, analyze it, and decide whether to intervene in some way by approaching the designated roles with direct accountabilities.

The Taxonomy of Indirect Accountabilities: Service Giving, Service Requesting, Contract Servicing

There are other kinds of roles with indirect accountabilities for the outputs of others. However, these roles are not expected to take the initiative to determine whether some action is warranted. Instead, they must respond to authorized requests from others who have direct accountabilities. Many organizations refer to these kinds of roles as "internal suppliers" and the roles with direct accountabilities as "internal customers." This is fraught with all sorts of negative consequences. However, they can be avoided.

A good example of a service-giving role is a CAD-CAM operator, who is accountable for responding to a request from a mechanical engineer to make a digital representation of his engineering diagram. The engineer is accountable for the output (i.e., quality of the engineering design), not the CAD-CAM operator who is providing a service. The problem with calling the CAD-CAM operator an internal supplier is that whenever a "true" supplier (i.e., external vendor) experiences increasing levels of demand for his service from customers, he will raise prices, add more staff, or select which customers are in his own best interest to serve. The service-giver role does not—and should not—have those authorities. Those resourcing and priority decisions should reside at a higher level, most often with the ubiquitous "process owner."

Service-giving accountability does not need to take the initiative to identify when and where to intervene. However, service-giving accountability must respond to authorized requests for services.

When a business-unit head encounters situations that prevent him from subordinating a necessary mainstream business function within his own organization, there needs to be an accountable mechanism for him to be able to depend on the precise quantity of resources that either are centralized or reside within another business unit. Service-giving accountability and service-requesting authority do not provide the level of certainty that those resources will be available when needed. At the same time, a service-giving manager cannot create excess capacity merely based on the possibility that additional services may be requested. Therefore, in these circumstances, we create a contract-servicing accountability, where the business needing resources from another entity commits—in advance—to cover the cost of the intended quantities. In reality, the business is buying capacity up front.

The Taxonomy of Direct Accountabilities

In this chapter, I have explored the types of indirect accountabilities some roles carry in relationship to other roles with direct accountabilities. In addition, I have examined the notion of direct accountability "process owner" or process-accountable manager roles. These roles have the full decision-making authority over a process (i.e., authority to decide on the process's structure, policies, methods, limits, resources, and frameworks for subordinate decision-making). I have also differentiated process-accountable managers from subordinate process or system stewardship roles.

DIRECT ACCOUNTABILITIES: VERTICAL WORKING RELATIONSHIPS

Category	Accountability	Authority	Qualifying Conditions
Direct Process Accountabilities	Accountable for the Process (AC)	Full decision-making authority over a process (i.e., the process's structure, policies, methods, limits, resources, and frameworks for subordinate decision making)	This is the true "process owner" who defines and changes the processes, within which subordinates must function.
	Limited Accountability within Manager's Framework (AC/F)	To make limited input-output decisions, within larger processes of the manager, affecting one's colleagues, but within frameworks set by the manager	This is necessary to ensure timely, optimal, and accountable cross-functional decision making, below the process accountable manager
	Accountability for Sub-Processes (AS) or Work Steps (AW)	To deliver one's own required outputs into the process flow upon which the process depends	This is simply an accountability for direct outputs—being held accountable by ones own immediate manager

Managers are accountable for the outputs of their subordinates and all roles subordinate to them. To enable timely decisions between subordinate roles working across the same cross-functional process, the "crossover" accountable manager can assign limited authority to a role—one or two levels down—to "make the call" that best supports the accountable manager's intentions.

DIRECT ACCOUNTABILITY: "PROCESS OWNER"

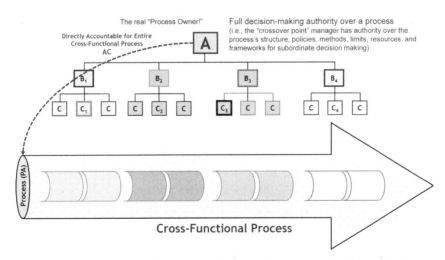

A "process owner" is the first managerial role up the hierarchy that has authority over every role with some accountability for the process.

As one moves down the organization from a process-accountable manager role, there may be lower level sub-process-accountable manager roles that have nearly full authority over sub-processes within a larger cross-functional process, constrained only by the "parent process" input and output requirements. As one continues down the hierarchy toward procedures, we eventually find roles with direct accountability for process steps.

Managerial systems are accountability hierarchies where every manager is fully accountable for his subordinates' outputs, effectiveness, and adherence to policy and process limits.

One additional scenario can benefit from a process-accountable manager delegating limited accountability and authority to a subordinate role in the service of efficient and timely cross-functional decision-making. This situation exists when the coordinating indirect accountability is felt to be too time-consuming to resolve differences of opinion between roles that are working on common processes and consuming resources in common. A failure to collectively persuade others would normally require delaying action and elevating the decision, which may still need to be elevated further.

When the process-accountable manager, in concert with his team, develops a decision-making framework (DMF), which captures his perspectives, principles, and priorities around the types of bottlenecks that could occur, he may choose to delegate to one subordinate quarterbacking-type authority. This means that role can "make the call" that in his judgment best reflects the intentions captured in the DMF—as long as it will not prevent anyone else from being able to meet his accountabilities.

I refer to this hybrid direct-and-indirect accountability as limited accountability within the process-accountable manager's framework.

Improving Process Effectiveness (without Violating the Laws of Accountability Gravity)

The age-old struggle in managerial systems since the beginning of the Industrial Revolution in the 1700s has been to find the proper balance between releasing human creative initiative and ensuring process control and discipline. The pendulum of management fads swings back-and-forth between these two extremes every few years, yielding a few short-term gains. However, it always overreaches and eventually creates new problems as well as unintended consequences.

The solution lies in understanding that managerial systems are dynamic human judgment and accountability hierarchies. It is neither one nor the other. It is both. By establishing the expectation that employees are accountable for, simultaneously, keeping their word, no surprises (process control), and earning their keep (creative initiative), and creating the means for clarifying "who is accountable for what in relationship to whom," we can regulate that balance.

Furthermore, decision-making frameworks ensure the optimal and accountable running of cross-functional processes; they are powerful productivity multipliers. They ensure that people will work together to find the best-possible solutions that support an organization's overarching strategy and goals. As this chapter has pointed out, there exists a hierarchy and taxonomy of indirect accountabilities and authorities that are not accountable for the decisions or actions of others with direct accountabilities and authorities. However, they are accountable for initiating action in relationship to others with direct accountabilities. In this way, managers avoid the chaos and conflict attendant with matrix management and similar solutions, which defy "the laws of accountability gravity" by suggesting that an employee has more than one manager.

CHAPTER 9

System Stewardship:
How to Defeat Matrix Management

"THINK LIKE AN OWNER, not like an employee!"

This frequent management exhortation is communicated—and interpreted—in countless ways in thousands of companies every day. Employees should endeavor to always maximize profit. They should always minimize costs. They should always minimize waste. They should feel responsible for doing the right thing. Unfortunately, the slogan is usually invoked when managers have abdicated their role in holding subordinates accountable for keeping their word, no surprises, and earning their keep.

Nevertheless, I believe it is useful to translate the mindset of someone who "owns" an asset into concepts that apply to managerial hierarchies. If I ran a solo personal services business and bought a critical piece of equipment, I would want to make sure it was well maintained and in peak operating condition. I would want to ensure that I had been trained to use it correctly to avoid errors and customer complaints. I would want to use it as often and as efficiently as possible to get the best return on my investment. This is what it really means to think like an owner.

Whenever a manager delegates a resource to a subordinate, it should carry with it the same expectations that an owner would place on herself. While owners feel personally responsible for doing so, managers must hold their subordinates accountable for stewarding those resources.

Stewardship is the accountability of every manager and employee for taking optimal care of the resources delegated to him, continuously finding ways to improve on their capabilities, and deploying them as effectively and efficiently as possible to create the greatest value for the organization.

At higher levels of an organization, managers are accountable not only for stewarding their tangible assets, but for all of the systems and processes they "own" and for ensuring that employees working within their units operate within the requirements of those systems. When a number of interrelated processes subordinate to a process-accountable manager exist, that manager may assign system stewardship accountability to a subordinate in order to support the capability, integrity, and control of those cross-functional systems (i.e., collections of related processes, policies, procedures, and structures).

System stewardship refers to a unique type of subordinate role established primarily to support the manager's stewardship accountabilities. The system steward accomplishes this by studying and making recommendations on the system framework; by coordinating system implementation; by service giving; by regulating opportunities, obstacles, and limits; and by studying and making recommendations on system improvements.

Providing Solutions to the Multiple-Boss Conundrum

A significant challenge for companies that have multiple entities (e.g., business units, manufacturing plants, service centers, distribution centers, etc.) is how to achieve consistency of processes and practices across each unit, without compromising clarity of accountabilities for and within any unit. The typical solution around the world is to create matrix organizations, where a line manager holds her employees accountable for their outputs and dotted-line managers hold the same employees accountable for safety, quality, and delivery performance.

This often creates both confusion and internal conflicts over priorities for those employees. Frequently heard defenses by employees who have failed to satisfy the expectations of one of their "managers" is "don't blame me, blame my other boss."

These types of hybrid solutions undermine the central property of accountability in managerial systems. A "true" manager role is simultaneously accountable for its subordinate employees' effectiveness in role outputs *and* adherence to process and policy.

Consequently, if any employee has more than one manager, then no one manager can be held accountable for that employee. The same problem exists when we say an employee can report to multiple managers. If we mean they are simply accountable for providing reports, no problem. However, if we mean that each one of those managers can hold them accountable, we once again short circuit the accountability hierarchy.

If any employee has more than one manager, then no one manager can be held accountable for that employee.

An immediate implication of this reality is that managers can no longer simply pressure their subordinates to maximize outputs at any cost because they are—and will be—held accountable for ensuring their subordinates also adhere to process and policy when working on those outputs. This properly puts on the shoulders of managers the need to consider and balance the effects of all policies and processes when they are delegating assignments. They must weigh the impact of particular demands on their employees' ability to concurrently adhere to limits.

Context Is the Means for Communicating This Balance

Managers' thinking then needs to be effectively conveyed to their subordinates both while setting context and in accurately defining the Rs in QQT/Rs. As we have discussed, effective and accountable delegation must be clear and specific when defining assignment parameters. Outputs should be described in terms of both quantity and quality (Q, Q). The maximum time (T) allowed for completion needs to be specified to enable employees some discretion when prioritizing and sequencing each of their deliverables. And resources and resource constraints (R) must spell out which limits, policies, practices, etc., must be strictly adhered to and with which constraints the employee can exercise discretion.

The setting of context surrounding the managers' rationale for these relative priorities is particularly important. It equips their subordinates with a logical framework when considering alternative courses of action.

> *"I know I am accountable for producing N outputs over T time and that I am also limited in the number of contractors I can hire, the amount of overtime I can pay our employees, the number of hours per week I can expect employees to work safely, and the speed with which I can ask them to run their equipment. But since my manager was clear about the overall priorities and the absolute limits within which I must operate, I can develop two or three options for proceeding, each of which could succeed. I may even need to alternate among them. No matter what, any plan must reinforce my manager's context about limits."*

Context is the "bread and butter" of effective accountability leadership and should be expected of every manager within an organization. The "A" for alignment in L.E.A.D. is critical.

Implications at Higher Levels of an Organization

However, as we move up an organization's hierarchy, the time required and the difficulty of explaining and overseeing adherence to all the policies, processes, and procedures expands considerably. A managerial role that has authority over all aspects of a process (structure, policies, methods, limits, resources, people, and frameworks) is the true process owner.

Keep in mind that the ultimate goal of organizational design is to (1) maximize the amount of opportunity for exercising creative judgment, initiative, and discretion for each role and to (2) ensure that when effective lateral working is required, all roles operate within the same context and boundary conditions. Every role carries with it some of these direct accountabilities.

To support managers in roles at Levels 4 and above, it is often useful to establish subordinate roles that are accountable for stewarding various systems, subsystems, and processes on behalf of the managers who "own" them, such as finance, HR, legal, engineering, and IT.

For example, it is the CEO who is the process owner of the organization's financial system—not the CFO. The CFO can only steward the corporate financial system on behalf of the CEO, because that role does not have managerial authority over the CEO's other subordinates who are accountable for working within the financial system. These other executives need to be held directly accountable for adhering to the financial system's requirements by the CEO with the stewardship assistance of the CFO.

System stewardship carries four primary types of accountabilities:

1. Supporting the "system- or process-accountable manager" in the continual improvement in the capability, efficiency, and accountability of the system. This includes: ·

   - Identifying opportunities for improvement
   - Leading study-recommendation efforts to design potential improvements (to be decided by the accountable manager)
   - Leading implementation-coordination efforts across the organization

2. Providing services to units in the organization to

    ■ Provide training designed to enhance the effective application of the system's processes and procedures within those units

    ■ Respond to requests for studies or recommendations regarding system issues

3. Exercising the full gamut of indirect accountabilities, both influencing and regulating, to ensure the optimal application of the system's processes and procedures

    ■ Informing: Advising and Recommending

    ■ Persuading: Monitoring and Coordinating

    ■ Instructing: Auditing and Prescribing

4. Directly overseeing aspects of the system

    ■ Running processes

    ■ Maintaining best practices

    ■ Mentoring system-related talent pool

There is one critical difference between a matrix solution and a stewardship approach for balancing the dual needs for control and discretion. System stewards work to ensure process consistency and control, on the one hand, while respecting the need for an unambiguous managerial accountability hierarchy, on the other. Again, this is based on the simple principle that every employee has only one manager holding her accountable for outputs, effectiveness, and adherence.

A system steward is not the accountable manager of an employee in a different function—who must nevertheless operate within the requirements of that system. The employee's immediate line manager is the role that holds him accountable for adherence. The steward supports the system-accountable "owner" for ensuring the system is optimally designed, the employees are effectively trained, and the appropriate indirect accountabilities relative to employees are exercised to assist them in being fully informed, to persuade them to avoid risky courses of action, and to prevent them from acting outside of limits.

Stewardship roles and functions often exist at many different levels within the same organization. For instance, a Level 7 CEO will have a Level 6 CFO subordinate executive who stewards the enterprise-wide financial system on behalf of the CEO. The CEO may also have three Level 6 regional division executives who each must operate within different regional financial regulatory constraints. The division executives will likely need their own Level 5 regional CFOs to assist them in designing and overseeing each of their regional financial systems. Nevertheless, the Level 6 corporate CFO needs to ensure that each of the Level 5 regional CFOs designs regionally appropriate systems that still adhere to the overarching requirements of the corporate financial systems. This cascading of systems, subsystems, and sub-subsystems requires stewards at each level. This is analogous to a series of Russian Matryoshka nesting dolls of decreasing sizes, one placed inside the other.

The corporate CFO is not the dotted-line manager of the regional CFOs; the regional presidents are their accountable managers and their only managers. Nevertheless, the corporate CFO does have, and must exercise appropriately, a number of indirect accountabilities in relationship to her regional division head peers and their regional CFOs. When the corporate CFO hits a roadblock with the regional CFO and business heads, the corporate CEO must intervene and hold them accountable for operating within the corporate system requirements.

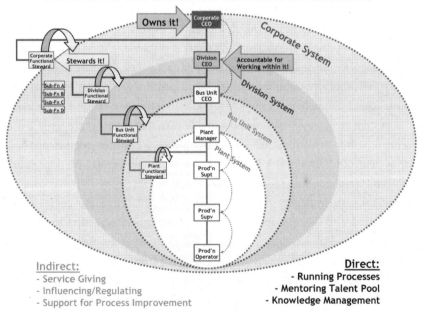

System Stewardship
Nested Direct and Indirect Accountabilities

Indirect:
- Service Giving
- Influencing/Regulating
- Support for Process Improvement

Direct:
- Running Processes
- Mentoring Talent Pool
- Knowledge Management

"True process owners" can delegate system stewardship authority to subordinate roles—with a combination of direct and indirect accountabilities—to assist in maintaining the integrity of the owner's systems and to support their continuous improvement.

Recognizing and Designating Stewardship Roles

Not all roles that have indirect accountabilities and authorities are stewardship roles. It is when they are also accountable for supporting continuous process improvement and the direct running of system processes—combined with the other indirect accountabilities—that they become system stewards.

An additional complication in designing system stewardship roles is one of critical mass. When an organization has multiple and similar functional units but does not have the quantity of employees to justify establishing stewardship roles within each unit, the "parent" stewardship role will often develop its own staff to provide stewardship-like services to the heads of each of the subordinate units.

This can create a conflict when a unit head expects this service-giving role to function like her own immediate subordinate. However, it is the "parent" steward who is the immediately accountable manager of the service-giver. This common ambiguity often results in a struggle for control.

In these instances, it is important for the heads of the units to be able to count on the service-giving roles to function as if they were members of their teams and their own stewards. Otherwise, those roles will most likely be shut out. Moreover, they often assume more policing postures or, worse, become redundant.

A Final Word

System stewardship is a critical element in designing and implementing strategically aligned accountability leadership managerial organizations. The stewardship role itself requires a holistic view of work organizations.

It often functions as the conscience of the process-owner managers whom they support. These roles require people who are comfortable with having limited positional authority but enjoy exercising their personal authority. That authority must be earned by listening carefully to the problems and tensions expressed by people frustrated with the systems they steward, understanding their constraints thoroughly in order to express genuine empathy, formulating creative solutions (either temporary or permanent), and pulling in the process owner only when necessary to resolve a roadblock.

CHAPTER 10

Human Resource Systems

THERE IS AN ACTIVE debate about whether the human resources function is a genuinely professional discipline like engineering. Or is it a collection of tactical activities related to staffing, development, compensation, safety and health, and employee and labor relations?

Since a discipline is a body of work built upon a scientific foundation, I would argue that the principles and practices presented in this book should serve as the basis for human resources becoming a critical strategic discipline. And here, I will attempt to prove it!

Science requires definitions, measurement, principles, methodologies, and the ability to predict outcomes without first applying trial and error. Here is a synopsis of the criteria I have established so far.

DEFINITIONS

Work is the application of judgment and discretion to the completion of an assignment.

Assignment is the delegation of an output (characterized by quantity-Q and quality-Q) to be completed within a certain time-T and within defined resource-R and policy constraints.

Accountability is the obligation to both keep one's word, no surprises, (QQT/Rs can be measured), and to "earn one's keep" (effectiveness can be assessed).

Functions are broad categories of accountabilities.

Processes are a series of actions or steps one is accountable for taking in order to achieve a particular end.

Roles are economic constructs to be filled by an employee selected with the capabilities to meet its work requirements, in terms of complexity, functional, process, and role-relationship accountabilities.

Effectiveness is the judged aggregate value of an employee's contributions relative to the standards for his role's degree of complexity.

Potential is the level of a person's innate capacity to handle complexity and is a necessary capability for being qualified to fill a role with a defined level of complexity.

MEASUREMENT

Timespan of a role is the length of time targeted for completion of a role's longest accountability and defines both the degree and level of complexity for that role.

PRINCIPLES

The proper **distance** of one level separating manager and subordinate roles is necessary to ensure both add the value for which the role was created.

Potential continues to mature and grow at predictable rates throughout most of an adult's lifetime.

Trading business units are optimally established as Level 5 entities around a defined market and resourced with all of the mainstream business, resourcing, and control functions.

METHODOLOGIES

Establish the **timespan and level of complexity of the most senior role** in order to determine the **optimal** number of levels beneath it.

An employee's **future potential** (in a specified period) can be accurately predicted based on his maturation curve identified from his assessed current potential and age.[1]

ABILITY TO PREDICT

Here is an example of prediction after one day of data gathering about a merger of two comparable businesses (with a combined total of 7,500 employees).

Whatever new structure finally emerges will reduce the time it currently takes for making decisions by 25 percent. Moreover, they will be better decisions.

Clue: The timespan of the newly combined division head role required Level 6 role complexity. Both legacy organizations had eight levels, so the new organization will need two fewer levels. Eliminating those two levels will increase the speed of decision-making by 25 percent. It will also significantly reduce the amount of non-value-adding bureaucratic noise currently created by the extra levels.

What are the elements found in HR functions that can now be designed into an integrated, comprehensive, strategic HR system, all based on these common sets of scientific platforms?

- Strategic alignment principles and architectures driving organizational design;
- Role establishment precisely reflecting each role's complexities, functional and process accountabilities, and direct and indirect working relationships;
- Highly capable managerial and teamworking leadership practices;
- Talent assessment and development systems for continually improving employee effectiveness, current potential, and other capabilities in direct relationship to role requirements;
- Accurate selection decisions enabling a systematic search for qualified employees across the company;
- Strategic recruitment with an eye for, simultaneously, optimally, and accurately filling vacant roles and identified "holes" in the talent "pipelines of potential";
- Finely tuned staffing planning with rich data about critical competencies at risk; and
- Sophisticated succession planning based on accurate mapping of talent pipelines and accountable career mentoring.

HR Systems Are the Foundation for Healthy Psychological Contracts

As set out in Chapter 2 on leadership, the critical multipliers in achieving high levels of employee engagement and commitment are the strength and integrity of the psychological contract between employees, their managers, and the organization. The more that employees experience their managers, and company's commitment to their own personal and work success, the stronger they will reciprocate by working enthusiastically to support the company's success. The more they trust that their managers are accountable for helping them achieve their full potential, the more they will focus all of their creative energies on helping the company achieve its full potential. They will not need to conserve their energy to protect themselves from an unfair and untrustworthy company.

HR Systems Are like a Double-Strand Helix

Managerial systems are inherently purpose-driven work organizations. They exist to create the value necessary to achieve their owners' purpose and mission. Strategy represents the short-, mid-, and long-term steps deemed necessary to accomplish those goals and, in turn, requires both a strategically aligned system of work and capable people to fill its roles and make the necessary decisions. Cascading manager-subordinate hierarchies are the means by which authority and resources from the owners are delegated successively down the organization and by which employees are held accountable by their managers for both keeping their word, no surprises, and earning their keep. Leadership represents the managerial work necessary to engage people's commitment, align their judgment, and develop their capabilities—all within an accountability framework.

A double-strand helix, which is the structure of a DNA molecule, is a perfect metaphor for the core concept underlying HR systems. A DNA molecule consists of two strands that wind around each other like a twisted ladder. Each DNA strand within the double helix is a long, linear, hierarchical molecule made of smaller molecules that form a chain. There is a one-to-one connection between the molecules of each chain at the same level. Consequently, this holds both chains together into a single functioning entity.

The HR system consists of two interlocked strands, as well. One strand contains hierarchically arranged roles with defined accountabilities for specific functions and processes. The parallel strand consists of employees—attached to each of these roles—who possess the required capabilities to make effective decisions, add the appropriate level of value, and meet their delegated accountabilities. Each of the attributes of the roles and people must be stewarded by HR systems in a capable, efficient, and accountable manner.

The two main streams of HR systems that work to achieve that optimal alignment are (1) organizational design and development and (2) talent assessment, deployment, and development.

Strand #1: From Organization Design to Role Establishment

The process of organizational design explained in Chapter 5 involves the scientific translation of strategy into the required levels of role complexity, the necessary functions and points of functional alignment, and the optimally capable and efficient processes. The art of organizational design lies in arranging each of these three multipliers in relationship to each other, so that accountabilities are clear, unambiguous, and aligned with the requisite authority.

Chapters 6 through 9 elaborate on the properties of each of these multipliers and Chapter 11 describes the methodology for integrating them into a cohesive, whole system of work. Keep in mind there are many different ways to design and construct a bridge, but every one of them must comply with the laws of gravity and material science.

Once the organizational design is completed, then creating a role specification is as simple as documenting the hierarchical intersections of each role's specific functional and process accountabilities. A role can now be characterized by its level of work complexity, its types of work (specific accountabilities for functions and processes), its nature of work (e.g., managerial, individual contributor, team leader, analytic, execution, service-giving, etc.), and its working relationships (hierarchical as well as direct and indirect cross-functional relationships).

The process of role establishment needs to be understood through the lenses of managerial accountability. When a manager A creates a subordinate manager B role, A has a conception of the types and volumes of QQT/Rs that will be delegated to B, many "chunks" of which B will need to delegate to his subordinates at the C-level. With that in mind, A needs to decide how many C-level subordinates B will need to support him in delivering on all of his QQT/Rs.

There are three different kinds of QQT/Rs that A can delegate to B. Some will be direct output support (DOS), namely assignments that require B to personally analyze information and make recommendations back to A to support A's own decision-making.

Other QQT/Rs will require B to create direct outputs (DO), namely, to apply his own time and capabilities to work on assignments by himself and deliver them directly to the organization or to the external environment. Both

DOS and DO accountabilities will take up a portion of manager B's time and thereby leave less time to effectively manage his subordinates.

The third type of QQT/Rs that A will definitely delegate to B are delegated direct outputs (DDO). These assignments—for which B will be ultimately accountable—require that B first develop his overall plans for completion and then delegate "chunks" of those plans to his subordinates as their QQT/Rs. B remains accountable for his subordinates' outputs, but he should not be spending his own time making the actual decisions to complete them. However, he will need time and proximity to them in order to monitor their work, assess their effectiveness, coach them, and hold them accountable.

With this in mind, manager A must estimate the amount of time that each subordinate manager will likely need to spend directly on administrative matters and DOS and DO assignments. Then A must gauge the likely scope and volume of B's delegated DDO assignments, the amount of B's planning time for each, the amount of context-setting time and delegating time for each, and the amount of time monitoring B's subordinates' progress and coaching them.

ROLE SPECIFICATION AND QQT/Rs

At the very least, a role specification document should include the following information:

1. The role's primary purpose and its level of role complexity.

2. Its direct accountabilities. Owns the process or function and is fully accountable for the output.

3. Its indirect accountabilities. Affects the decisions of others.

4. Its stewardship accountabilities. Supports process integrity of a process owned by one's manager.

5. General accountabilities. Specific to all subordinates, all managers, all managers of managers, and all managers of a major function.

6. Metrics. How the accountabilities for the role will be measured.

7. Major thrusts. Long-term themes or initiatives to be embedded in the multiple specific objectives (below).

8. Specific objectives. List tasks, assignments, projects, programs, initiatives, etc., (in QQT/R format).

Accurate and comprehensive role specifications eliminate non-value-adding ambiguities that often require employees to "work the system." They free up employees to fully apply their judgment and creative initiative to do their "real work."

Collectively, these analyses should yield the number of subordinate resources B would likely need to address all of his accountabilities.

Whenever B requests additional subordinates to meet the demands of his role, B's manager A must take into account how well B's current employees are filling each of their roles. If B has a team of weak subordinates—and has failed to enhance their effectiveness at a reasonable rate—then adding additional subordinates to help B fulfill his accountabilities could be counterproductive. "If you cannot effectively manage the eight subordinates (you already have) to complete the work they should be able to accomplish, how are you going to have the time to effectively manage two more subordinates?"

The B-level manager can only recommend to his own manager the establishment of new subordinate roles. It is his manager, A, who is accountable for determining and delegating the level of resources (the "R" in QQT/R) that B requires.

Strand #2: From Role Establishment to Role Filling

Whenever making selection decisions, the challenge for every organization is to balance or reconcile the need to simultaneously:

- Present to the "selecting" immediate manager a slate of qualified candidates to choose from;

- Ensure that those qualified employees who—along with their mentors—have identified roles of this nature that are desired next steps in their career development and will be seriously considered;

- Provide timely developmental opportunities for those highly effective, high-potential employees who are critical for implementing the long-range succession plan;

- Ensure proper representation of candidates from diverse backgrounds and geographies; and

- Strategically distribute top talent across the organization to support managers in being able to meet their accountabilities.

Since we have now defined each of the dimensions of work roles, we can apply the same lenses when assessing the capabilities of every employee. Once that is completed for the entire pool of organizational talent, the widest possible net (i.e., search) can be cast for every vacancy or newly created role to identify employees who possess the full set of capabilities required for the role.

As additional criteria are added to the search, the net gets narrower and allows the organization to identify the optimal intersection of the multiple individual and organizational needs.

I am often asked which of the five capabilities is more important than the others when making selection decisions. First, the employee's current innate potential must minimally be at the level of complexity of the role to be filled. It is the minimum price of entry, a necessary but—by itself—insufficient requirement for filling every role. To select an employee who lacks the innate problem-solving capacity to master the levels of complexity for which the role was established ensures that he will diminish the scope of the role to a size he can handle.

There are some caveats to this principle. An employee whose potential is far greater than the role's complexity will often begin like a blaze of fire, identifying opportunities to add value that others never realized. However, given the

ALIGNING PERSON TO ROLE

Populating Roles with Capable, Motivated Talent with the:

- **Potential** to Handle the Complexity of Work of the Role
- **Skilled Knowledge** to Master the Types of Work of the Role
- **Commitment to** and **Valuing of** the Nature of Work of the Role
- **Natural Aptitudes** for the Types and Nature of Work of the Role
- **Maturity** to Effectively Manage the Role's Working Relationships

By precisely defining each role's work requirements (complexity, types, nature, relationships), it becomes possible to accurately assess and select employees with the precise capabilities (potential, skilled knowledge, work valued, aptitudes, and maturity) needed for each role.

limited authority in the role to address many of these challenges, the employee will often become bored, frustrated, and demoralized.

Another problem occurs when an employee who has a great deal of "headroom" in her current role is promoted to a role more than one level higher without having first experienced and mastered some of the breadth of work at the interim levels. She may be intelligent enough but lacks the experience of the way people work and think at higher levels.

Second, one should consider excluding employees from consideration who have been judged to demonstrate appreciable degrees of disruptive behaviors and have not responded constructively to coaching and mentoring. These behaviors are often aggravated by promotion to more complex and stressful roles and the behaviors will have a greater adverse impact on more people the higher the employee rises. Being advised by one's mentor that future promotion is contingent upon getting these disruptive behaviors under control is often the most potent motivator to get employees to commit to changing.

Third are the various factors that predict for strong motivation to be successful in the role. Past performance is a powerful predictor of future performance. Employees who have consistently demonstrated exceptional commitment and high degrees of effectiveness in past roles should be given priority status. This is especially true when the nature of work in past roles was similar to work in the vacant role. Employees who have always had a strong work ethic and high levels of grit (i.e., passion and perseverance for long-term and meaningful goals) should also be ranked high on the list.

Paradoxically, skilled knowledge and experience are only fourth on my list but are often the first type of capabilities searched for in most companies. A baseline degree of skilled knowledge about a role's functions and processes is, of course, necessary, but should not be the "first cut" in a search to fill vacancies. Higher levels of the first three filters (potential, mature behaviors, and commitment) are ultimately more important predictors for success in a role than higher levels of skilled knowledge. Furthermore, as long as a candidate meets the minimum threshold of experience required to hit the ground running, greater brainpower and stronger commitment will accelerate the employee's on-the-job learning and acquisition of knowledge.

Finally, the presence of unique talents and aptitudes that might provide incremental nuances of understanding and accelerated mastery of a role should be considered. Here is an interesting example. In a cosmetic company client, there are two categories of employees who work in its "color creation" unit:

chemists and colorists. It was far easier to recruit for chemists than people who have a strong, intrinsic ability to discern gradations in an almost infinite spectrum of color shades. Only one in 10 candidates screened was able to meet the requirements. Not coincidentally, the successful candidates were also artists or involved in some artistic endeavors that required high levels of similar innate talents.

Back to the Beginning: Accountability and Assessing Effectiveness in Role

A central principle underlying highly productive managerial hierarchies is the need to ensure meaningful accountability that balances against the need for process control with opportunities to exercise value-adding creative initiative. Throughout the book, I have translated this requirement for each employee as "when you give your word, you must keep your word, no surprises," and "when you are in a role, you must earn your keep." In this context, earning one's keep means adding the aggregate degree of value—in a variety of ways—that falls within the range of value expected of all roles with that specific level of complexity.

Keeping one's word, on the other hand, is all about outputs and throughputs (i.e., adhering to limits). These artifacts can be measured. For example, the production line for a pharmaceutical tablet met its target for N pills per shift for the last three days. The production process quality metrics never exceeded more than one standard deviation from the centerline or mean for the entire period.

In contrast, earning one's keep is all about the exercise of judgment, discretion, and initiative in addressing all of the accountability dimensions of a role. This includes figuring out how to overcome obstacles to delivering QQT/Rs without exceeding limits and making continuous adjustments when working on one's QQT/Rs to support one's teammates in ways that best support the manager's context. This also includes minimizing the utilization of delegated resources wherever possible and taking the initiative to identify ways to further enhance resource capabilities. These actions can be observed. Their value can be assessed, but not readily measured.

A fair and trust-inducing culture of accountability is never actually achieved until employees receive feedback from their first "honest" and accurate effectiveness appraisal that was also tied to appropriate consequences—whether they are positive or negative.

There are myriad problems associated with most organizations' performance management systems, enough so that many corporations are abandoning them altogether. These problems stem from the fact that genuine effectiveness appraisal is inherently subjective. Few organizations have figured out how to achieve internally consistent, reliable assessments of every employee across the entire organization against the same high standards. Most surveys reveal that when managers rate their subordinates' performance by themselves (i.e., without calibration conversations), three-quarters of employees are rated in the top quartile. Obviously, "our people are all above average" is an oxymoron.

Other companies do not trust their managers to render accurate individually rendered performance assessments. Instead, these companies require that their managers "force rank" their subordinates' performance. A major problem with this approach is that employees are not being assessed against the requirements of their roles; they are assessed only in relationship to each other. It is often the case that the lowest-ranked subordinate of a very effective manager—who has developed a high-performing team over time—may be much more effective in his role than the highest-ranked subordinate of a poor manager with a weak team.

Assessment of employee effectiveness (earning one's keep) must reflect the degree of value contribution one demonstrates relative to the range of value expected of the role he currently occupies, not relative to others.

A Pragmatic Approach to Evaluating Effectiveness Accurately and with Internal Consistency

With 40 years of experience working around the world with managers at every level of their organizations, I have devised the following hypothesis of how employees add and subtract value in their roles. Since employee "value-add" per se cannot be measured, a model is required that accounts for the subjective experience managers have about who their most and least effective employees are.

Such a model must be congruent with other models that assign value to entities in order for it to feel natural to the managers doing the assessments. It must recognize that different managers have different standards for what constitutes effectiveness. Not surprisingly, all managers have at least some bias about certain individuals or groups of individuals. Somehow, these differences and biases must be made explicit and then offset or diffused. Ultimately, there needs to be a way of establishing a common high standard to be applied to the assessments of all employees in an organization and for the managers doing the assessments to be "kept honest" by their own managers and their peers.

One helpful analogy is to look at the way in which stock markets assign economic value to publicly traded companies within each of their own industries. Companies that deliver products and services consistent with the industry norm, which have evolved technologies also consistent with industry norms, and which manage their businesses effectively enough to achieve levels of free cash flow and ROI consistent with industry norms, will likely trade at values midpoint in their industry. Companies that fail to achieve these norms will likely trade at lower multiples. Companies that have exceeded industry norms in any of these areas will create greater value for their shareholders and consequently trade at higher multiples.

THREE COMPONENTS OF EFFECTIVENESS

That results in the creation of
"incremental value above and beyond" the basic role

INTENSITY + INTEGRATION + INNOVATION

EXTRAORDINARY VALUE

That "delivers results consistent with the effective application"
of the assessed levels of skilled knowledge mastery

VERTICAL WORK + LATERAL WORK + MANAGERIAL WORK + CULTURAL BEHAVIORS

BASIC ROLE MASTERY

That has an "adverse effect" on
the overall contribution of the employee

DISRUPTIVE EXTREMES

Assessing the effectiveness with which an employee fills her role is inherently subjective. Nevertheless, managers can be expected to provide anecdotal evidence of how well each subordinate has mastered and delivered the value required of the basic role, how well any subordinate has contributed incrementally greater value by virtue of extraordinary commitment, and whether the employee has reduced the value of his contribution due to exhibiting disruptive behaviors.

Applying similar logic to roles within the same level of complexity (analogous to the same industry), the employees in each role (analogous to each company) could be assessed as to whether they have fully mastered each of their roles' requirements (i.e., learned and applied all of their functional, process, managerial, and cultural skills). The degree to which they have not yet fully applied the expected knowledge to get the expected results is the degree to which they would fall below the midpoint in their roles' range of required effectiveness—the degree to which they have "failed to hold the role up."

And whether or not they have fully mastered their roles' core accountabilities, have they exhibited extraordinary initiative in ways that generated incremental value—value not expected from role mastery alone? The degree to which they have actually "pulled the role up" would be additive to whatever value was created within the core or basic role.

Finally, the degree to which they may have exhibited behaviors that disrupted their own effectiveness or that of their team—i.e., "pulled the role down"—would be subtractive from their overall rating.

Establishing Standards, Minimizing Bias, and Ensuring Internal Consistency

Since the assessment of effectiveness is inherently subjective, it is necessary to ensure the judgments made by managers of their subordinates are filtered in a variety of ways to align or "gear" their frames of reference. To begin, managers must defend the bases of their assessments to their teammates and their immediate manager by providing anecdotal evidence of strengths and gaps. They must also take into account input about their subordinates from their peers. All of this is in full view of their common manager, who—as the steward of the standard set by the CEO—must continually set context for his team about how their expectations may be deviating from the intentions of the CEO.

We have found that the best way to facilitate this process is for the manager leading a "gearing" session to begin by reviewing the defined levels of complexity of the roles. It is important to remind the evaluating managers about the way in which roles with different functions, but the same level of complexity, are expected to add comparable value to the company—each in its own way.

Next, the gearing manager needs to lead a benchmarking session where each of his own subordinate managers assesses one of their immediate subordinates. In this discussion, he has the opportunity to directly challenge the personal standards used by each of them as they offer anecdotes as evidence to justify their opinion of their subordinates' overall effectiveness. He needs to continually reference the standards set by the CEO until satisfied that all of his managers interpret the evidence the same way with their benchmarked subordinates.

Both the benchmarking and subsequent larger-scale gearing assessment processes use the following criteria and narrative:

"These subordinates of yours are all occupying roles with level N complexity. Let's begin by discussing how well each of them has mastered the skilled knowledge required of their basic roles and has fully applied that knowledge to deliver the kinds of results and level of value expected from a solid employee. Although each role has different specific accountabilities, each has defined accountabilities for its functions, processes, leadership, and culture."

1. What is your sense of the overall degree of basic role mastery for each (i.e., holding the role up)?

    ■ Solid, requiring little or no supervision (i.e., the complete package).

    ■ 90 percent, able to deliver on nearly all of the basic requirements, but still needs some coaching.

    ■ 67 percent, mastered two-thirds of the role's "levers," but still needs active development and oversight in the other areas.

    ■ 33 percent, mastered only one-third of the role's "levers," and needs active development, direction, and oversight in many areas.

    ■ 10 percent, has not yet mastered any of the role's major levers, but is responsive to direction and actively seeks support when unclear as to how to proceed.

    ■ 5 percent, still getting oriented to the role and needs active supervision and monitoring.

    ■ 0 percent, not meeting the minimum requirements of the role, although may be adding the kind of value expected of a less complex role.

2. Next, have instances of incremental value-add (i.e., above and beyond what would be expected from mastering the basic role alone) been demonstrated by any of these employees as an outcome of their exercising extraordinary initiative (i.e., pulling the role up)?

   ■ Untangling and resolving extremely complex and difficult problems successfully by virtue of taking personal initiative, combined with intense focus, persistence, perseverance, and effort.

   ■ Resolving gaps in delivery performance due to process breakdowns by taking personal initiative and leading the efforts to identify and mobilize all relevant stakeholders and drive agreement and commitment to work together toward a solution, even when it is not one's accountability.

   ■ Add significant, incremental value by taking the initiative to think laterally, identify novel opportunities, and innovate.

3. Finally, do any of these employees exhibit behaviors that have been disruptive to, and undermined, their own personal effectiveness and their ability to interact appropriately with others: clients, suppliers, peers, managers, and subordinates (i.e., pulling the role down)? Keep in mind that these are not statements about unusual or eccentric behaviors. Rather, they are about those extreme behaviors that have an adverse effect on how people are able to function. These behaviors can be episodic, persistent, or extremely disruptive.

Typical disruptive behaviors may include:

■ Occasional episodes of detracting behaviors: mild, but with noticeable impact on others; tolerable, but annoying.

■ Consistent episodes of detracting behaviors: impact still mild and tolerable but having a "cost" to others.

■ More persistently disruptive behaviors: impact is stronger and requires active efforts to counter.

■ Persistent disruptive behaviors: having a consistent and profoundly negative impact on the organization's effectiveness.

■ Unacceptable behavior! Grounds for immediate termination.

■ The expectations for appropriately mature behaviors include the ability to "self-regulate" one's reactions under stress, to be reasonable and exhibit reasonable responses to pressure, and to maintain perspective under difficult circumstances.

Having applied the gearing manager's common standards as their reference for the benchmarked roles, the managers return for the final gearing session having reassessed their remaining subordinates' effectiveness. This is when a systematic review of all subordinates' assessments takes place, calibrated and defended with anecdotes about each component: holding the role up, pulling the role up, and pulling the role down.

This process serves many purposes. First and most importantly, it is the most tangible way for a CEO to accurately communicate to every manager and employee what constitutes "earning one's keep." It ensures—as much as is humanly possible—that personal biases are surfaced and challenged and that all employees are evaluated based on the value they contribute, not on personal attributes. It creates a culture of transparency where managers are kept honest about describing and assessing their subordinates with anecdotal evidence, which they can subsequently use when providing feedback and coaching them. And when consequences (recognition, pay, promotability, etc.) are tied to the level of value each employee has contributed, it reinforces and validates an organizational culture of trust and fairness.

Coaching: Developing Employee Effectiveness in Role

A primary accountability of every manager's role is to ensure that her subordinates fill their roles effectively. Therefore, managers are accountable for coaching their subordinates to continuously enhance their effectiveness. Coaching, at its core, begins with clarifying for one's subordinates all aspects of their roles, which must be mastered within a reasonable period. This means clarifying the functional and process knowledge they must become fully skilled at and apply consistently to get the expected results and value-add. By providing and appreciating specific behavioral examples of one's subordinate's strengths, the manager can reinforce them. By providing examples indicating a lack of mastery of a particular function or process step, the manager can develop plans with her subordinate for additional training, feedback, or apprenticing.

As their subordinates grow in their roles and approach nearly full role mastery, the emphasis of coaching needs to move toward encouraging them to exercise additional extraordinary initiative in tackling some of the toughest problems, taking the lead when things go wrong (even if they are not accountable for doing so), and identifying opportunities on their own for innovating and improving process capabilities and asset capabilities.

The aspect of coaching that most managers dislike and tend to avoid is calling their subordinates' attention to behaviors that undermine their effectiveness or the effectiveness of the unit. Managers make all kinds of excuses. "I don't want to hurt or demotivate them." "I don't want to make them angry or start blaming me or others." "I feel guilty that I'm part of the problem."

Often, employees with disruptive behaviors lack insight and self-awareness about their behaviors. Therefore, this aspect of coaching requires describing observed behaviors accurately and encouraging the employee to recognize them and their adverse impact. By realizing that these behaviors will have a negative impact on their effectiveness ratings, compensation, and career options, employees will often become motivated to change—sometimes quite rapidly. Most become more self-aware and begin to identify and practice more constructive, alternative behaviors.

A critical difference in the way coaching occurs in a genuine accountability hierarchy is that it is no longer optional for managers to be actively engaged in continuously improving their subordinates' effectiveness. Managers who are observed by their own managers to fail to develop their people and whose people show little improvement over time will be called to account. I find it both tragic and amusing how quickly managers, who have previously shown little interest or willingness to provide feedback and support to their people, get quite serious about working with them to overcome gaps and build on their strengths.

Potential: The Rest of the Story

In Chapter 4, I defined the upper limits of complexity any employee can get his "mental arms" around as his current potential. I also refer to it as one's current maximum capacity or CMC. I also asserted that this problem-solving ability is innate—in the sense that the color of one's eyes is innate. It is one form of biological expression of the DNA we were conceived with. While experience and skilled knowledge can improve the effectiveness with which we apply our potential, they do not modify the underlying degree of potential.

Similarly, four profound discoveries by Dr. Elliott Jaques have transformed this concept into four powerful productivity multipliers.

1. Managers who understand the construct and practical application of establishing discrete organizational levels of complexity are able to gain remarkable agreement about which employees have the "raw potential" to work at what levels, independent of skilled knowledge, commitment, and maturity.

2. When casting a net to identify appropriate candidates to fill a vacant position with a defined level of role complexity, one can use the existing assessments of employee current potential to serve as the first filter.

3. Employees whose potential has been reassessed repeatedly over time demonstrate actual growth of their potential. In fact, it is so predictable that Jaques was able to map a series of maturation curves. These curves look just like pediatric growth curves (of height, weight, and head circumference). Instead of tracking just the first two years of life, Jaques reliably mapped them from age 20 to well into their 70s.

4. The ability to project any employee's future potential at specific time intervals going forward enables far more accurate career-development mentoring and succession planning, and talent pool modeling becomes possible. Organizations can consistently and reliably map their current and future "pipelines of talent potential."

A Pragmatic Approach to Evaluating Current Potential and Future Potential

As part of the same evaluation process for assessing employee demonstrated effectiveness, a gearing manager with his team of subordinate managers will pose the following hypothetical question about each of their subordinates:

> "If today, this subordinate—whose current role has x.y level of role complexity—had already acquired all of the skilled knowledge and experience required for a more complex role and were strongly motivated to advance and could eliminate any disqualifying disruptive behaviors, how big a role do you feel he could handle today?"

Over a decade of research exploring the correlation between employees' observable and recordable thought processes (when debating a point of view) and managerial assessments of their current potential (using the method just described) shows a 95 percent correlation. Without realizing how, most people form a remarkably accurate sense of others' potential; however, they lack a language and framework with which to describe it.

Managers who have been working with employees for a period of months unconsciously collect all sorts of data about them, including how clever their thinking is, how effective their problem solving has been, how closely their work approximates the required "way of working" relative to their roles' level of complexity. Without overtly realizing it, most managers have developed a keen sense of "radar" about people's innate abilities. Once they understand the nature and levels of role complexity, they are able to use that as a yardstick for describing at what level they believe their employees *could* potentially work at today.

The gearing manager then asks similar questions to each subordinate manager about each of their subordinates:

"Thinking about how 'innately capable' this subordinate is, relative to his current role, do you feel he has any 'headroom' today? Could he get his 'mental arms' around the work of a role at a higher level of complexity IF he had already developed greater skilled knowledge, were strongly committed, and were free from disruptive behaviors? If you do feel he does have headroom today, would that be for a role only degrees higher than his current role's complexity or in a role at even a higher level? What level of role complexity do you sense would be the upper limit to his current potential today?

"If you don't sense this employee has capability greater than his current role (i.e., no headroom), do you feel he has the right level of potential for his current role or is he already in over his head? Is the complexity of his current role greater than his current potential?"

Typically, during the initial gearing session, each assessing manager is hesitant and unsure about the first few people he is asked to evaluate.

"Do you really mean how smart he is? Are you asking about his raw brainpower, the speed of his processor? How would I know?"

After the first half hour or so, something clicks in for most of the managers and they are able to understand and to more quickly render an assessment.

They are also able to provide relevant anecdotes that illustrate their points of view. The gearing manager next asks his subordinate team of managers to compare each of their employees' initial assessments of current potential against the other employees' assessments.

"When you look at these five employees who we initially judged to have level m.n current potential and compare those individuals against each other, do any of them seem to have greater or less raw potential than the others? Which ones? How much higher or lower?"

The gearing manager then adjusts the representative icons on the appropriate levels grid.

"Does that feel more accurate in terms of their relative current potential?"

This process needs to iterate up and down the levels until there is consensus about the assessments being accurate, both for each person and relative to the others.

The next step is to use the curves—initially mapped by Jaques and validated by others—to illustrate what the managers' assessments of their subordinates' current potential would predict for their future potential. This can be done either by advancing employees' potential ratings along the curves in 10-year, 20-year, and even 30-year intervals or by illustrating what the "career end" potential for each employee would be if not further modified.

"When you examine where the curves would place these employees' future potential at age 65, do their projected potentials seem plausible? This is not to say that they will actually progress into roles at these levels within their careers, but can you envision their capacity to handle complexity eventually reaching these heights? If not, where would you consider their future maximum capacity more likely to peak? Does the subsequent adjustment of their current potential (because they would now be on a different maturation curve) make sense in light of this?"

This process needs to iterate up and down the levels until there is consensus that the assessments of both current and future potential are relatively accurate and internally consistent.

There are two important caveats worth mentioning at this point. The initial assessments of the current potential of young, high-future potential employees are often over-inflated because they stand out so clearly from the others.

However, the predicted career-end potential for many of them seems unrealistically high. When they adjust that rating (to fall on a lower curve), the degree to which the current potential rating drops eventually makes sense to them.

The other difficulty regularly encountered is when managers are asked to evaluate the potential of bright, but disruptive employees. It is very difficult for them to envision many of these people advancing in the organization because of their behaviors and that makes the assessing managers reluctant to acknowledge their innate capabilities maturing. In these instances, we force the issue by asking the following.

"Imagine he had a life-altering event that erased all of his disruptive behaviors. Under those circumstances do you feel by career end he would have the 'raw mental power' to solve problems at the level predicted by his current potential curve?"

Effectiveness and Potential: Two Very Different Creatures

In many ways, the assessment of potential is less complicated and takes less time than the assessment of demonstrated effectiveness.

A person's potential or innate problem-solving ability is a physical manifestation of his brain's current state of maturation; it is an actual property of the person's being. Furthermore, the evidence proves that given enough interaction with others, we can intuitively and relatively accurately gauge their current innate thinking ability.

What is required to more precisely assess their potential is the yardstick of levels of complexity and enough experience to understand what kinds of thinking are required to successfully work at each level. We then compare our sense of the person against the kinds of thinking required by people appropriate for work at different organizational levels.

Effectiveness, on the other hand, is a construct. It reflects the notion that roles are established as entities into which people are hired to do work, to deliver outputs, and to create value in a variety of ways. Therefore, each organization's conception of what constitutes creating value must be articulated and translated into granular enough language that can both be communicated to its employees and then serve as the basis for assessing them.

The phrases and definitions used earlier in the evaluation of the effectiveness components (basic role, extraordinary initiative, and disruptive behaviors) are still merely helpful definitions. The standards against which those definitions are compared must be set by the CEO at the outset when he evaluates his immediate subordinates and when he gears their assessments of their own subordinates. Each of those executives, in turn, become gearing managers with their own subordinate managers and must use the CEO's standards when taking them through the assessment process. And this process cascades down and across the entire organization. It is in this way that the CEO can ensure the same high standards are applied in the evaluation of every employee in a transparent and equitable manner.

> *Potential is innate capability. Effectiveness is applied potential.*
>
> *Potential is governed by nature. Effectiveness is a product of nature and nurture.*
>
> *Current potential is most critical when first "sizing" a person's fit for role.*
>
> *Future potential is valuable when developing people for future roles and in developing the organization's future "pipelines of potential."*
>
> *Effectiveness is what we need to get things done and create value today.*
>
> *Effectiveness is what we must hold people accountable for and reward accordingly.*

Mentoring: The Accountability of the Manager-Once-Removed

Earlier, I explained why coaching to enhance employees' effectiveness in current roles is the accountability of their immediate managers. It is one of the axiomatic properties of accountability hierarchies. Managers are accountable for continuously improving the resources they control.

The next logical question is, "What role should be accountable for developing and preparing people who could fill bigger roles in the future?" Should it be the accountability of an employee's immediate manager to also develop him and others to replace the manager when his role becomes vacant? Or should it be the manager's manager (manager-once-removed or MoR) who should be accountable for identifying and developing the pool of employees two levels down who have the future potential to be promoted up a level? This translates into the future potential to become one of the MoR's own immediate subordinates.

After all, the gearing manager (the MoR) drives the assessment process of employees two levels down. This provides him with great insight and hands-on experience into who the effective employees are today who also have the potential to move up levels in the future. The MoR is in the best position to understand what existing roles and potential new roles will be required in the future and what capabilities will be needed to effectively fill those roles. Therefore, from an organizational accountability perspective, it is the MoR who should be accountable for career planning and mentoring of subordinates-once-removed (SoRs).

It is important to ensure that the mentoring conversation focuses on the employee's future potential and aspirations and developmental needs. It should not be allowed to undermine the relationship between that employee and her immediate manager. So, it must be made explicitly clear that employees cannot use their mentoring sessions to complain about their immediate managers nor can the MoR use the sessions to spy on his subordinate manager.

Mentoring: Developing Employee Effectiveness for Future Roles

The role of the MoR in mentoring their SoRs is to first communicate and discuss the most recent assessments of their current potential. Our experience is that over 85 percent of the time the SoRs' perception of their own potential is the same as the MoR's initial assessment. The MoR should provide anecdotes that surfaced during the gearing session to illustrate the basis for the assessment when there is not agreement and should arrange for opportunities over the coming year to personally observe his SoR in action.

The next step is to explore the nature of work the SoR values and the types of roles he aspires to both in the near-term and long-term. This would ideally lead to a discussion of areas of development necessary to qualify for next steps and work experiences necessary to progress in his career. Any examples of disruptive behaviors that were identified during the gearing session should also be discussed. The MoR should place special emphasis on correcting them in order for the SoR to be considered for promotion.

One of the most valuable aspects of the mentoring sessions is providing perspective about the demands and constraints associated with moving up within the organization. It is important to encourage employees to take a serious look at their expectations of work-life balance and the demands on their time outside of work before committing to rigorous and ambitious career-development plans.

The development plans, risks, desired next steps, and readiness for next steps need to be documented to be available whenever the SoR's name shows up during a "capability search" for filling a vacancy. Presumably, if the mentor agrees that the nature of the vacant role would be useful for the SoR's career and that he is qualified, that should enable the SoR to progress onto the next filter.

Employees whose assessed career potential was consistent with executive-level roles should also be considered "corporate property," in that the executive team and the board need to be aware of them and provide input into their career paths and velocity.

This discussion of future highly capable and experienced employees, not surprisingly, leads right into a discussion of selection and succession-planning processes.

Selection: A Major Advance in Decision-Making and Diversity Inclusion

With the assessments of demonstrated effectiveness and current potential residing in the company's HR database, a company's leaders can now undertake straightforward Boolean searches whenever building a slate of appropriate internal candidates. Each role should be methodically characterized by the complexity of its work, its types of work (functional and process accountabilities), its nature of work, and its working relationships.

The capability search criteria flow naturally from the role's requirements: current potential, skilled knowledge, aptitudes, commitment, and maturity. I am often asked about the relative priority and weighting for each of these capabilities. The first positive capability should always be current potential, which needs to be at least at the level of the role's complexity. If an employee lacks the capacity to get his "mental arms" around the complexity of work of the role, he will have no choice but to "whittle the role down" to the size he can handle. However, while high enough potential is a necessary capability, it is by itself insufficient.

An important variable here is whether a candidate's current potential is equal to or slightly greater than the role's level of complexity or if it is significantly greater. The more "headroom" a committed employee has relative to his role, the more quickly he will be able to identify the critical "levers" for creating incremental value, and the less relevant experience becomes. In fact, when intending to drive transformational change in a unit's ways of working, it is often useful to select (into the role driving the change) an employee with potential a full level higher than the role will require once the change is completed.

At this point, I find that ensuring respect for a just and trust-inducing culture and mature behaviors is the next most critical requirement. As I alluded to earlier in this chapter, the higher an employee rises in an organization, the greater the adverse impact of disruptive behavior on those around and below him. Since a healthy psychological contract is key to employee engagement and commitment, the presence of disruptive behaviors (i.e., negative capability) . should prevent employees from being considered for promotion and, therefore, these employees should be "filtered out."

The second positive capability that should be weighed heavily is commitment, work ethic, valuing the work of the role, and a history of high effectiveness ratings, particularly in "pulling the role up" by virtue of extraordinary initiative. If an employee is mature, bright enough, and highly committed, he can get up to speed quickly by rapidly acquiring the skilled knowledge required by the role. He would need to have enough baseline skilled knowledge for the work of the role. However, strong commitment outweighs depth of knowledge as a predictor of ultimate success in a role.

Once a search has identified employees with high enough potential, strong commitment, and few (if any) disruptive behaviors, then greater depth and breadth of skilled knowledge is often a useful predictor for success. From many years of business consulting, my concern, however, is that when a vacancy needs filling, often the first (and occasionally, only) criteria chosen focus on skilled knowledge and experience.

Finally, in some roles there exist subtle nuances that are best perceived by employees with unique aptitudes or talents and can lead to better decisions and results more quickly and intuitively. In these situations, I believe we should consider the possibility that those aptitudes can be advantageous. However, they are usually not as essential and important as the other capabilities.

Succession Planning: Shaping Talent Pools into a Competitive Advantage

I hope you can now weave multiple strategic, organizational, and talent multiplier threads together to align your company's talent systems with its strategic organizational requirements. A central premise of this book is that leaders should always design managerial systems around the work. In particular, the managerial systems should be designed around the work required to deliver on the organization's strategy.

When a strategy becomes clear enough to anticipate what the business would ideally look like in five, 10, or even 20 years, it becomes possible to translate the work of those periods of time into the structures and processes needed to do the work. Once we identify the roles required by the organization at each time interval, we can then quantify the number and functions of roles at each level by complexity and function. This then determines the number and capabilities of employees we would need to fill those roles. When we project our existing "pipelines" of potential talent forward into those times, we will have our first clear opportunity to see how well our existing talent pipelines could fill those roles, at least in terms of having enough people with the potential required.

This completely changes the paradigm for succession planning from the usual "replacement planning" model, where A retires and B goes into A's role, and C goes into B's role, and so on down the line. This approach tends to anoint employees for their next role and, consequently, is a winnowing process with winners and losers. It also creates real vulnerability for the organization if an anointed successor leaves or is too critical in his current role to be promoted.

The alternative is to proactively develop pools of talent, people who would be capable of filling several different roles at each level of complexity appropriate for each timeframe. Having mapped the pipelines, it becomes possible to identify the future pipeline strategic gaps in raw potential and the likelihood that the existing talent could qualify for future roles, based on their current assessed effectiveness, skilled knowledge, commitment, and maturity.

Not only does this open up many more career options for more people, but it also informs the organization how it can be increasingly strategic in its recruitment plans. By accurately identifying the gaps in the pipeline by age and current potential, leaders and managers can be more specific about all of the ideal candidate attributes when recruiting externally.

Requisite HR Systems as a Strategic Planning Tool

A powerful case illustration occurred when I was working with a Level 5 business unit in Venezuela. The business unit was part of a global Level 8 company.

The Level 7 SVP over all of the South American businesses asked the Venezuela president to assess the feasibility of creating a combined entity that would include the entire Andean Pact region, consisting of six countries where products were sold only via distributors. Using requisite design principles, we concluded that the new regional entity would require one Level 6 president and six Level 5 country heads and 45 to 50 Level 4 functional heads. At that time, the Venezuela business had two Level 5 roles (one was a rotating development role for U.S. executives) and 11 Level 4 roles.

The Venezuela business unit was clearly the "best show in town" for employment in this remote community, so the most capable talent was more than happy to work there, even though they were mostly underemployed relative to their potential. When we completed their potential assessment process, we realized that Venezuela already had three managers with Level 6 potential, 12 with Level 5 potential, and over 60 with Level 4 potential. In effect, the one existing business unit had enough capable managers to populate the entire regional business if necessary.

This is just one of the many HR system capabilities that can ensure the HR function can earn an important seat at the strategic table.

A Final Word about Requisite HR Systems

The most powerful motivators for all human beings are to be successful, to realize their potential, and to create value with purpose. When the workplace systematically places employees in roles they value, for which they are qualified and continuously developed, and provided with clear context and assignments coupled with the requisite authorities, they experience the organization and their managers as committed to their success. When, in addition, their managers help them understand what their future potential and career options are and provide the mentoring and development opportunities to pursue a meaningful and successful career, they become motivated to do whatever they can to support their managers and company to be successful in return.

CHAPTER 11

Implementing a Strategic Organization

ABOUT 2,300 YEARS AGO, Aristotle purportedly said that "The whole is greater than the sum of its parts." In other words, when individual parts are connected together to form one unified entity, they create more value than if the parts were deployed separately. This is especially true when implementing the productivity multipliers presented in this book. Each multiplier provides incremental productivity value when applied on its own, but the full expression of each multiplier expands exponentially when connected and integrated with the others.

Embedded at the core of each of the productivity multipliers are the concepts of work and complexity, accountability and engagement, trust and fairness, and adaptability and control. These are foundational and must be communicated and modeled accurately during the implementation of a Strategic Organization transformation project. It is critical that employees understand the primary goal of these initiatives is not eliminating roles per se, but removing the "noise" in the system that interferes with people's ability to work effectively and be successful.

Genuine strategic alignment of a leadership system requires:

- Designing market-centric business and functional structures, with value-adding managerial levels;

- Supporting capable, efficient, and accountable processes;

- Resulting in roles with clear accountabilities aligned with requisite authorities;

- Being populated by capable, motivated talent;

- Being led by value-adding accountability leaders;

- Being supported by fully integrated, comprehensive HR systems, which support meaningful accountability and a culture of trust and fairness; and

- Being implemented with a comprehensive technology platform, based on—and requiring—fully requisite principles and practices.

The transformation process begins with understanding an organization's strategy and identifying the perceived barriers to its ability to execute it effectively. With that as a backdrop, the next step is to systematically translate the structure as it is formally described (organizational charts, job descriptions, etc.) into requisite formats.

The goals are to:

- Help an organization's managers realize that what they "say they have" (the manifest structure), what they "think they have" (the assumed structure) is not what they "really have" (the extant structure); and

- Design and implement "what they really need" (the "to be" or requisite structure), to implement strategy and release full enterprise value by applying the principles of leadership and organizational science.

Getting Started

The transformation process begins with systematic and cascading interviews, beginning with the CEO. Organizational charts are redrawn to illustrate levels of role complexities and functional accountabilities. Timespan of discretion is the longest period of time during which an employee has a continuous, uninterrupted accountability for exercising judgment and discretion toward the completion or fulfillment of some target or outcome. The timespan for each role clarifies its level and degree of complexity. Each role's primary, secondary, and tertiary functional accountabilities should also be clarified and labeled.

Accordingly, there are two types of initial structural analyses: positional alignment and functional alignment analysis.

- Positional analysis includes analyses of role compression and role vacuums, and spans of control.

- Functional analysis includes analysis of business-unit functions and corporate and sector functions.

Strategic Organization Methodology

PROBLEM IDENTIFICATION

Clarify Strategy and High-Level Goals	Organizational Analysis

STRATEGIC ALIGNMENT

Identify Root Causes: Structure, Process, Systems	Design Strategically Aligned Organization

TALENT ALIGNMENT

Assess Talent Potential and Effectiveness	Deploy Talent into New Organization

ACCOUNTABILITY LEADERSHIP DEPLOYMENT

Cascade Leadership and Teamworking Training	Implement Accountability System

SYSTEMS DEVELOPMENT

Map and Define Lateral Accountabilities	Establish Accountabilities for System Stewardship

ONGOING ORGANIZATIONAL AND TALENT DEVELOPMENT

Talent Pool Development System	Continual Monitoring and Improvement

Strategic Organization Transformation can be systematically achieved by first applying sound engineering principles to assess the current state of structure, processes, systems, and talent. It then requires the application of those principles to design, and select from, alternative organizational models and to accurately fill each role with talented and motivated employees. All managers and employees then need solid grounding in accountable managerial and teamworking leadership and collaboration practices. Finally, HR and talent systems need to be designed and deployed to ensure the integrity of the accountability culture, the continuing growth of each employee, and the development of well-developed pipelines of potential to meet the organization's future strategic needs.

Compression and Vacuum

The requisite organizational chart with levels of role complexity should clearly display instances of role compression (manager and subordinate roles within the same level of complexity) and vacuums (manager and subordinate roles separated by more than one level of complexity).

Compression often gives rise to reduced managerial value-add, because managers and their subordinates are both operating with the same type of mental complexity. This blurs decision-making authority, because it is often unclear which role above the subordinate has the "real" accountability for making decisions. It also precipitates a sense of management's being rigid and unresponsive, because the extra layers typically delay getting decisions made.

Compression is rarely indicated, except when a step-change transformation in structure, process, and technology is required. In these instances, one may create a role to lead the change that is one level more complex than the ultimate role required once the change is completed.

I have found that there are myriad reasons why instances of compression may emerge. Geographically dispersed roles—subordinate to a common manager—may have required local oversight. This usually results in creating additional layers, rather than establishing a peer-level coordinating role.

One example is functional misalignment where "line of business" heads lack their own subordinate business functions. To compensate, they create roles to manage those functions from other areas of the organization. Other examples occur when the organization creates a new layer of management to address spans of control issues or to provide a promotion for a key employee to prevent him from leaving the company.

There are a number of possible solutions to compression. Realign the structure to achieve proper spans of control and to create local "coordinating" roles. Realign functions within lines of business or create a better mechanism for sharing functional resources. Instead of solving a manager's broad span of control by creating additional subordinate manager layers, one should consider creating another peer-level role to the manager and transferring half of her subordinates to the new peer. Or consider consolidating the compressed two or more roles into one.

Here is a textbook example of role compression. I was working with a $1.5 billion plastic container manufacturer owned by a private equity group. The company was the result of two merged companies, and had missed its targets for 18 consecutive quarters. I spent two hours eliciting the timespan and level of complexity of the CEO role. I, then, translated the organizational charts into presumed requisite structures. Understanding at only a high level the number and breadth of manufacturing facilities, I was able to predict that the "to be" structure would collapse 10 organizational levels into six levels. Think of the ramifications of that!

Vacuums, too, may give rise to reduced managerial value-add because the complexity distance from managers to their subordinates is too great for the manager to be able to communicate context in terms the subordinates can readily understand. As a result, their subordinates are often "flying blind." Concurrently, managers often complain that they are "pulled down into the weeds" to do the work of their subordinates. However, in reality, they are doing the work of a missing subordinate-level manager.

Private Equity Property with Compression

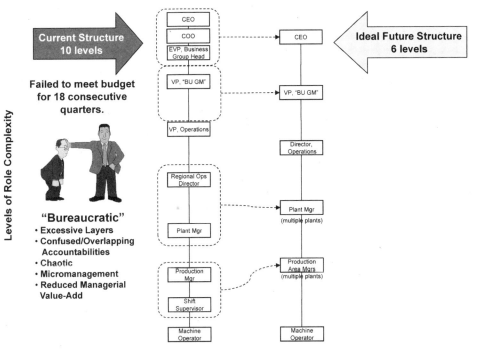

Applying the "science" of levels of work complexity enables the rapid identification of excessively layered hierarchies and helps to model the optimal layering required. The notions of role compression (roles too close) and vacuum (roles separated too much) are foundational in organizational design.

However, there are several conditions where vacuums may actually be appropriate. One is where subordinates are providing technical or analytical decisional support to their managers. These are DOS-type (direct output support) roles where individual contributors are providing support to managers. Another is with administrative support roles.

There are several underlying causes for the emergence of vacuum manager-subordinate relationships. One is a lack of critical mass for a function to justify a more complex subordinate role. Another is recent rapid growth of a manager's accountabilities leading to its being redefined at a higher level, but without elevating its subordinate's role. Manager-subordinate vacuums may also occur because of excessive and often random downsizing of subordinate organizations.

Potential solutions to vacuum relationships include subordinating the role to another immediate subordinate of the manager (e.g., subordinate a Level 2 role of a Level 4 manager to one of Level 3 subordinates) and reassessing the functional alignment to consider consolidating two or more functions, creating a larger role (without vacuum) if there is legitimate need for the more complex work.

How Certain Spans of Control Can Cause Difficulties

Spans of control that are too broad or too narrow are often identified as suspect.

Whenever a manager is seen to have three or fewer subordinates (i.e., a narrow span), one needs to investigate whether there is so much critical individual contributor work on the manager's plate that he simply does not have time to effectively manage more people or they just do not need more than a few subordinates doing DOS (direct output support) work to support their own DO (direct output) work.

The kinds of problems that emerge with narrow spans of control are too much "structure" (i.e., overhead) for the function, and when functions are too fragmented, especially when there are other similar functional managerial roles with narrow spans. This suggests the need for consolidation.

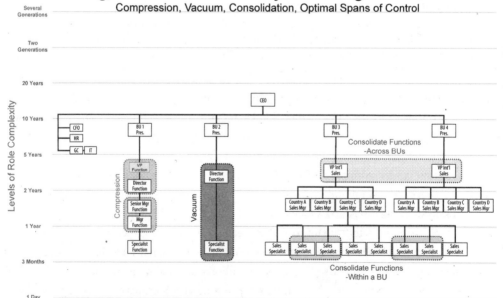

Solid, commonsense "organization engineering principles" both simplify and accelerate the organizational diagnosis and design process. They enable modeling that can predict and mitigate potential problems with alternative designs.

As indicated previously, a narrow span of control may be appropriate for high-level individual contributors that need only a few analysts to support their work. It may also be appropriate when creating a new function with plans for significant growth, but not enough work in the early phases to justify additional subordinates.

As just indicated, narrow spans may exist appropriately when the manager role is a high-level individual contributor. On the other hand, this may be a consequence—and a clue about the existence—of compression at a higher level, resulting in the classic "one-over-one" findings (i.e., where a manager has only one subordinate role). Conversely, it may be a consequence of too broad a span of control at the next level up. In either case, the resolution requires understanding both the historical rationale for its presence and rethinking the optimal three-level structure to support the processes.

Too broad a span of control exists when a manager has more subordinates than he can effectively manage—given the non-managerial accountabilities that position also has in its basket. This frequently results in "disconnects" when the manager is unable to spend the time necessary with his subordinates to ensure their individual and team effectiveness. Consequently, a lack of managerial control emerges over its subordinate function. This state is never requisite.

It may emerge with rapid growth of a function without reassessing the managerial leadership implications. It may also emerge with excessive downsizing of the manager's peer organization consolidating all of their subordinates under the remaining manager or when there exists too narrow a span of control the next level up.

A counterintuitive response to a manager requesting that he add an additional (non-requisite) layer of subordinate managers to reduce his broad span of control is to create a new peer-level manager role and transfer half of the requesting manager's subordinates to that new role. It is understandable that managers may be reluctant to have their team cut in half, but the manager's manager is accountable for maintaining the integrity of the discrete levels of role complexity.

Another response may be to correct a misalignment of functions within the current structure. This leads into the second category of organizational analyses.

Functional Alignment

As I explain in Chapter 7, "doing business" requires accurately characterizing marketplace opportunities and threats, creating new and improved products and services that provide incremental value to its customers, providing quality products and services in a cost-effective and safe manner, and engaging current and potential new customers around the value proposition of those products and services. Having the authority to lead and integrate all of these mainstream business functions is critical for a business-unit head to be accountable for the business results.

By mapping the distribution of functional accountabilities (including primary, secondary, and tertiary functions and sub-functions for each role) in the current, actual organization, it becomes clear whether a business head has the requisite authorities to be held accountable. By observing the alignment of functions within the business, one can visualize whether there is clarity about "who is accountable for what in relation to whom."

Translating Strategy in Business-Unit Structures

The first step in designing the "to be" organization is defining the markets around which the business units will be structured. Ask yourself the question, "What component of my company is its driving force?" Identifying which dimension of an organization is its driving force (i.e., technology, natural resources, production capacity and capabilities, products and services, sales/marketing methods, distribution methods, customers, industries, geographies, size) is a key element of strategic thinking. It will help you to decide how to structure your organization's business units.

A business unit wants to compete on its own terms based on its unique strengths, not the way the competition defines and approaches the market. The noted management consultant Michel Robert said that the choice of a market-based strategy is critical to "permanently tilting the playing field in your favor."

Once defining the business unit's market, the next step is to model alternative Level 5 business-unit structures containing all of the necessary mainstream business functions (market development, product/service development, product/service provisioning, and sales), together with the resourcing and control functions necessary to sustain them. The functional architecture does not necessarily equate with the ideal actual structure as long as the functions are present and within the managerial authority of the business-unit head role.

Once several models have been created, the next step is to examine the clarity and alignment of accountabilities and authorities for the critical cross-functional processes. The objective here is to opt for simplicity in the workflow decision-making, requiring the fewest number of indirect accountabilities to maintain process optimization and control. The near-final "to be" business-unit structure should be the one that has the optimal intra-business synergies and trade-offs between capability, efficiency, and accountability.

The process of modeling structure-and-process business unit options is iterative and requires "pressure testing" each option against all three attributes.

The work of the Level 5 business-unit head is to develop an integrated business model, incorporating all of the environmental and internal information into a coherent plan to penetrate, "own," and even dominate its chosen marketplace. That role relies on its Level 4 business, resourcing, and control managers to provide input into the model, translate the eventual model into operational terms, and then delegate the tactical implementation of those streams of work to their Level 3 managers. The actual conducting and transacting of business over the next two years occurs at this level.

Building Corporate Structures

As described in Chapter 7, Level 6 corporations will generally be more successful by establishing, resourcing, and integrating subordinate Level 5 business units, each with its own mainstream business functions, than by centralizing all of those functions at Level 6. The work of the Level 5 business-unit head is translating longer-term corporate strategy into the five-to-10-year business-unit model for attacking and dominating its own marketplace in ways that deliver the maximum amount of free cash flow and ROI.

A marine metaphor may be informative. It is often useful to think of the Level 5 business-unit head as steering his ship, adjusting course as necessary, enabling the seamless collaboration of the different functional members of his crew, and holding them accountable.

The Level 6 corporate head, on the other hand, should not be directly involved in directing the business functions. Instead, he should focus on acquiring and divesting businesses and establishing the targets and investments for each of them to optimally grow their asset value.

The Level 6 corporate head should also focus on finding synergies across the business units and, where there is insufficient critical mass within one business unit to justify a fully developed function, find ways to support that function from the other business units.

Level 5 business-unit heads create models with which to run their businesses in order to maximize free cash flow, market share, and customer retention.

Level 6 corporate heads make investment and asset allocation decisions to maximize the asset worth of the entire company.

When designing Level 7 corporations, the initial challenge is to identify a number of Level 6 market sectors containing multiple, related, but distinct business markets, around which one could establish Level 6 portfolios of strategically aligned Level 5 business units. Examining sectors requires analyses similar to those in determining a business unit's driving force. And once a sector is defined, one still needs to model alternative market definitions for the business units within the sector portfolio.

Inter-Business Unit Synergies

The process of modeling corporate structure-and-process options is also iterative. It requires "pressure testing" each option against all three attributes in the same way as modeling business-unit organizations. It is not unusual during this phase that potential synergies are identified across business units—within and across sectors—that may require further modification of the business units to fully exploit. The most complex aspects of this phase involve:

- Deciding which sectors and business units should be accountable for developing new technologies and product components that would be utilized by other sectors and businesses; and

- Deciding how to orchestrate commercial strategies that combine products and services from multiple businesses.

An acquisition by a Level 6 division (within a Level 8 corporation) of another Level 6 company with complementary technologies and customers required a ground-up reassessment of the optimal structure and business model for the combined organization. After analyzing the extant levels and functional alignments of the antecedent companies and exploring a variety of options for defining markets for its new Level 5 business units, the decision was made to organize around specific customer industries. The first design included new product and technology development functions in each business unit, but that would have led to considerable overlap and redundancy. The next iteration was to clarify which specific technology was "core" to each business unit and then create processes to "contract out" the development of non-core technologies to the other business units. Finally, they clarified that foundational or platform new technology development should reside in yet another Level 5 role immediately subordinate to the Level 6 division head.

Structuring Business Unit Resourcing and Control Functions

Until now, I have focused primarily on the mainstream business functions, business units, and business sectors as entities. The design of resourcing and control functions at every level of a corporation creates an additional set of issues that were discussed in Chapter 9 on system stewardship.

Resourcing functions are not primarily involved in "doing business," but rather are accountable for obtaining, creating, and distributing the resources required by the mainstream business functions. They develop, recommend, and oversee policies and processes that ensure those resources are managed appropriately and facilitate their continuous improvement. They provide support and services to managers in the business functions and monitor the adherence by those managers to the system's limits. However, they are not accountable for the decisions and actions of those resources. That resides with their immediate line managers.

A general principle for structuring resourcing functions within business units is that they should be made subordinate to the business-unit heads, not to higher-level sector or corporate resourcing roles. They are integral to the analyses and decision-making support required by the business-unit head when she is developing business models and deciding what resource types and quantities to delegate to each of his mainstream business functions. I find it useful to think of the resourcing functions (finance, HR, process and technology development, legal, etc.) as the business unit head's "brain trust" and resource acquisition "agents." Not surprisingly, many of the actions of one involve related actions from the others.

For example, the recommendation by a technology function to acquire a new type of technology to support the business must also involve the finance function around the investment analysis and the HR function to assess what retraining of existing personnel or recruitment of new employees would be required to operate the new equipment.

The resourcing functions should be plugged into the business unit head's modeling-brain-function to help him model "what if. . ." scenarios.

Control functions are not primarily involved in "doing business" either. They exist to ensure the proper use of the resources delegated to the mainstream business functions. They provide monitoring and, occasionally, auditing over-sight of resource utilization and well-being. The control function monitors the budget. It identifies deviations from plan, determines whether they are by design or by neglect, and ensures they are brought to the attention of the appropriate people. The HR function similarly monitors the application of health and safety policies and practices and utilizes their indirect accountabilities to address risks. Similarly, the QA function monitors the integrity with which defined processes are adhered to and raises the flag when discrepancies are identified.

The control functions should be plugged into the business unit head's analytical-brain-function to help him identify problems with "what has already transpired."

Ancillary Support Functions

Where the resourcing and control functions are intimately engaged in helping senior management model resource requirements, and then obtain, deploy, and protect them, they have traditionally provided some services that are more like ancillary commodities. For example, personnel and payroll administration, accounting and computer services, medical services, facility services, etc.

The governing design principle for generic ancillary services is to choose whichever mechanism that provides the required quality and reliability of those services at the lowest cost. This means centralizing them at a corporate, sector, geographic, or business unit level, or outsourcing them.

Translating Structure and Process into Role Specifications

Once the high-level structure has been decided, it is time to create the role specifications, including level or role complexity, functional and process accountabilities, and role relationships. From this, the nature of work of each role can be determined.

ROLE RELATIONSHIPS	TYPES OF WORK	TYPES OF ACCOUNTABILITIES	PRIMARY FOCUS
Managerial	Analytical	Direct	Internal
Individual Contributor	Execution	Indirect	External
Teamworking	Service-giving	Stewardship	Supplier

ROLE RELATIONSHIPS	TYPES OF WORK	TYPES OF ACCOUNTABILITIES	PRIMARY FOCUS
Cross-functional Working	Resourcing		Market/ Customer
Project Management	Controlling		Regulatory Technical Relationship

Finally, other attributes of the role may influence role-filling decisions, such as subtle nuances that might predispose to an employee with unique talents geographies that might require local languages, etc.

A Systematic Role-Filling Optimization Process

Especially during a major restructuring with many newly created and redefined roles, it is wisest to adopt a "clean slate" approach to role filling. This means that no employee being considered for selection "owns" a role, including one that may be unchanged from his existing role. The objective is to satisfy multiple needs at the same time.

So, the senior manager overseeing a large-scale NFL-type draft must reconcile (1) each manager's first choice for a particular role, (2) the closeness of fit between person and role, (3) whether there are better roles for that person or (4) better people for that particular role, and (5) addressing organizational diversity, geographic transfer, and other objectives.

The expectation is that all of the existing talent assessment and development data will be available to the selecting managers, who will be asked to list their top five or six choices for each role to be filled. We have found that the sports draft model with successive rounds of selection decisions is extraordinarily useful. It requires the selecting managers to "defend" their choices to the senior or crossover-point manager and each other, and it enables each manager to come up with the best chance for ending up with a strong team. The crossover-point manager needs to continuously look across the entire organizational unit and weigh the impact of any particular choice against the criteria listed above.

At the end of each round, it is useful for the managers to review the remaining employees not yet selected and consider revising their top five or six choices for the next round of selection decisions. By tracking the attributes of those already selected in real time, it also becomes possible for the crossover manager to focus consideration of those qualified employees who would support succession planning, diversity, and geographic rotation targets.

The crossover manager needs to make clear that selecting an employee into a role means the manager is "on the hook" for that person's being able to do the work of the role. It will not be an acceptable excuse for the manager who fails to deliver on his QQT/Rs to say he was not able to choose an effective team. This means that roles for which there are no qualified candidates remaining in the draft pool will require external recruitment.

Managers are accountable for ensuring each subordinate role is effectively filled and, as such, need to veto appointment of candidates to fill vacant roles when the manager deems them unqualified.

Implementing an Accountability System

Designing strategically aligned structures, processes, and systems creates the organizational conditions for reliably and sustainably releasing full enterprise value. Accurately filling its roles with employees who have the full range of capabilities required creates the opportunity for sound decision-making. However, unless managers leverage the full potential of their subordinates by actively engaging their commitment, aligning their thinking with strategy and each other, and continuously developing their capabilities, the degree of value created will fall short. The final cornerstone for delivering full value, safely, reliably, and sustainably, is for managers to hold and reward every subordinate accountable for keeping his word, no surprises, and earning his keep.

Effective and accountable managerial leadership in such a system is not optional. There are many moving parts that managers need to understand and master in order to effectively implement their own leadership accountabilities. The full gamut of practices inherent in the L.E.A.D. model can be efficiently taught in less than a week and should involve the managers of each group being taught to reinforce the importance of "living" these practices every day. These managers of managers must make it clear that every manager's leadership effectiveness will be continually assessed and that managers will be called to account when they fall short.

Many elements contribute to establishing a trust-inducing and fair accountability system. The core organizational credo always begins with "accountability without authority is fantasy and stress." Employees need to see evidence every-where they turn that the accountabilities of their roles are clearly defined and aligned with the decisional authorities required. They need to see that the Rs (resources) in their QQT/Rs are commensurate with the outputs they have been delegated. They need to experience that the people they must collaborate with are also being held accountable for collaborating effectively with them. They need to see evidence that their own managers are being held accountable for adding L.E.A.D. value and for helping to set them up for success.

Implementing Phase 1: Keep Your Word, No Surprises!

Under these conditions, most employees "feel committed to and responsible for" meeting their accountabilities and need few instances of being "called to account" to want to do their jobs well. Nevertheless, even highly responsible people are frequently subjected to extreme pressures that simply make it impossible to meet all of their accountabilities on time and as specified. The importance of "no surprises" is critical at this point. Employees are accountable for alerting others to whom they have made commitments about potential problems with delivering and renegotiating with them, if possible. Issues that cannot be resolved laterally must then be elevated to one's manager, because the manager is fully accountable for her subordinates' outputs.

It is in this sequence of actions that process control can be maintained, not in a rigid, bureaucratic way, but by deploying a series of conversations and judgments about mitigating problems. Managerial employment systems are inherently human judgment systems, so the goal when confronting obstacles is to get people together to decide how to craft the best possible solution to achieve the original objectives, while still maintaining process integrity. To ensure that this occurs, every employee needs to understand that failing to alert someone in time is not just a sign of ineffectiveness, it is actually an act of insubordination. It undermines process and it betrays trust, so it must be dealt with applying some form of discipline. Remember, the requirement is not "keep your word, no excuses." It is no surprises.

Discipline can occur in gradations from a verbal warning, to written warnings, all the way up to dismissal for cause. In my experience, this construct represents such a dramatic shift in cultural expectations for many companies that we have found it valuable to have a period of amnesty when first rolling it out. For a pre-defined period of time, whenever an employee fails to give a "heads up" when it is warranted, his manager should meet with him to explore why not, why it is so important to do in building the new culture, and what the consequences will be after the period of amnesty expires. This not only softens the blow for future failures to alert, but it also creates a climate of transparency and willingness to help people make the transition to a new way of thinking and behaving.

Implementing Phase 2: Earn Your Keep!

As important as keeping one's word, no surprises, is for maintaining process control, earning one's keep is the key to innovation and value creation. The phrase "earning one's keep" is not new; it has been around since the 1800s. Earning one's keep originated as an expression for satisfactorily performing services in return for remuneration, room and board, or other benefits.

Too many companies use bonuses tied to measurable outputs as their primary mechanism for encouraging employees to improve their productivity. It assumes, as Harry Levinson explained in his book *The Great Jackass Fallacy*, that employees are like donkeys and will only move into action when bribed with carrots or threatened with sticks. Moreover, Dr. Levinson goes on to demonstrate that people "would rather be in an organization that provides them with an opportunity to demonstrate their competence and proficiency than in those that test their ability to run a managerial maze successfully."

This is as true today as it was when Dr. Levinson wrote it in 1973. Employees are far more motivated by opportunities to apply their creative initiative, when they have the authority to exercise judgment and discretion and experience the gratification of achieving results, and the pride of mastering new skills. The problem is that one cannot readily measure this work and how it results in value creation.

As I have explained throughout this book, effectiveness in role cannot be measured. Managers can and must observe how well their subordinates go about overcoming obstacles and identifying and exploiting new opportunities in their roles. When assessing how well an employee is filling his role and creating the corresponding value, managers should be able to defend their judgments to their peers and their managers by offering incidents as anecdotal evidence. Because these are judgments, an internally consistent process of calibrating these managerial judgments against the same criteria and a common high standard is required. I describe this in detail in Chapter 4.

Closing the Loop on Value Creation: Rewarding Employees

The next step in reinforcing a culture of trust and fairness is to ensure that employee rewards and opportunities are commensurate with their assessed degree of effectiveness in filling their roles. If one thinks of a role—with a minimum and maximum range of salary—as an entity designed to deliver value, an employee's degree of value contribution within that role should determine the level of pay he receives within the pay range. If the process of evaluating effectiveness is experienced as fair by the employees of an organization, then using one's assessment as the basis for differential pay will also be perceived as fair. I fervently believe this is the only means for achieving a transparent meritocracy.

However, reward is not just about pay. The formal organizational and managerial recognition of the value of one's contribution is meaningful, rewarding, and consistent with a culture of fairness. Tying one's eligibility for challenging assignments and promotability to one's demonstrated effectiveness is another way in which employees can feel fairly recognized and rewarded for their contributions.

The Accountability System: Details Matter

Each phase of organizational analysis and design—beginning at the top— needs to establish the architectural principles and high-level structures and processes for the next two levels down. There needs to be enough specificity about accountabilities and requirements for each role to enable an accurate process of role filling. However, there remains a great deal of detail that needs to be thought through and worked out, including the direct and indirect accountabilities for processes and sub-processes. Once the newly created roles are filled, those employees need to undertake a more granular analysis to define and structure these processes in a way that ensures the optimal balance between process capability, efficiency, and accountability.

It is at this point that the crossover-point managers (i.e., the actual process owners) need to be engaged in thinking through with their teams and documenting the decision-making frameworks that will govern the trade-offs that those working in the process flow must make and agree to.

Establishing Stewardship Systems

There is a major logical flaw in organizations that resort to matrix management solutions, where multiple managers hold an employee accountable for different aspects of his work.

The fundamental property of all managerial accountability systems is that one's immediate manager is accountable for not only his subordinate's effectiveness and outputs but also for ensuring his adherence to the limits prescribed by many different systems.

The problem that matrix management solutions attempt to mitigate is that managers are so often under the gun to have their subordinates deliver greater numbers of outputs at an ever-faster pace that they ignore or overlook the process limits their employees are required to respect. Too often, safety, machine maintenance, and quality specifications are viewed as having lesser importance, so senior management creates parallel hierarchies to hold those employees accountable for adhering to specific process limits. This frees up their immediate managers to focus only on output performance. The assumption appears to be that managers are not capable of balancing the calculus of getting many things done by their subordinates while, simultaneously, adhering to boundaries.

Managers can and will manage both subordinate outputs and adherence, but they need a number of practical means for being readily informed when their subordinates are beginning to deviate from prescribed process standards. To enable this, the CEO, who is the overall "owner" of all organizational systems, needs to establish roles that will steward these systems on his behalf. Higher-level stewardship roles develop policies and, with the CEO's approval, convey them throughout the organization. They work with their peers to understand the policies and develop practices that allow them to hold their own subordinates accountable for working within those policies.

The system and process stewards do not directly hold subordinates of other managers accountable for adherence to their processes, but they do support those managers in doing so themselves.

Designing and Implementing Fully Integrated HR Systems

Although many of the elements of a fully integrated HR system are deployed early in the organizational design and implementation process (role establishment, talent assessment and deployment, etc.), it is useful to wait until much of the implementation is well established before designing and implementing a full-scale HR system.

While the talent assessment process is invaluable early on in establishing standards and expectations for all employees, my experience is that training managers in, and facilitating the process of, authoritative coaching and mentoring takes more time and is best rolled out to each lower level every year.

What is important at the outset, however, is to fully and transparently communicate the full complement of HR systems and how they are all geared toward systematically developing employees to be able to work to their full potential. When employees experience each of these aspects, it always reinforces the psychological contract, which, in turn, enhances engagement and increases retention.

HR and Talent Pool Development Systems

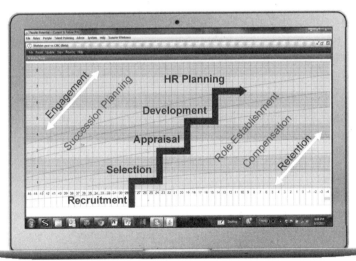

Strategic Organization principles and practices enable the only fully integrated HR and talent system that begins with a common model for role establishment, role requirements, and capability assessments. This leads to far more accurate fit-for-purpose selection and recruitment decisions. It also simplifies and makes more accurate the development work of coaching, mentoring, staffing, and succession planning. When combined with a system of requisite (i.e., felt-fair pay) compensation, the entire system ensures optimal engagement and retention.

Successfully Leading the Process of Change

Implementing a Strategic Organization Transformation represents an enormous change in almost every aspect of a company's work environment. And it is especially true because it is such a transparent system.

For this reason, it is useful to now examine aspects of human nature that strongly affect how people respond to major demands for change, i.e., when confronted with a crisis. Most people are creatures of habit. When they find things they can do well, they tend to repeat them to feel competent and confident. The sum of these habits becomes fashioned into their identities. *"This is what I do, so this is who I am."* People become rooted in these habits; the habits become sources of continued affirmation. People tend to avoid challenges for which they are not yet prepared in order to preserve their self-confidence. This is not true of all people, but it is true of most.

The more we are challenged, the more alert we become (physically, mentally, and emotionally) and we begin to process more information, imagine more possible scenarios, and try to find solutions that will bring us back to a more comfortable state of mind. We can become more effective than usual for brief periods and we can cope with increasing pressures up to a point, but we no longer feel comfortable. And if those pressures are too intense or too prolonged, we can unravel quickly and become poorly reactive to even mild demands. This is human nature. Green Berets, Navy SEALs, and mountain climbers thrive on pressure, but most people are not Green Berets, Navy SEALs, or mountain climbers. Most people prefer a more comfortable steady state.

In addition, most employees have evolved over time a set of implicit expectations of their relationship with the organization and its managers: "If I behave and respond to your requests in these ways, I have learned that you will behave and deal with me in those ways." This has become their psychological contract. However, when the organization and its manager suddenly behave in new ways and create new expectations of its employees, they experience a violation of the psychological contract as either abandonment or betrayal. It usually results in a loss of trust and confidence in management.

When driving critical new ways of working, people feel loss of the familiar and comfortable things that made them feel competent and confident. Suddenly, they are confronted with new demands that threaten them with failure. On top of that, they feel the very psychological contract that enabled them to depend on their managers is now broken. The work of leadership during critical change, therefore, is to help people contend with the losses, prepare for the new demands, and renegotiate a new psychological contract based on the new realities.

It is useful to think of this change leadership process as requiring five distinct types of communication. These are informing, clarifying, modeling, seeking input, and setting limits.

From nearly 40 years of observation and consultation, I have found that the best organizational leaders communicate in five specific ways to successfully implement organizational change.

1. First, leaders need to communicate and provide cogent information so that their people will understand that change is necessary, it is reasonable, and it is desirable. They begin by outlining the current situation. "Here is the problem." "Here are my assumptions about the future." "And here is why change is needed."

   Challenges and existing problems are presented clearly and understandably. Nothing should be left to the imagination. A roadmap or guide to the future is then articulated. "This is exactly what we need to do differently." "These are new skills and new technologies we need." "This is how we need to structure and operate differently." They also candidly express the rationale for change—the "how," the "why," and the "when." This is where transparency may be most important.

   Then, leaders dig deeper and go into detail in terms of the decision-making process that led to the specific plan for change. How did we arrive at these decisions? What alternatives were considered and what were the advantages and disadvantages of each? Then, they discuss the logic behind the decision-making process, how exactly the mandate for change was arrived at, and the desired outcome that will be realized.

   ## DESIRED OUTCOME: REALIZATION

   This change is necessary.

   This is a reasonable decision.

   This is a worthwhile plan.

2. Second, leaders provide clarification about the implications of the change decision in order to encourage trust. In other words, there are no surprises! They talk in terms of the status quo and intended future with regard to purpose, values, and cultures. In particular, they provide an overview of what will endure, what will have to change, what will be discontinued, and what will be incorporated into the new way of doing things.

   In response, employees are encouraged to consider their own values, purpose, and degree of commitment. Then, as employees clarify these issues for themselves, they are confronted with two probing questions. What changes can they accept? What changes can they not accept and why?

DESIRED OUTCOME: TRUST

The change decision was made with integrity.

"I can live with it. It fits with my values."

3. Next, leaders model trustworthy behavior to encourage greater identification with the immediate manager, with top management, and with new organizational goals. They share information and solicit questions. They also invite personal discussion about the professional and personal impact of the changes. In addition, good leaders also acknowledge the profound toll that change takes.

   As they model behavior, leaders also have to be realistic in their expectations. They should expect mature commitment. At the same time, they have to recognize temporarily decreased productivity and acknowledge employee needs for support, training, and resources. Leaders should be patient; they should expect to support experimentation with new skills and new processes.

DESIRED OUTCOME: IDENTIFICATION

With the leaders as "worthy"

With the organization's goals, via the manager

4. Next, leaders seek input and advice and incorporate their employees' ideas wherever possible. This way, people will see their own imprint on the blueprint and become genuinely committed to supporting the change. Specifically, they accept and seek out employee involvement in the logic, strengths, and weaknesses of the strategy and plan. They also seek out employee involvement regarding opportunities to improve the plan. In addition, they accept and seek out employee involvement in the plan's implementation with regard to such issues as timing, planning, and providing resources.

Good leaders also authorize teams of subordinates to study and recommend changes and to delegate tactical implementation of the plan.

Desired Outcome: Commitment

To master new tasks and accountabilities

To genuinely and unequivocally support the change

5. Finally, leaders set limits to encourage appropriate behavior and mutual respect. They define, monitor, and enforce the limits of appropriate behavior in two ways. One, they create opportunities for open and healthy expression of distress and disagreement for individuals and groups. Second, they work to prevent and ameliorate dysfunctional extremes of behavior.

Good leaders act decisively when employees are overwhelmed, psychologically impaired, and firmly oppositional. Overwhelmed employees are either reassigned or released. Psychologically impaired employees are urged to seek professional help. And firmly oppositional employees are given ultimatums and often terminated.

Desired Outcome: Mutual Respect

The leader's credo sometimes becomes, "You may not like these changes, but you must behave maturely and act constructively to support them."

Similarly, the effectiveness of the organizational change implementation itself will depend on several closely related variables.

Obviously, the plan needs to be a good plan. It must apply the essential principles of L.E.A.D., ensuring that structure and process are fully aligned with strategy, that accountabilities are clear and fully aligned with authorities, and that people are aligned with the requirements of their roles. The people who will implement the plan must come to accept that the plan is necessary, good, and reasonable. They must come to a point of personal ownership of the plan. They need to be convinced it will help them and the organization to succeed. And it is worth repeating that managers must set clear limits around what is acceptable and desirable behavior by employees during the change.

Moving Forward

Managerial leadership systems are complex accountability, complexity, and judgment hierarchies that when properly organized and activated can yield enormous gains in productivity, as well as human satisfaction. Achieving maximum organizational productivity is possible! Using leadership and organizational science to design, implement, and lead strategically aligned managerial systems that release their full enterprise value is no longer a "black art." Many of the management fads that come and go every few years do contain a few kernels of useful tools that can be found in some of the multipliers in this book but are in fact simplistic when promoted as total solutions.

As with any serious endeavor, one needs to weigh the investment (in time, focus, energy, and consistency, even more than money) in relation to the rewards. Our clients have achieved extraordinary gains in productivity, market share, free cash flow, ROI, and stock price. Along the way, they have achieved enormous employee engagement and retention levels because of their commitment to develop and support people to work to their full potential.

CHAPTER 12

Leadership in Healthcare Systems

UP TO THIS POINT in the book, I have focused on understanding leadership in the world of managerial work organizations. When we move into other types of work organizations, the nature of decision-making, authority, and accountability changes significantly.

Managerial systems are accountability, complexity, and judgment hierarchies and have unique properties, especially with respect to the nature of managerial leadership accountabilities and authorities. As I have said many times throughout this book, managers are accountable for their subordinates' effectiveness, outputs, and adherence to limits. The following are other fundamental concepts found in managerial systems that may not apply to other types of work organizations:

- Accountability without authority is fantasy and stress.
- In a matrix organization where an employee has more than one manager, no one is accountable for that employee.
- Similarly, joint or shared authority means no one is accountable for the outcome.
- Team accountability is a myth; it short-circuits the accountability hierarchy.

Many physician clinicians will also assume leadership roles during their careers. If I had known 50 years ago what I now know about leadership in different types of work organizations, I could have been a far more effective practicing psychiatrist, medical director of a mental health center, hospital department head, president of a hospital medical staff, and CEO of a mental health HMO. Therefore, I am hoping to spare each of you having to make the same mistakes I made.

Leaders in Non-Managerial Work Organizations

The managing partner of a partnership is not the accountable manager of the other partners. That role may have managerial authority over the administrative staff of a partnership, although typically those employees complain that each partner acts like their boss. The managing partner functions more like an elected leader of a political entity who governs processes. However, the key decisions really are made by consensus involving all of the partners, who collectively are the owners. If there is a problem with a partner, it is the entire partnership that has to vote to hold him accountable—not the managing partner.

Similarly, the dean of an academic department in a university is not the accountable manager of the tenured professors in the department. He may be appointed by the chancellor, but has limited authority with respect to the professors, who have been granted membership in the university faculty. If a professor engages in too much disreputable behavior, misses class too often, and fails to do research and publish, the dean may be able to rebuke him, but not much else.

This is also true of elected and appointed leaders within a hospital's medical staff. They do not have managerial authority over members of the medical staff. Medical staff members have been granted privileges to practice in the hospital by its board of directors, based on the recommendations of the medical staff credentialing and privileging boards. A medical staff specialty department chairman also lacks managerial authority over the physicians in that department. If a clinical physician has too many patient and staff complaints, is too inefficient, and has too many adverse clinical outcomes, the department head may be able to bring that physician to a medical staff review board and it may choose to suspend him. Otherwise, physician leaders of physician clinicians do not have the authority to hold them accountable for the effectiveness with which they practice medicine.

The Dilemma of Evaluating Physician Clinician Effectiveness

There are many reasons for this. In the United States, physicians are licensed to practice medicine by a state's board of medicine, which grants them broad discretion in how they treat patients and provides little oversight unless there is clear evidence of malpractice or illegal behavior. Furthermore, there is little objective evidence and few clear practice standards with which to determine and prove how well a physician treats her patients overall. Even though there are more and more guidelines governing evidence-based medicine practices, these are generic guidelines providing a wide range of what is considered acceptable practice. Additionally, each patient is a unique individual with a complex nexus of biological, psychological, and social factors operating in his life. This, by itself, has a major impact on the patient's medical outcomes, independent of the quality of the clinician's care.

Forget, for a moment, about existing measurable patient outcomes and prescribing limits. They include medical outcomes, which may or may not be a consequence of being treated by a highly effective physician . They also include patient satisfaction survey results, which can be skewed positively toward doctors who give patients lots of time and prescribe whatever the patients request. In addition, they require physicians' adherence to policy, which all physicians should be expected to do anyway.

When you reflect on some of the most effective physician clinicians you know, what is the basis of your assessment of their effectiveness?

- The ways they think? The kinds of decisions they make?
- The actions they take? The ways they behave?
- The skills with which they diagnose, plan treatment, and prescribe?
- The ways they interact with patients, families, colleagues?
- Their expression of compassion tempered by objectivity?
- Their focused attention, tenacity, and resilience?
- Their efficiency and mindfulness about costs?
- Their leadership and compassion among physicians, other professionals, administrators, and community services?

I think this long list of capabilities and behaviors makes it clear how difficult it is for anyone to fairly evaluate the overall effectiveness with which any physician clinician practices medicine.

The Sanctity of the Doctor-Patient Relationship

This difficulty is further compounded by the confidential nature of the doctor-patient relationship, which is an intimate personal relationship requiring great sensitivity on the part of the physician. "This quality in the doctor-patient relationship is undermined if doctors are organized in manager-subordinate relationships" in hierarchies.[1] Confidentiality cannot be preserved if whoever is the doctor's manager is to be accountable, for she must be able to check upon what is being done. It becomes an economic transaction and loses the quality of being a complex social transaction.

These difficulties can be overcome by retaining clinical freedom for hospital doctors to use their clinical judgment in diagnosis and treatment without managerial review, so long as they stay within the law, within professional regulations and standards, and within the limits of sanity.

This is not an issue for physicians in training (medical students, interns, residents, and fellows) because it is expected that their professors require information that may be of an intimate nature in order to evaluate their training and development needs.

The rest of the professional services in a hospital (e.g., nursing, PT, OT, lab technicians, etc.) can readily be organized into an accountability hierarchy. These services, mostly highly professional, do not carry the accountability for deciding the diagnosis and the general program of therapy, nor for confidential discussions of the prognosis with the patient. They simply do not require the clinical autonomy carried by the physician.

A New Paradigm for Physician Leaders

There is an old adage for acquiring knowledge in medical school, "See one, do one, teach one." This can be applied as well to learning how to lead a clinical team. Very few physician clinicians have had any formal education in leadership. They have, instead, relied on emulating whoever were their role models during their training. Furthermore, in most instances, physician clinicians lead teams of non-physicians (nurses, assistants, lab and x-ray technicians, PT and OT specialists, etc.) where prescribing and moral authority and general protocol offer them positional authority. "If I prescribe a regimen of therapy, you are accountable for administering it on my behalf." In the clinical setting, physician clinicians are in control. Lives depend on it.

As a clinical leader, physicians are the undisputed experts. They expect others to follow their orders without question. For them, the "system" is not the organizational system. It is the patient's body and they have been trained to understand the properties of optimal biological systems and human health. They are the experts at diagnosing known syndromes and prescribing known treatments. When making decisions, they usually choose from among many well-defined solutions that achieve—for the most part—predictable, quantifiable results.

The moment physicians move into leadership roles in a healthcare system (as opposed to a clinical leadership role), they discover that decisions are often arrived at by consensus and negotiation. They find themselves no longer in charge but acting as a contributor with one area of valuable expertise. They can no longer demand to be followed but they hope others will consider their ideas and suggestions respectfully.

In the current world of healthcare, the organizational system is usually a multi-dimensional array of complex and ill-defended interdependent open systems, where they must learn about and behave in ways that align with the properties of social systems and work systems. "Diagnosis" in this context requires making sense out of a complex cluster of organizational symptoms, and "therapy" requires collaboratively crafting novel, incremental, and previously untested solutions. Moreover, these solutions may have only modest effects, often with unintended consequences, requiring the patience to cope with delayed and often-undetectable results.

Physicians who assume leadership roles in healthcare systems need to adopt an entirely new paradigm and develop a dramatically new personal and professional identity. It requires more flexibility than grit, more listening than prescribing, and more willingness to share authority than to wield it. Developing personal authority and credibility as a useful and collaborative contributor to the healthcare leadership team is more important than expecting to receive the authoritative respect due a physician clinician.

The *Harvard Business Review* pointed out in 2018 that "physicians are neither taught how to lead nor are they typically rewarded for good leadership. Even though medical institutions have designated 'leadership' as a core medical competency, leadership skills are rarely taught and reinforced across the continuum of medical training."[2]

Similarly, below are some of the realities faced by physician leaders who attended "Leadership for Physician Executives," a five-day seminar that I led for many years that was accredited by Harvard Medical School.

- Healthcare organizations are challenging environments in which to lead and manage (skewed accountabilities, politically charged systems, silo-based structures, etc.).

- Traditional criteria for advancement in medicine regard clinical and academic skills much more so than leadership or management competencies.

- Many physicians are not inclined to collaborate and follow.

- Up until recently, little attention has been given to training physicians regarding leadership and management competencies. However, this is beginning to change. As I write this, about 60 percent of healthcare systems in the U.S. have at least some kind of executive leadership or management program, even if limited.

Developing Physician Leaders' Ability to Persuade

Physician leaders must abandon their inclinations to prescribe. Instead, they need to enhance their abilities to persuade. I have found it useful to borrow from Aristotle to create a useful model or taxonomy for the different types of persuasion. Aristotle differentiated *logos* (appeals to reason) from *pathos* (appeals to emotion) from *ethos* (appeals to character).

Logos builds on rational, logical argument. It describes the thoughtful leader who lays out all the facts and openly leads the discussion toward a shared perspective and common goals. It makes use of two types of logic: inductive and deductive. One exercises inductive logic by offering up similar examples and then drawing from them a general proposition. This logic is straightforward. "If you accept this, that, and the other thing, then you will accept this conclusion." On the other hand, deductive logic requires offering up a few general (presumably, reasonable) propositions and then sequentially drawing from them a specific truth.

Pathos appeals to our sense of identity and self-interest and exploits common biases. We naturally bend in the direction of what is advantageous to us, what serves our interests or the interests of any group we believe ourselves to be a part of. By appealing to one's emotions, you can establish a state of reception for your ideas.

One example of pathos is reciprocity where people tend to return a favor, similar to the way a politician works to build up power by "collecting chits." Another example is social proof where people will do things that they see other people are doing. They will find the parade and get in front of it. A third example is commitment and consistency. Once people commit to what they think is right, they are then more likely to honor that commitment, even if the original incentive or motivation is subsequently removed. They connect a new idea or initiative to one already embraced. A final example is scarcity, because perceived scarcity will generate demand. It will emphasize a real or imminent constraint to create a "burning platform" sense of urgency.

Ethos has more to do with earning respect and positive regard. Our perception of a leader's character influences how believable or convincing we find what that person has to say. We are naturally more likely to be persuaded by a person who, we think, has personal warmth, consideration of others, a good mind, and solid learning. People will tend to obey authority figures, even if they are asked to perform objectionable acts. Therefore, at times, it can be useful to play up one's recognized authority or stature to "speak authoritatively" about another area. Additionally, people are easily persuaded by other people whom they like. That is, a friendly, charismatic leader can be irresistible. As a young physician, when elected president of a 250-bed community hospital, I often mobilized several senior respected physicians to help me deal with problematic physician clinicians, who otherwise would have simply dismissed my intervention.

Healthcare Systems Are Hybrid Organizations

Most healthcare systems consist of, at least, two distinct, but highly interdependent and symbiotic organizational entities: the hospital managerial hierarchy and the medical staff association. The hospital CEO has a traditional hierarchy beginning with her immediately subordinate executives: some are clinical (nursing, laboratories, x-ray departments, etc.) and others not (CFO, HR, engineering, etc.). The medical staff consists of physicians who have been granted privileges by the board of directors to practice medicine in the hospital and to prescribe treatments which hospital personnel must administer.

The tension arises when the medical staff expresses a need for new equipment or additional hospital personnel on a unit and the CEO declines, potentially for a number of legitimate, practical reasons. It also occurs when the hospital needs physicians to alter their practice routines so that it can more efficiently deploy its nursing staff or improve on its operating room scheduling. Leaders in neither entity have the authority to demand changes in the other. Furthermore, even if the medical staff leaders agreed with the hospital's requests, they also have limited authority to demand and enforce changes from the members of the medical staff.

It is especially frustrating for chief medical officers (CMO) who are employees of the hospital, often directly subordinate to the CEO. Hospital CEOs often expect that their CMOs should just demand changes of the medical staff leaders and members just as the CEO can demand that his other executives can demand changes of their subordinates. The problem, of course, is that the hospital executives have managerial authority over their subordinates, whereas the CMO is not the accountable (i.e., positionally challenged) manager of any of the medical staff members.

The picture is further clouded by the fact that hospitals have purchased many of the medical practices previously owned by the physicians on their medical staff. Moreover, many of these physicians are now "employed" by the hospital, so the CEO tends to view them as the same as any other employee. Even though the IRS may view these physician clinicians as employees, the reality is that they function more as independent contractors, who have agreed to practice medicine under the hospital's umbrella.

Nevertheless they do not recognize their leaders' authorities to evaluate the effectiveness with which they practice medicine. Hospitals (as well as medical partnerships and other healthcare entities) have worked around this by choosing to compensate practicing physicians based on the revenue they generate, categories of illnesses they treat, productivity indices, reoccurrences of their patients' illnesses, and other metrics. But this is not the same authority that truly accountable managers have to evaluate and reward the effectiveness of their subordinates. Instead, it introduces a counterproductive management approach, The Great Jackass Fallacy, by shaping physician clinician behavior with "carrots and sticks." This emphasizes productivity over quality and, ultimately, effectiveness.[3]

Developing Physician Leaders' Ability to Negotiate Collaboratively

Even though the hospital and medical staffs live under one roof, when it comes to making decisions and implementing decisions that involve both entities, it is useful to think of them as separate entities that need to negotiate agreements and agree to mutually oversee their implementation.

I find it useful to understand there are four different types of negotiation strategies that can be viewed from two axes. One axis is the criticality of the outcome for each party. The other is the importance of building and maintaining an effective working relationship.

When neither the outcome nor the relationship is of critical importance to a party (entity, company, etc.), it is often easiest to just concede to the requests of another party. "I may lose something of little value but I won't lose any sleep over it or resent the other party, because they mean so little to me. It is better to conserve my time and energy, concede, and move on."

When the relationship is important and I am willing to accept a somewhat less satisfying outcome, people will try to negotiate a compromise. "Look, I realize that you are not in a position to negotiate some items that are important to me but are able to negotiate others. So, I'm willing to compromise on some of my demands and agree to some of yours in order to maintain our working relationship."

When the outcome is all-important but there is little need for or interest in an ongoing relationship, people will compete furiously and take every advantage they have to get all that they can, and not worry about how the other party feels about them afterwards. "Look, I am interested in buying your property, but I have others that will suit my needs. I know you are close to bankruptcy and have had no other interested buyers, so I am going to bid only 60 percent of your asking price. Take it or leave it!"

Finally, when maintaining a healthy, trusting, and just ongoing relationship is important and being able to achieve one's most important objectives is also critical, then collaborative negotiation is the most important category to deploy.

> *"Instead of approaching this as a bargaining exercise, let's start by sharing the problems each of us is trying to solve so we can learn what the other is up against. Then, instead of 'opening our kimonos' to reveal what each of us might be prepared to offer, let's help each other explore what potential solutions to each of our problems would look like and how supporting those solutions could be beneficial to the other (i.e., by helping to solve the other's problems).*

> *"We can then define the shared principles that should be the basis of our eventual negotiation and explain them to the stakeholders whom we are representing. Once we get agreement from them about the principles, we can begin to construct potential solutions—which would involve exchanges of resources—until we identify the one that best solves each of our problems and feels fair to both of us."*

This process of collaborative negotiation serves multiple purposes. Working together, the parties often come to a better understanding of the root causes for each of their problems; this enables more elegant and accurate solutions. Working together to understand each other builds mutual caring and trust, the basis for a healthy psychological contract. Being part of each other's solutions creates greater investment on everyone's part in the successful implementation of the negotiated agreement. And it can bring both parties closer together to discover even more ways in which they can collaborate in the future and contribute to each other's success.

In healthcare systems, with two interdependent organizations needing to function as an integrated whole, I have found that collaborative negotiation is the best vehicle for driving alignment of decisions, implementation, and shared investment in the success of the entire enterprise.

A New Vision for Physician Leaders

Physician leaders need to define and communicate the healthcare system's "rules of engagement" by developing clear boundary conditions about working relationships, prescribed limits, and consequences for failing to adhere.

They need to gain personal authority to lead by simultaneously:

- Identifying the collective aspirations of the medical staff "political" entity by discovering and acknowledging the aspirations of its individual members;

- Providing their own integrative visions of purpose and mission for the organization and their own personal aspirations for the physicians to identify with;

- Setting context ("big picture") to condition the ways in which people go about their work; and

- Defining limits within which people must work (and mechanisms for enforcement).

Physician leaders need to exert more personal and political leverage than managers in accountability hierarchies, who also have the authority to delegate tasks to subordinates and hold them accountable. Physician leaders need to develop and continuously enhance their ability to persuade and negotiate. They also need to harness the power of group cohesion and physician personal responsibility in order to encourage them to increase their own personal and teamworking effectiveness.

Finally, physician leaders need to make clear to the hospital hierarchy that, although they are leading a different type of work organization than their CEOs, they are eager to engage in ongoing collaborative negotiation to deliver the greatest possible value to patients, to the community, and to all other stakeholders.

Physician Leaders as Catalysts for Positive Change

From 1984 to 2018, Levinson and Co. led a joint venture with Harvard Medical School to train over 3,000 physician and other healthcare leaders in these and other leadership concepts and practices. Almost all of the seminar participants stated that being a physician healthcare leader was in many ways far more complicated and mentally and emotionally challenging than being a physician clinician. They felt far less professionally confident and competent in this new role and were eager to learn more to be able to lead more effectively.

The intriguing question for me—also as a physician—was why they would voluntarily subject themselves to roles that made them uncomfortable and often unpopular, at least for the first few years. The answer was always the same: they wanted to have a greater impact on the overall quality of healthcare to their communities that treating individual patients and families alone did not provide. Many of them loved being clinicians. However, their value systems still drove them to seek more leverage over improving the quality and access of healthcare.

I can think of few nobler aspirations!

CHAPTER 13

Anatomy of a Leader

IN OCTOBER 2006, *Canadian Business* magazine chose Denis Turcotte as its "CEO of the year" for taking Algoma Steel from its second bankruptcy to become one of the most profitable steel companies in North America.[1] Since I originally conceived of the idea for this chapter, Turcotte has gone on to accomplish many more impressive challenges.

Turcotte is currently a managing partner and chief operating officer at Brookfield Asset Management's Private Equity Group, responsible for all business operations. He joined Brookfield (with over $540 billion in assets under management) in 2017, bringing expertise as a member of the BAM Private Equity Advisory Board for 10 years and a member of the Brookfield Business Partners' board of directors from 2016 until 2017. He provides operational and financial oversight for portfolio companies within Brookfield's Private Equity Group. Prior to joining Brookfield, Turcotte held several roles, including principal with North Channel Management and Capital Partners, CEO of Algoma Steel, and president of the Paper Group and EVP, corporate development and planning, with Tembec.

Turcotte holds a bachelor of engineering degree from Lakehead University and an MBA from the University of Western Ontario. He received the Engineering Medal in Management from the Professional Engineers of Ontario.

As COO of Brookfield's Private Equity Group, Turcotte has introduced the concepts and methodologies described in this book as foundational to both the due diligence of new potential acquisitions and the organizational reform of companies once acquired. He believes that organizing their work in a disciplined and efficient manner based on the leadership and organizational science from Levinson by Pariveda is the most effective and timely way to extract full enterprise value from their portfolio companies.

An Exemplary Leader

In this chapter, I explain Turcotte's success in terms of his understanding and exercise of three dimensions of leadership:

- Personal leadership;
- Accountability leadership; and
- Strategic organizational leadership.

I can do this because of my firsthand experience with Turcotte and the three of companies he has managed since he led a group of employees that partnered with Tembec (a global forest products company based in Témiscaming, Quebec) to purchase the Spruce Falls Paper Company from Kimberly-Clark and the New York Times Company in 1991. In providing executive counsel, organizational consultation, and leadership training to him and his managers and employees over this period, my staff at Levinson and Co. and I have learned as much about leadership as we have taught.

Personal Leadership

Denis Turcotte has several distinctive personal attributes and characteristics that help to explain his successful career. He is extremely bright and intellectually curious. He possesses a clear moral compass, yet he is intensely competitive. He is analytical and committed to operating from first principles and logic, but he is not afraid to make far-reaching decisions based on the information at hand.

Most importantly, Turcotte values what they call in the U.K. "man management." He genuinely believes that, as capable as he is personally, his organization's capability depends on fully leveraging the potential of all his employees working effectively together. In addition, Turcotte enjoys challenging his employees, engaging them around ambitious goals, holding them to high standards, and rejoicing in their successes. He demands a lot, but he gives a lot.

Part of Turcotte's strength is his willingness to ask any type of question without worrying about it revealing his lack of knowledge. He has enormous confidence in being able to figure out solutions to complex problems. Therefore, when his executives and managers would tell him how things worked, he would ask them why. When they could not defend their explanations with data and principles, he challenged them to look at things differently. When they would assert, "this is the way it has always been done," invariably he would probe until he got to the underlying principles. In this way, he simultaneously earned their respect and forced them to think.

Accountability Leadership

When Algoma Steel came out of its first bankruptcy, the board made a number of agreements with the union leadership in order to extract financial and other concessions to restore the company to profitability. The two most important were the unionization of all specialists and first-line managers, and the involvement of union members in nearly all managerial decisions. These decisions amounted to veto authority over managerial business and employee-selection choices.

The net effect of these concessions was decreased management authority and accountability, and a culture of consensus and entitlement. Managers who expected clarity and accountability were shunned; they were considered abrasive, non-team players.

Turcotte bluntly and directly addressed the status quo when he began his tenure as president and CEO of Algoma in September 2002. "Algoma exists to deliver top value to the shareholder," Turcotte asserted. "The company will survive, endure, and prosper only if we deliver value that exceeds what they could get elsewhere." He stated that as CEO, he was accountable for making that happen and he could achieve that only by holding each of his subordinate executives accountable for delivering their part.

Furthermore, Turcotte made it clear that employment was a privilege, not an entitlement. All employees would be expected to keep their word and earn their keep. Functioning accountably was no longer optional for anyone who wanted to continue to work at Algoma.

Strategic Organizational Leadership

Turcotte was drawn to the principles of Strategic Organization when he first began working with The Levinson Institute in the 1990s. The leadership practices not only resonated with his own experience, but they provided a framework and language for teaching and aligning the entire organization with his approach. Additionally, Turcotte saw the power of being able to rationally align organization with strategy, using the lenses of levels of complexity, functional alignment, three-level-unit processes, and system stewardship. He also realized that a software-enabled system of talent-pool assessment and development, tied to compensation, was the most reliable way to establish and implement consistent, high standards for effectiveness.

Algoma's existing strategy was to sell as many tonnes (metric tons) of steel as possible, usually at the lowest price, in order to fully load its production capacity. Turcotte reasoned that in a cyclical commodities market, this strategy was a recipe for bankruptcy. While it was important to load the fixed-cost production engine as fully as possible, he believed that a value-oriented sales approach could be consistent with a more intelligent production loading-and-planning process. To reconcile and optimize these two needs, accountability for production loading needed to be aligned with sales, not manufacturing. Similarly, the accountability for production planning needed to be aligned with steel finishing, not steel making. This necessitated major functional and process realignment at Algoma.

To create a value-oriented sales strategy, Turcotte needed to create metallurgically unique products and services. This required creating a product development capability, which had been eliminated years earlier during the period of financial cutbacks. This, too, required implementing significant organizational functional and process realignment.

In evaluating the manufacturing organization, Turcotte identified seven or eight levels in a function that required only five levels. He also calculated that a competitive ROI for shareholders required a total payroll consistent with 25 percent fewer employees. He next engaged a knowledgeable industrial engineering group to evaluate process efficiency and identify where roles could be eliminated without reducing productivity—and perhaps even improving it.

The most dramatic change in culture and productivity resulted from Turcotte's immediate implementation of a rigorous process for assessing employee effectiveness and potential. Because of his long experience with The Levinson Institute's talent-pool process, he understood that the systematic assessment of employee effectiveness was the best way to simultaneously communicate and calibrate high standards and implement meaningful accountability for people to earn their keep.

Lessons Learned from Denis Turcotte

No one can deny that Denis Turcotte is an exceptional leader. He understands the value of leadership and organizational consultation. Turcotte has applied the principles and practices—first developed by Elliott Jaques and now adapted and refined by Levinson by Pariveda—with enormous success in three different companies. He was recently quoted as saying that "Levinson consulting was fundamental to getting the right structure, integrating our efforts, and driving home accountability. Within 36 months out of bankruptcy we drove $152 million in annualized improvements, and over $1 billion of equity value."

However, Turcotte's success does not stem from the intellectual prowess of his consultants. Rather, it derives from his own personal leadership, accountability leadership, and strategic organizational leadership. Not only does this story prove that one person can make a difference, but it also proves that leadership itself can make a difference. Sound, moral, enlightened, and confident leaders can leverage the full potential of any work organization.

What then are the six characteristics of strategic leaders? Here are six that I have found correlate strongly with the kinds of values practiced by Denis Turcotte.

1. Strategic leaders value managing and leading people; in other words, they value getting work done through others. If they are in it just for the power, prestige, or strategy, they will not create long-term value, because the sustained, effective implementation of strategy must involve every employee. Senior managers cannot lead mechanistically with carrots and sticks and expect to be successful.

2. Strategic leaders are intellectually curious. They are always seeking new ideas and are receptive to trying new ways of thinking and working. They know there is no simple formula for winning and thus continuously strive to discern the underlying principles that will allow them to leverage every resource within their control, including their entire pool of talent.

3. Strategic leaders "walk the talk." They continuously set context with their own subordinate managers about the bigger picture and how each of their functions must work together to support the company's overarching goals. This is how strategic leaders achieve genuine

alignment and enthusiastic engagement—not by taking people on ropes-and-ladder courses or by white water rafting together.

4. Strategic leaders recognize that they can never figure out all the answers by themselves. They seek input from their people, share their thinking, and encourage debate in order to get to the best possible understanding. Then, they push for action. They model a delicate balance between the need for proper reflection and a bias for action. Thirty-five years ago, Harry Levinson, founder of The Levinson Institute, wrote a noteworthy book entitled *Ready, Fire, Aim: Avoiding Management by Impulse.*[2] Dr. Levinson proved that strategic leaders engage their entire team in taking aim before they pull the trigger.

5. Strategic leaders are comfortable with their positional and personal authority and never shy away from holding their subordinate managers accountable for keeping their word, no surprises, and earning their keep. They establish high standards, recognize and reward success, and confront failures to adhere to policy and/or commitments with appropriate discipline. In addition, most importantly, they hold their subordinates accountable for being effective, value-adding managers themselves.

6. Finally, strategic leaders understand that to deliver full value, every aspect of the leadership system must be aligned with strategy: structure, processes, people, and human resource systems. It is worth reiterating that every element of a strategic organizational system is inextricably linked to every other element.

Work organizations are powerful forces in the lives of managers and employees. The degree to which managerial leaders can create the organizational conditions in which people can succeed is the degree to which they can have a positive impact—on employees, their families, and, ultimately, society. For you, the manager, I hope Denis Turcotte's story will act as a catalyst to help you renew your own commitment to identifying, developing, and promoting personal leadership, accountability leadership, and strategic organizational leadership.

CHAPTER 14

Sustainability:
The Purpose-Driven Organization

PARIVEDA SOLUTIONS, INC., is an employee-owned, strategic services and information technology consulting company whose business model is to recruit, develop, and deploy highly talented people to significantly improve its clients' performance. Pariveda places special emphasis and has particular expertise in solving complex enterprise problems that create high value for its clients and provide major growth opportunities for its people.

Pariveda was founded in 2003 with the purpose of developing people toward their highest potential. As a professional services firm, it does so by attracting, hiring, and nurturing the best people to co-create valuable solutions with clients, resolving their most challenging dilemmas. With the addition of Levinson and Co., Pariveda is strengthening its ability to provide holistic organizational, talent, and leadership solutions to companies.

On January 30, 2020, I got together in Dallas with Bruce Ballengee, Pariveda Solutions' president and chief executive officer, and Kerry Stover, Pariveda's chief operating officer, for a casual, yet probing, conversation about a powerful topic: those elements that sustain the best organizations over the long term and the very long term. What follows is an edited transcript of our lively, thought-provoking, and occasionally humorous discussion.

Discussion Playbook

Gerry Kraines: The title of this book is *Management Productivity Multipliers.* Each of the individual components of a strategic organizational system goes into my model. We call them *multipliers*. And they are dynamic and synergistic. The more multipliers you get connected with each other, the greater the aggregate value they create.

For me, it always has to start with accountability, because I am talking about managerial hierarchies. It then moves on to leadership, complexity levels, and the notions of potential and effectiveness. What are all the different things that go into designing organizations; how do you fit those together? Then, looking at teams, different types of teams from an accountability point of view, functions, cross-functional working relationships, system stewardship, human resource systems, and then implementation, and finally variations on the model with healthcare systems.

Healthcare systems are hybrid organizations. The hospital, absent the clinician physicians, is a managerial hierarchy. The medical staff is an association; it is inherently a political entity. How do you bring them together? Because physician leaders cannot hold other physician clinicians accountable in the same way that a manager can hold a subordinate accountable. It requires creating personal authority and skill in collaborative negotiation.

Bruce, how does this fit into your vision of an organization that will last 1,000 years? I thought it would be useful, first, for you to articulate your general thinking about the nature of design, about design in nature, just your general thinking about it. Then, Kerry and I will interact with you.

Nature of Design Systems (NODS)

Bruce Ballengee: People hear "nature of design" and they say, "Just what does that mean?" I call it *nature of design systems* or *nature of design school,* because that makes the acronym NODS. You could nod off to sleep thinking about this. I like things like that—double entendres.

Nature of design is the idea that, "Hey, if you want to be sustainable, if you want to see what works, then we have a fabulous example that we can look to." That is our universe. It is the oldest, most complex thing that we know about. And we know that it has worked for a very long time—five billion years. It occurs to me that no matter what theory you use, it is probably good for another five billion years.

So, what can we learn? There are a lot of repeating patterns that we see in nature. The universe is nature. And we see those things repeat at all levels of the universe. They repeat in some form at the galaxies and universe level, at the star systems and a galaxy level, at the planets in a single solar system level, at the level of a planet, at the level of an organism, and at the level of a molecule. Then, you can get into questions at an atomic level and then we get into the world of quantum mechanics. That is just beyond my ability to integrate.

There also appears to be a limit to what the universe is. We cannot see outside the universe, probably due to some quantum qualities.

In addition, it is not prescriptive. We don't say, "This is the right way." We say, "Look at these patterns that appear to work consistently." And we can copy. We can reuse aspects of that to make things that work; however, there are limits to that. The first airplanes attempted to recreate a bird wing. Other people followed for hundreds of years. Yet none of this worked.

However, the fundamental is valid. You have to go below that apparent level to the level down and deconstruct what is really going on. A system of lift and a system of aerodynamics led the way to things that work. However, there are limits and not everything works all the way.

And then, there are some other really cool things. We might not be able to postulate what the purpose of the universe is. It thinks its purpose is to exist. In other words, the agnostic NODS. Then there are beliefs that a greater thing than the universe created the universe with a purpose. It works either way.

However, everything has a purpose. And living things have purposes. And certainly, sentient things have purposes. And so we see that repeated over and over again.

Applying NODS to Business Organizations

Bruce Ballengee: A business enterprise is a complex system that interacts in a complex ecosystem. It needs to have a purpose. And each component in that enterprise needs to have a purpose. That would be another aspect of it.

At Pariveda, we take a humanistic view of it, a human-centric view of it. So, when we're thinking about a business enterprise, it is important to think about it, I believe, as being human centric. We have to start with the smallest component of an enterprise in human terms. And that is the individual, not the collective. And we have to think about aligning the purpose of the enterprise with the individual.

Most organizations—most enterprises—do not intend to do that directly. They do not intentionally design their enterprises for alignment. They are seeking other purposes. However, for ethical, moral, good business-sense reasons, they basically add on other aspects and other things so that the individual is protected and supported, which is really not a pure NODS view of it.

A pure NODS view would say we start with the individual, and we think about how individuals come together collectively and collaborate. And we use those actual things to think about how we organize, how we organize people.

There's the Elliott Jaques Requisite Organization label that is used a lot and in a much more specific way about roles, role complexity, and people and their abilities. But there is a broader enterprise view. What are the requisite components of all the components of the enterprise? And so, some of those come from the individual who is the employee. However, some of those come from the individuals in the C2C world, so we think about the "little C" customer. And in the B2B world, we think about the "large C" customer. However, sometimes we forget that there are little Cs who are making the decisions for the big C.

For a business enterprise to be requisite, it needs to understand the nature of the individuals within its boundaries and how it interacts with the individuals outside its boundaries and in its ecosystem (suppliers, customers, competitors, regulators, etc.). And so that's a very fundamental difference that comes out of NODS that we don't see in other places. I think it is very, very consistent and aligned with the kinds of things that The Levinson Institute has always been about, consults on, and is learning about.

Helpers, Heroes, and Sages

Bruce Ballengee: What do individuals need? They need to self-actualize. How do they go about doing that? How does that happen? What is the environment that needs to be provided?

In the professional services world, which we happen to be in at Pariveda, it's a good fit because it's easy to see the generative power of that employee. It's relatively easy to think about empowering the "little C" customer or client and the "big C" customer. It's doing the same thing, self-actualizing.

In many ways, this way of approaching things is very fundamental to human civilization. Joseph Campbell (the late American author, editor, and teacher whose work on comparative mythology and folklore examined the universality of recurring myths in human culture) said that all narratives are variations of a single great story. The first story they had was *Beowulf* and that established the whole idea of the person being her own hero or heroine. In order to do that, people need various things. They need helpers. They need a sage.

So how does one become a sage? One becomes a sage by being an effective hero. To be a sage, you have to be a hero. That falls back into what is requisite for the individual. The individual is striving to become a hero, first, and eventually, a sage, who can be the advisor to someone trying to be a hero. And before they have that experience, they can help. They can be a helper, which is also a hero.

Think about the meaning of the word *leader* coming from Germanic, German. The aspect of suffering for others fits in there pretty conveniently, at least in my view of the world. And then, there are a lot of other things that flow from that fundamental . . . going back to the individual.

The Origins of Purpose

Gerry Kraines: How do you envision purpose in the universe?

Bruce Ballengee: The purpose of things in the universe? Or the purpose of the universe?

Gerry Kraines: You asked, "Is there a purpose to the universe?"

Bruce Ballengee: Having the view of there is a god. For me, having to think about that, there is God who creates universes. And universes were created so that everything could find its purpose. They need a safe space. Everything needs a safe space to find its purpose or to be its purpose. The gods fill the universe to fulfill its purpose. The star needs a space in the galaxy. There are some wandering stars in parts of our galaxy. But the trouble is that they can't get very good planets unless they're thrown off. They need to have dead-star supernovas to make the elements that they need to have very good planets.

How does sentient life grow? It takes a galaxy. It takes a galaxy to get to sentient life. At that point, then, there is choice, and sentient life chooses its purpose. I don't know if it answered consciously or unconsciously. They just never question it.

Gerry Kraines: So, it's a teleological view (the argument for the existence of God from the evidence of order) when you talk about purpose? The purpose of the universe is to create its subsets? And the purpose of the subsets is to create more subsets?

Bruce Ballengee: Well, I put God in there. The non-God view would just say that stuff happens and the darn thing has a purpose of just existing.

If you want to exist for millions and millions of years, this is just the only way that we know how to do it. A lot of stuff went on in the universe and someone got lucky, and at least there is one universe. It is just pure randomness. And that's possible.

It's really complicated. It's really a complex way of thinking about it. And for a simple answer, I just use God, and then I don't have to worry about the complexity of God.

Gerry Kraines: But, again, I'm trying to draw the connections here. Is this a fair conclusion or corollary that the notion of Strategic Organization, which looks at a subset of human work organizations as a system . . .

This is where I'm trying to understand that you say that you have to start with the individual. But what you've done with the universe is to go past the individual all the way down to quantum mechanics.

Bruce Ballengee: That's right. I came back to these things in the middle.

I think this would help. For an individual to achieve a purpose, there are many things that one can do on his own. A farmer or want-to-be farmer can clear a field of rocks. It might take years but they can build fences or maybe be able to make a plow on their own or just get a stick and dig. They might be able to find some plants they could reproduce in the nihilistic hunting-and-gathering world. And that was fairly advanced technology that happened over time.

However, it is not possible for that farmer to sustain. They need some things for them to reproduce, which is a basic thing about living things—sentient or not—is that they need to reproduce. Now, I can grow. I'm a farmer and I am out here to reproduce. I have a spouse. I have a family. If we're going to support that, then we're going to need more farms.

Eventually, now we need other specialties to emerge like baking bread. . . things like that. In addition, other things start happening. Maybe not on the farm. But as those specialties happen, now we have a village. Now, we have a village with a bunch of farms, and there are others who just come to take. Their purpose is, "We just take stuff."

At our size, we can't all be warriors; we can't be farmers all the time. We need some people to specialize.

Gerry Kraines: Central to the notion of NODS is that each element has a purpose?

Bruce Ballengee: Yes. Whether conscious or unconscious, each element has a purpose.

Gerry Kraines: Humor me. Is there a purpose in sustainability? Is sustainability a purpose?

Bruce Ballengee: I think that purpose could be an oversimplification. The key driving thing of all living things is that they generally want to live as long as they can. And they want to have primacy. They want to perpetuate themselves, or their species, or their race or however you want to think about it—with varying degrees of balancing out self and other living things.

Take a colonial species—ants. Individual worker ants don't reproduce, but they're thinking about helping the colony to reproduce . . . helping the queen. So, the colony keeps going.

The Sustainable Organization

Gerry Kraines: Let me put this to Kerry then. What is your interest in pursuing the magic sauce of sustainability? Because I know that you have been looking at it in a very serious way for several years.

Kerry Stover: I'm deciding where to start. My idea of an enterprise is a collection of individuals seeking to accomplish something for the benefit of society. Ideally, society finds value in what they do, what they produce, enough that the value they give to the enterprise is more than the cost of producing and running the enterprise. If the company fails to benefit society, it goes out of business. That is the natural tension.

Bruce talked about not having found many companies that keep people at the core of its purpose. So how do you organize and keep purpose that lasts?

Sustainability then becomes important. Deciding not to be sustainable, one argument is, is that you end up not needing the purpose of developing people because you have some other end in mind that you want to go toward. So lacking sustainability, people will naturally move to other benefits from the organization.

Man has constantly searched for a way to live longer. It is in the nature of man to not want to die. He will fear death. Organizations are filled with people who seek to have an answer as to, "What are we trying to do?" "What are we trying to achieve?"

So, making sustainability a core tenet answers the question with perpetuation, rather than an end game, for individuals.

Bruce Ballengee: Why is it so important to Pariveda? Because we are a requisite enterprise built on the fundamental component of an individual in a professional services organization. That's a great testament. Hey, that is a long career and there is a long period of development for people to achieve their full potential. So, people need a safe space to achieve that.

Therefore, a straightforward way, a process for them to do that, would be sustainable. Ergo, we want our organization, our enterprise, to be sustainable.

The first leg up we have is that we tend to select people who are sustainable, i.e., people who are resilient and adaptable. That's a big leg up. That's just one element, though. It doesn't talk about structure, which is mostly what buying up Levinson and Co. has been about. Then, there's the element of the process/technology. Those are interchangeable words really: the process or the technology. At Pariveda, we seize both. I think that's easier for people to get and it serves our brand and marketing purposes more conveniently than saying they are the same thing. . . at least for now.

So, we want to get through that. That means that we've got to be worried about encountering cycles in professional services. That is something that can really kill a professional-services enterprise. And so we do things with people, structure/organization, and process to deal with that internally. And we do things externally: in how we think about customers, how we think about market, and how we think about the relationships that we maintain with our customers.

For example, we want to develop lifetime relationships. Again, this speaks to the little "e" employee and the little "c" client, and how we want to foster lifetime relationships at both those levels. And at the enterprise level, we want many "e"s and "c"s, so that it is a robust relationship—a stronger bond. A compound bond is stronger than a single bond. It takes a lot more energy.

This takes us back to the sage-hero, hero-sage, and teams of heroes and teams of sages.

Gerry Kraines: Let me see if I can reframe.

The ultimate purpose for individuals is to realize their full potential. And the goal is to create an organization, which can promote their realizing their full potential. That organization needs to give them a safe space for development to acquire capabilities. That way, individuals can qualify for bigger and bigger work that challenges their potential.

But the organization also needs to form a relationship with the environment, which is both cyclical and unpredictable. The key to that is forming more than a lifelong relationship with its customers. It is continuing strong relationships with its customers, even where the people are replaced as they leave, but where the relationship with the customers and their people remains and grows. This is essentially the organization's root system. It allows the organization to weather the tough times and to grow more quickly when good times return.

However, it all gets back to the purpose, which is to create an enduring environment in which people can realize their full potential.

Kerry Stover: In the case of Pariveda, it's interesting designing that way. But I think there are other ways. And that's what leads to the necessity for teams. Once the necessity for teams is recognized, we also need structure/organization.

Bruce Ballengee: I would say purpose and sustainability. Because it's easy to translate creating a safe environment into some timeline that future executives may choose to think and to tell people nothing has changed. But, in fact, for internal purposes, individual executives someday may need to monetize the company. And so by putting sustainability as congruent with purpose, it becomes an important factor not to just say, "what about building people," but, to use your choice of words, enduring. It gives the enduring nature front and center that people will see that we're committed not just to cash out, but also to build leaders who will build leaders, who will build leaders, who will build leaders . . . the regenerative nature of our leadership development.

Kerry Stover: In the historical coming together of Levinson and Pariveda, there is this aspect of "I can achieve that for myself" and "I can help others along the way." But as far as transferring all that knowledge and capability so that it can pass from generation to generation, that's another reason I need to be sustainable. Because I can't really be fully fulfilled unless I achieve all these things.

Bruce Ballengee: Your output transcends your lifetime for future generations!

Kerry Stover: It's a bit of, "Hey, I've got some immortality" outside of the realm of God.

Gerry Kraines: I keep joking Bruce is like Hari Seldon. Hari Seldon from Isaac Asimov's *Foundation* series. He keeps coming back every 100 years or so as a hologram.

Kerry Stover: He's a psycho-historian who is manipulating the entire progress of humanity. Fortunately, there is a sentient robot named R. Olivaw that decides that that's what his purpose ought to be. So R. Olivaw pulls it off for 1,000 years.

Asimov died before he could write the final book of how R. Olivaw was going to regenerate himself, and it wasn't looking good at the end. And then, Asimov died. Perhaps he was writing the last book, *R. Olivaw Must Live*.

Gerry Kraines: Elliott Jaques died before he could finish his trilogy books. *The Life and Behavior of Living Organisms* was supposed to be the first of three books, which he originally was going to title, *The New Theory of Life*.

Bruce Ballengee: But he decided that it wouldn't sell books. The wrong kind of buyers would buy the book!

Helping People to Reach Their Full Potential

Gerry Kraines: What is hitting me is that this is what Harry Levinson worked on in the 1950s. The purpose of human endeavor is to realize one's potential.

The purpose of organization is to provide a sense of transcendent purpose. People both attach to and contribute to the sustainable purpose of the organization. And they are sustained by the organization.

Elliott Jaques approached it differently, but still with the same goal. He focused much more on the notion of potential itself. And that if people do not use their full, in this case, mental potential, they will wither.

So, in a managerial system, we focus on how to help each individual realize his full potential. Now, that is different from a professional services firm that has the possibility of an infinite number of roles for people who could match their potential. Whereas a managerial system really cannot.

Our approach is to ask the organization to be thoughtful and proactive about estimating and communicating with each employee his current and future potential. We work to help employees develop a career path that, if they earn the right, can still let them realize whatever their individual full potential is.

See, that's where the commonality is.

Bruce Ballengee: Let me offer this one. A dry cleaner can be differentiated with high touch and with high care. It's not complex. Historically, it's the industry with the most millionaires in it. It's very interesting. The plan of this business was to go find the undereducated, the poor with good hand skills and strong work ethics. And let's help them own and operate dry cleaners and go across the country. And they will do all sorts of things. They are, for example, not too proud to stitch a new button on a shirt.

Kerry Stover: The dry cleaner we use is in a little place with a service station next to it. And they even know me, when I walk in. It's dirt cheap, but it's the quality of the people.

Bruce Ballengee: Those kind of folks are not going to cure cancer. They're not going to be the captains of industry. They're not going to advise presidents or anything like that kind of stuff. But, do you know what they can do?

They can reach their full potential and they can own their own home. They can live comfortably, and send every child, if not every grandchild, to college. That is the basic value proposition.

And that can spread all over the United States. It is more a developing world kind of thing. However, that could lift huge portions of humanity out of the poor or lower-middle class or worse into the solidly middle class.

You know how to operate a dry cleaner. You know how to do great customer service.

Gerry Kraines: So I think you're saying that we're aligned, whether it's a requisite organization or it's an approach to social progress.

Bruce Ballengee: Yep.

Gerry Kraines: The goal is that the world will be better served by creating situations in which people can realize their full potential. That's the common thread.

Bruce Ballengee: Yes, taking that requisite approach, one can create, I believe, a more sustainable enterprise in any industry than someone who doesn't do that. Someone who's thinking about, "Hey, we're about profit and growth." We can trash that; we can crush them. "Hey, it's not all about profit and growth, it's also about values." We can crush them, too.

Gerry Kraines: But that's what their value is, profit and growth.

Bruce Ballengee: That's right. Then there's this emerging practice that says, "Oh, some of these core values and purposes, it's like yes, that's better." That's the green organization.

But, wait. Think about the universe and what works, and what the basic building block is. It is the individual. And so, there are whole masses of individuals of all kinds and sorts. And you match up those individuals that fit your product or service; that creates the money. It's the Disney thing. "We make movies to make movies; we don't make movies to make money." So, that's the return.

The 1,000-Year Company

Gerry Kraines: So what you were explaining to me over the last week or two of conversations, Kerry . . . in order to have a sustainable organization for 100 years or 1,000 years, a necessary component or purpose is sustainability.

Kerry Stover: Yes.

Gerry Kraines: Which means?

Kerry Stover: You should establish a congruency. Purpose is sustainability. You call it enduring. My perspective is people can separate that by just looking at the words . . . a safe space to develop people. Nothing about the enduring nature.

You can only develop people through having a safe space that lasts for a very long time. Safety cannot be founded by years or decades.

When I joined and was listening to the stories about what Pariveda is, Bruce agreed to do it. Only fill a consulting company by developing people. It was focused on developing people. It had to be different. It had to be about developing people first.

The second thing that he said was I thought that it had to be interesting. It had to be an ESOP (i.e., a company with an employee stock ownership plan). That was really a proxy for another phrase that he used, which is that it has to be a 1,000-year company. Which again gets people looking past their lifetime, past more of an infinite game.

And so, it's harder for people to think about developing people in the way that Bruce thinks about it if you don't parallel it with the sustainability notion. Because they don't see the development requiring anything. It is good to pull it out and share it.

Similarly, we use transparency as another core component of developing people. We pull it out because most companies hide it. They share what they want to share and they don't share what they don't with people. In fact, people value knowing a lot of stuff. And they're better developed by giving them more. And assuming that they are capable of handling it and developing them when they're not capable of handling it, in a way, that is how the organization grows.

In some of our presentations, we put those three as the core tenets for the founding of Pariveda. And those, too, are really part of developing people.

Bruce Ballengee: To me, sustainable can just be that. Well, we're entirely sustainable. If we wind up consuming the world, that doesn't work. So we have to sustain our clients. And sustain our customers. When we macro that, we have an office model, that's another integral part of what's requisite, for metropolitan areas. So we need to help sustain the metropolitan areas that we're in. All of those things feed off of themselves.

If there's a glacier and another Ice Age, then we're no longer sustainable in New York. Because New York is not sustainable. We so care about the next Ice Age. We care about climate change. Conversely, they can't keep building a dyke around Manhattan, which is their current plan.

Gerry Kraines: Are you saying that ESOP, transparency, enduring relationships, saving metropolitan areas, those are all the sustainability ingredients?

Bruce Ballengee: You need sustainability to achieve the purpose. In other words, given our purpose, we need to be sustainable.

If we said that we were going to be an organization that was trying to help jockeys be everything that they could be, we might be able to put some stuff into R&D to extend the useful life of the individual, but we could only go so far. There isn't going to be a 60- to 75-year-old person on the field, short of some huge advances in medical technology that we don't have yet.

Kerry Stover: Or changes in the game. Jockeys are not necessarily driven to live in metropolitan areas. Cities only die by natural events. Towns die. Cities don't die. There are very few examples of cities dying, other than by a volcano eruption or manmade devastation.

Bruce Ballengee: The Romans took care of Carthage.

Kerry Stover: Cities don't die; they tend to thrive and grow. And talent tends to want to be around other talent.

Bruce Ballengee: There is another aspect of it. The alternate view is that people are a resource like sand or timber or iron or coke. And that's not valid.

Gerry Kraines: It's not valid if the purpose is developing people to their full potential?

Bruce Ballengee: And it's not valid if you want to be sustainable.

Gerry Kraines: But, if you want to make a lot of money and then retire quickly, it could be great.

Bruce Ballengee: That's right, that's right. And then celebrate. Committing suicide as an enterprise. The enterprise isn't celebrating, but the leader is feted, celebrated, and honored. "Yes, I led my enterprise to commit suicide. I sold it to another company."

Kerry Stover: You made a bunch of millionaires, and hurt many, many people along the way.

Bruce Ballengee: But hurt them at the end, because that enterprise died.

Gerry Kraines: How do you address the issue that the business that has these twin values—helping people realize their full potential and being sustainable—may cause the competition to go out of business and those people suffer?

Bruce Ballengee: Two things. One, it's a big tent so it can get bigger. It's worked so far. There's another one that says, there are no secrets here.

Gerry Kraines: There are no secrets from the competition?

Bruce Ballengee: From the competition.

Gerry Kraines: They have choice.

Bruce Ballengee: They have choices. Just like Southwest Airlines, where everybody says, "You know what? We can do better than that."

And you've got to think about the whole thing and think about their purpose. We should be able to let someone travel in the air on our jet from A to B for the same price that it would cost them to put their family in a car and drive. And so, they're pretty darn requisite as an airline, and they can crush.

Gerry Kraines: But their purpose isn't to help people realize their full potential?

Kerry Stover: They put that in there. Because in order to keep their costs down, they know they need to take care of people. Otherwise, the unions get out.

Bruce Ballengee: They pay pilots and mechanics well . . . and here's a whole bunch of Southwest stock for your union. And then, you can go out and individually manage . . .

Gerry Kraines: I'm trying to think about how to view this. This is what you need to do to grow your business. One piece of it is a system that supports people realizing their full potential. But that's not the driving purpose of most of the businesses that will be trying to implement what's in this book.

What I could then say is, here are the 12 percent of the companies that were in the *Fortune* 100 a hundred years ago that still exist. If part of your purpose is to be sustainable, then your driving purpose has to be to develop people to realize their full potential.

Kerry Stover: With the right definition of sustainable . . .

Gerry Kraines: Tell me more.

Kerry Stover: Sustainable is a word that people have different definitions of. Sustainable for a period of time? What does it mean to be sustainable, like we can live through one generation before it changes? Sustainable, going back to the founder? Is it a green organization?

Bruce Ballengee: Can it survive a murder? Sustainable by acquiring somebody else?

Gerry Kraines: So what's the qualifier I need to put in there?

Bruce Ballengee: You can look at the Rothschilds. The Rothschilds had some rules. You can have a piece of the action, but you don't have a piece of the decision-making. They were fractured for a few decades. Some of the top patriarchs and matriarchs had a spat. But then they had negotiations to come back together.

Gerry Kraines: You know what happened with the Rockefellers? There were 74 descendants who owned Rockefeller Center. They couldn't agree on what to do, so they had to sell it to a Japanese company.

Bruce Ballengee: They did not put in place a robust and resilient and adaptive structure and governance. You have to have equal. To be adaptable, you have to have structure. You have to have process. And you have to be adaptive and resilient. And if you've got the other two, you're probably going to come out OK.

Gerry Kraines: There, you're talking about the family wealth as opposed to the organization that they were selling.

Kerry Stover: I can get you the details, but there are less than a thousand 100-year-old companies. Ninety percent of them are family-owned businesses that have passed through generations.

Bruce Ballengee: The oldest ones are, there's a 1,400-year-old Japanese construction company, Kongō Gumi Co.

Kerry Stover: The next one is about 1,100 years old. There's a Swedish company about 800 years.

Bruce Ballengee: We can reset a record if we pass 1,400. I will be watching!

Size and Scale of an Organization

Kerry Stover: In some ways, they have a very narrow sense of people development. If you're a vineyard owner, I want this to pass from generation to generation and for it to be inbred. It's an organization of fewer than 300 people, because it's a size of society that can collectively work toward this purpose and feel that they're benefitting from it. They know the names and faces. You can look at how many hundreds and thousands of companies have come and gone for all these years.

Gerry Kraines: That is reminiscent of Elliott Jaques's mutual recognition unit. You have mutual knowledge of up to 25. You know people; you know who their kids are. A mutual recognition unit has maybe 200 or 250 people. You see them at a football game and you recognize everyone who is an employee. And that was a great limiting factor for how many people a manager of managers could manage.

Bruce Ballengee: It's like [Albert] Dunlap's number. He had something like that. There's a scalability angle to it. The reality is that it is very individual. As individuals collect as small teams, and then collections of small teams . . . These are the best practices and the rules of how you design, model, and make decisions about how you design in order to be scalable or not.
If you want to be sustainable, you also need this stuff.

You may not care about people's development. I just want to last long enough. You have committed to short-term scale. You have no hope otherwise. You will collapse if you don't understand the individual. You don't have to take care of them. But you do have to understand them. There is a tribal nature to it. And that is largely what happens.

Gerry Kraines: It's like this book's chapter on cross-functional teams. (See Chapter 8.) Context can be accurately conveyed from A to his subordinate manager Bs and each of the Bs to their subordinate Cs, enabling the Cs in two different teams to work effectively together. Yet the essence of the context doesn't translate meaningfully to one more level. Thus you need to structure three-level units, when you need to have effective cross-functional working relationships. And that's another variation of what you just said.

In fact, if you follow Chapters 1 through 13, you have a highly effective organization that will be extremely productive, will support people working to their full potential. But if the purpose of your organization is not primarily to help people realize their full potential, it will likely not be sustainable beyond one or two generations. But if the goal is sustainability, then the purpose has to be just that.

Self-Actualization

Bruce Ballengee: I think you said that it was Dr. Levinson who talked about the alignment of people to purpose, and the company aligned with its entities, so I think there's a sense of purpose. You don't really talk about it, but you could talk about where high-level engagement comes from; not only do you have the right structure in the organization, but to get highly engaged people, then you want purpose and alignment of people.

So, if you find people who want to save the world, and you have a company whose purpose is to save the world, you've got good alignment. OK? But that isn't what all people really want to do. Most people have a purpose of their greater self-development. So, our purpose is just a higher purpose than other altruistic purposes. But I think talking about achieving a more effective organization from employee engagement would be a nice touch.

[Harry Levinson on transcendent purpose:

Develop subordinates so that, as much as possible, they move toward their ego ideals by helping the organization move toward its collective, historical ego ideal, which I call its transcendent purpose.

The generative leader makes it possible for subordinates to confront realities and to act on them in a context of clear direction and accountability.

He keeps the common task as the focus of relationships with subordinates, opens avenues for problem solving, and supports people in the process of attacking and mastering problems.]

Gerry Kraines: Harry [Levinson] created a graphic in 1955 that depicted the purpose of every organization has to be to attack reality in one way or another to accomplish some value. You also need to align goals, means, and how you define goodness. You must engage people together in that attack, which means you have to authorize them and sanction them, and you have to support them.

Inherent in his notion of the psychological contract, simply stated, is that employees will commit themselves to the success of the manager and the organization in direct proportion to the degree to which their manager and the organization commit themselves to the employee's success.

Now, employee success may not mean realizing their full potential, depending on the industry you are in. It may be, as in financial services, that people define their success by making a lot of money.

Bruce Ballengee: The key is to engage. And engagement surveys look at, from the other perspective, how motivated and engaged employees are. So, when you said that it is up to the manager "to engage," it's actually up to the larger organization than just a manager.

Kerry Stover: Say a furniture manufacturer. There are factories where someone comes in as a journeyman, for instance. An apprentice is doing simple things on simple pieces of furniture. They develop through, if you think about it, increasing mastery. "Hey, you're a real master craftsman," in a manufacturing company. "I'm a master craftsman and I know how to do all these things about building tables. I have an idea for a table." So the manufacturer will say that we'll support you in that by providing the materials and the tooling, etc. And you'll be the person who makes these tables and you'll get a royalty from your team.

And so, when you think about that. There is really a lot of self-actualization in that, even though it may not be the same kind of self-actualization.

We talked about driving through a tollbooth on the Golden Gate Bridge. And that job has been eliminated. But the toll attendant was totally into it, about collecting tolls. This tollbooth attendant was in a state of self-actualization.

So it could be anyone. They may not be able to do it as frequently or for as long a period of time. Or in an exciting way. Or affect as many people. But everybody should have a right to attempt self-actualization. Someone who has mental challenges, by birth or whatever, should have a chance to become an independent person and live independently. They can even be in a marriage. That's huge. That level of self-actualization is huge when you think about it.

Go back to the "hero" thing. The overcoming, moving from the known world to the unknown world is dramatic! More dramatic than many other things.

Bruce Ballengee: We have talked for years that we are highly selective in choosing the more talented employees to work with. In our model, we did not build the model for the average. And it would really stress our current model if we chose to have the average mixed in with the talented; we would find contrast.

Kerry Stover: We would have a different scale. That's what would be different. We could even move from innate capabilities and not skills. One could move it to skills to make it.

Bruce Ballengee: Right.

Kerry Stover: . . . work at any level.

Bruce Ballengee: You could have most people working in a dry cleaner before one would say, "OK, some of you have a lot more potential than that." Now, you're into like Pariveda's, because this is the leadership track. This is what most companies do anyways. They say, "We have our chosen ones, the HIPOs and then everybody else."

Gerry Kraines: The POPOs, pissed on, passed over!

Kerry Stover: OK. It would be, what I'm talking about, is more like, OK, it may be repugnant to people, but Jaques is sticking to reality. Pointing to reality that different people are on different potential development curves and it's a matter of creating the structure that basically supports a person on each curve. Or how many curves they're going to jump through and how to do that.

So, it's more complex than what we have at Pariveda. We've simplified that. Because we don't need to take on the whole industry. It's a market share of a $20 billion business.

Bruce Ballengee: But what about future generations?

Gerry Kraines: Let me get from each of you what you would like the final message in this last chapter to be.

Kerry Stover: I want it to be from your heart and head. That's all I'll say. It's requisite that it should be an expression of you.

Bruce Ballengee: If you're writing the teaser, position it to five years from now. That's the way that I would position it.

You are now moving into a phase where you are in a different place. There is an additional component and there may be a story to tell after that.

Gerry Kraines: So this is like the last chapter of my book, *Accountability Leadership,* from 2001.

This has been great. Stimulating. Affirming for me.

Some Reflections on Consulting

Bruce Ballengee: Now, you see why our brand is so hard to talk about.

Gerry Kraines: I think for the uninitiated potential client, they are going to be less interested in how you get your [people] to be so effective. And more interested in what that effectiveness will yield for them.

Kerry Stover: They don't understand how; and they rarely ask. Their typical response is, "I must get the 'A' team every time." That is a pretty normal thing. And the other thing they would say is, "You can say that your people are better than the competition." And everybody says that.

Until they experience it . . .

Bruce Ballengee: The [consulting] market is so conditioned to expect platitudes and react cynically.

Gerry Kraines: I get that. I am trying. Your people have been challenged from the very beginning to look at any one problem through multiple lenses.

Kerry Stover: The challenge . . . they don't usually do that.

Bruce Ballengee: We're into marketing now.

Kerry Stover: Aspirational . . .

Gerry Kraines: The Pariveda Expectations Framework creates multiple lenses that require mastery.

Kerry Stover: It is? Not totally.

Gerry Kraines: They are challenged to look at things through multiple lenses. They've been given skilled knowledge with which to examine things through multiple lenses. But they have been challenged since the beginning to ask questions. To not accept any statement on its face value, but to always try to understand what the meaning behind that statement is.

They will be the people who come in and help you think through what is the unique solution you need. I have heard people say that.

[A skeptical potential client might say,] "How will they be better than others as a result of it?"

The Known Unmet

Kerry Stover: We have challenged the entire industry that is in complete cooperation with virtually every customer. As an agreed-upon way of doing business, they can simplify it by just saying we must have a request for proposal. That is essentially about defining the known unmet.

Gerry Kraines: I use that [term] a lot.

Kerry Stover: It's about finding the known unmet. And then, the suppliers like us, we're supposed to go in and show how well we meet their stack, how well we understand your business, and how compliant we're willing to be. But the goal of it . . . they're not going for purpose here. They're almost always going for value. They are going for sales and growth at some level. They're about efficiency and not effectiveness. And they want control.

And what they're doing is they just assume there must be a mountain over here. They're hill-climbing in an AI world. And it's a process [that] they let you climb a hill. It just so happens that they often climb the wrong hill. That's in the unknown unmet. And then, they frequently don't realize until too late that there is an unknown in that element. They were not really interested in us from the outset.

However, the people that stick with us: "When I have something ambiguous and complex and I need to trust somebody and I can work with them and they will guide me now that I know that I am on the edge of the unknown, that's when I really need Pariveda."

Gerry Kraines: But that's what I want to capture. That's exactly what I want to capture.

Kerry Stover: That's our market.

Gerry Kraines: I know it's your market. And the people who come to love you appreciate it. I'm trying to figure out how that 25 percent that will come to value it—who don't know you yet—can understand from the beginning why you make that statement. Why you can deliver on it.

This is one of the things I have learned about our clients as I have reviewed over 25 years of PowerPoints with over 125 clients, some as big as Ford Motor Co., and others as small as a 13-person Internet company. I am able to show that this is what clients thought they had before we worked with them in order to discover what they really had. This is the process of discovering what they needed. And this is how you implement it.

Here is an example from my consulting at Ford.

After two months with five consultants gathering data and just a week or two of analyzing it, we presented seven possible models for a new 83,000-employee structure, along with the requisite and non-requisite elements of each of them.

And then, two hours over lunch with the executive team every day for six weeks, we winnowed it down to what was the least bad structure for proceeding.

[It was] requisite in that the processes they needed to create value were structured at the right level with the right level of thinking integrated in the right three-level process.

Instead of having, as they did when we found them, patterns of five different roles with P&L accountability for the same thing, they learned how to create business units with only one role who had P&L accountability and authority. So, it's these principles and multipliers described in this book.

And it all derives from the basic truth that I believe that accountability without authority is fantasy and stress.

Kerry Stover: It's the people, the structure, and the profits. But mostly, it's the people. At this stage, it's mostly people. We lead with people, starting with working on the people part.

Gerry Kraines: It's the way you condition them.

Kerry Stover: No, the way we *develop* them. The way we put them on their learning edge, and we try to teach them as fast as they're learning. It's pretty stressful, some can't handle it.

Learning, Understanding, and Some Final Words on Consulting

Gerry Kraines: Let me just make one more attempt. There are two ways that people can learn. One is by being taught, by both training and by trial and error. And the other is by applying their own judgment to solve something for the first time.

Bruce Ballengee: And then experiencing whether they were right or not.

Gerry Kraines: And then, that becomes extant knowledge.

You, like [firms such as] Accenture, give people lots of training. But you give them more opportunities to have to figure things out for themselves. Things not covered by training alone.

Bruce Ballengee: That's right.

Gerry Kraines: Which then becomes an enduring value. They have a hunger for that. And that means that they will identify either problems with the customer request or more novel and effective solutions than the customer originally thought [were possible].

Kerry Stover: And the number-one tool that we have to do that is not making explicit expectations. It's making people . . . developing our leaders . . . to sell and deliver in small teams. Because if it's a small team, even the worst manager cannot stop the curious mind from doing all those things. In 30 years of experience, not even the worst manager can stop an inventive mind from thinking.

Bruce Ballengee: How can I make them more effective? I have seen them struggle. I just go off and learn from them. And the manager, it's not as though you "do" anything, but everyone wants you on the team.

Gerry Kraines: The Expectations Framework can be taught. The people have to discover how to do it.

Bruce Ballengee: NODS (nature of design systems) is just an offer to discover.

Gerry Kraines: For me, knowledge is sharing what someone else discovered. Training someone is not building the mind, it is just building tools.

Bruce Ballengee: It's not understanding. You can't teach understanding. You can share understanding.

Kerry Stover: The way it's taught. Whether it's the act of teaching or the act of absorbing.

Gerry Kraines: I think most people acquire knowledge and skill either by being taught or by trial and error, as opposed to actively inventing things.

Kerry Stover: What I'm saying is that you can teach, but people may not be taught.

Bruce Ballengee: Or they learn by being.

Gerry Kraines: That's true.

Bruce Ballengee: Experience is a basic form of learning and then logic can flow. The meta-systematic thinker is also an experiential thinker. If you experience reality differently than . . .

Gerry Kraines: My brain is going to explode!

NOTES

Introduction

[1] *Wall Street Journal*, February 20, 1996.

Chapter 1

[1] The use of QQT/R throughout this book comes from Elliott Jaques's definition of a task in *Requisite Organization* (Falls Church, VA: Cason Hall & Co. Publishers, 1998).

[2] Gerald A. Kraines, MD, *Accountability Leadership: How to Strengthen Productivity through Sound Managerial Leadership* (Franklin Lakes, NJ: Career Press, 2001).

Chapter 2

[1] The use of the term *psychological contract* throughout this book comes from Harry Levinson (with Charlton R. Price, Kenneth J. Munden, Harold J. Mandl, and Charles M. Solley), in *Men, Management, and Mental Health* (Cambridge, MA: Harvard University Press, 1962).

[2] Ram Charan and Geoffrey Colvin, "Why CEOs Fail," *Fortune* magazine, June 21, 1999.

Chapter 3

[1] Elliott Jaques, *Requisite Organization* (Falls Church, VA: Cason Hall & Co. Publishers, 1998).

[2] The use of *timespan* throughout this book comes from Elliott Jaques's definition of *timespan* in *Requisite Organization* (Falls Church, VA: Cason Hall & Co. Publishers, 1998) and in *Timespan Handbook* (London: Heinemann Educational Books, Ltd., 1964).

[3] The use of levels of role complexity throughout this book comes from Elliott Jaques's definition in *Requisite Organization* (Falls Church, VA: Cason Hall & Co. Publishers, 1998).

Chapter 4

[1] Elliott Jaques, *Human Capability* (Falls Church, VA: Cason Hall & Co. Publishers, 1994).

Chapter 7

[1] The structure of a strategic business unit used in this chapter is derived from Elliott Jaques's original work described in *Requisite Organization* (Falls Church, VA: Cason Hall & Co. Publishers, 1998).

[2] The terms direct output (DO), delegated direct output (DDO), and direct output support (DOS) come from Elliott Jaques's definitions in *Requisite Organization* (Falls Church, VA: Cason Hall & Co. Publishers, 1998).

[3] Michel Robert, *Strategy Pure & Simple II: How Winning Companies Dominate Their Competitors* (New York: McGraw-Hill, 1997).

[4] To protect client confidentiality in this case, I have used a pseudonym for the name of the company.

Chapter 8

[1] The taxonomy of direct and indirect accountabilities is based on Elliott Jaques's definitions of *task-assigning role relationships* (TARRs) and *task-initiating role relationships* (TIRRs) in *Requisite Organization* (Falls Church, VA: Cason Hall & Co. Publishers, 1998).

Chapter 10

[1] The curves referred to in this chapter (and elsewhere in the book) refer to Elliott Jaques's data progression curves described in *Requisite Organization* (Falls Church, VA: Cason Hall & Co. Publishers, 1998).

Chapter 12

1 Elliott Jaques, *A General Theory of Bureaucracy* (London: Heinemann Educational Books, Ltd., 1976), p. 346.

2 Lisa S. Rotenstein, MD, Raffaella Sadun, and Anupam N. Jena, "Why Doctors Need Leadership Training," *Harvard Business Review*, October 17, 2018.

3 Harry Levinson, *The Great Jackass Fallacy* (Boston: Harvard University Graduate School of Business Administration, 1973).

Chapter 13

1 Joe Castaldo, "Top CEO 2006: Denis Turcotte, Algoma Steel Inc.," *Canadian Business*, October 9, 2006.

2 Harry Levinson, *Ready, Fire, Aim: Avoiding Management by Impulse* (Cambridge, MA: The Levinson Institute, 1986).

INDEX

realization outcomes of change, 203
resources, accountability and, 12
resourcing functions, 117–118
    structuring, 193–194
responsibility, 10–11
results *vs.* effectiveness,
    accountability and, 8–9
Robert, Michel, 123, 190
role compression, 185–188
role filling
    clean slate approach to, 195–196
    role establishment to, 161–164
role relationships, leadership,
    24–25
roles
    categories of work and, 43
    commitment to, 79–80
    complexity level of, 87
    defining, human resource systems
        and, 6, 156
    effectiveness in, 18–19
    mastering, 43–44
    mastery, overall degree of, 168
    timespan and complexity levels
        of, 54–61
    valuing work of, 79–80
    work complexity of, 47–49
role specifications, creating, 194–195
role vacuums, 185–188

S

safety, personal, 33–34
sales and operating plan (S&OP)
    processes, 112
sales/product-service provisioning,
    110–113
selection processes, 178–179
self-regulation, judgment hierarchies
    and, 81–83
service-giving/requesting, indirect
    accountabilities and, 141–142

skilled knowledge, 73–78
    effectiveness in role and, 29
    vs. potential, 42
SONARIO˙, 3
spans of control, 188–189
Stover, Kerry, 225. *see also* purpose-
    driven organization discussion
    topics
strategic business unit (SBU),
    190–191
    accountabilities for near/
        mid-term, 115–117
    driving force as cornerstone
        of, 123
    functions, 119–120
strategic leaders, characteristics of,
    223–224
Strategic Organization
    implementation, 183–206
    accountability system
        implementation, 196–200
    ancillary support functions and,
        194
    business units, structuring,
        190–191
    change process, leading,
        202–206
    component relationships, 3
    compression and, 185–188
    corporate structure building,
        191–192
    desired outcomes of, 184,
        203–206
    functional alignment and,
        189–190
    HR systems, design and
        implement, 200–201
    inter-business unit synergies and,
        192–193
    leadership, 221–222
    overview of, 183–184

W

Wall Street Journal, 2
"what if. . ." functions, 117–118
work, defined, 155
work categories, employees'
    effectiveness and, 43

work complexity. *see also* complexity
    hierarchies
    potential to handle, 28
    timespan and, 50–52

Y

"Yes, but. . ." functions, 118–119

ABOUT THE AUTHOR

GERALD A. KRAINES, MD, is senior vice president at Pariveda Solutions, where he leads Pariveda's Strategic Organization and Organizational Change practice areas. In his role, Gerry consults worldwide to companies of all sizes. For forty years, he has helped to integrate and implement many successful cor¬porate reorganizations resulting from rapid growth, acquisitions, mergers, and consolidations. Gerry's clients have included Brookfield Asset Management, Centers for Medicare and Medicaid Services, Christie Digital Systems, ConocoPhillips, Eli Lilly and Company, FEMSA Coca-Cola, FEMSA OXXO, Ford Motor Company, GE Healthcare, Halliburton, Hexcel Corporation, Honeywell International, Morgan Stanley, Royal Bank of Scotland, the Social Security Administration, UBS, and Westinghouse Electric Company

Prior to joining Pariveda, Gerry was chairman and CEO of Levinson and Co., taking over from its founder, Dr. Harry Levinson, in 1991. Gerry was also on the faculty of Harvard Medical School for many years. Before becoming CEO of Levinson and Co., Gerry was the medical director at a regional mental health center. He also practiced clinical psychiatry for over fifteen years. His career has focused on enhancing leadership effectiveness: as an executive for healthcare organizations, as a teacher of leadership, as an executive coach, and since the 1980s, as a consultant to senior executives about leadership systems.

Gerry brings a systems perspective to Pariveda's research, education, and consul¬tation, where he is continuing Levinson's mission of disseminating in-depth knowledge about managerial leadership systems combined with the psychological aspects of leadership.

Born in Chicago, Gerry received an undergraduate degree from Oberlin College, a medical degree from Case Western Reserve, and a psychiatric fellowship and a postgraduate degree from Harvard Medical School. His critically acclaimed book, *Accountability Leadership: How to Strengthen Productivity through Sound Managerial Leadership,* was first published in 2001.